Environmental Planning
for Site Development

Environmental Planning
for Site Development

Anne R. Beer

E. & F. N. SPON
An imprint of Chapman and Hall
LONDON • NEW YORK • TOKYO • MELBOURNE • MADRAS

UK	Chapman and Hall, 11 New Fetter Lane, London EC4P 4EE
USA	Van Nostrand Reinhold, 115 5th Avenue, New York NY10003
JAPAN	Chapman and Hall Japan, Thomson Publishing Japan, Hirakawacho Nemoto Building, 7F, 1-7-11 Hirakawa-cho, Chiyoda-ku, Tokyo 102
AUSTRALIA	Chapman and Hall Australia, Thomas Nelson Australia, 480 La Trobe Street, PO Box 4725, Melbourne 3000
INDIA	Chapman and Hall India, R. Seshadri, 32 Second Main Road, CIT East, Madras 600 035

First edition 1990

© 1990 Anne R. Beer

Typeset in 10½/12pt Sabon by Best-Set Typesetters Ltd, Hong Kong
Printed in England by Clays Ltd., St. Ives PLC

ISBN 0 419 15300 4

British Library Cataloguing in Publication Data

Beer, Anne R.
  Environmental planning for site development
  1. Landscape design
  I. Title
  712

  ISBN 0−419−15300−4

Library of Congress Cataloging-in-Publication Data

Beer, Anne R.
  Environmental planning for site development/Anne R. Beer. − 1st ed.
    p.   cm.
  Includes bibliographical references.
  ISBN 0-419-15300-4
  1. Building sites − Planning.   2. Building sites − Environmental aspects.   I. Title.
NA2540.5.B44   1990
720′.28 − dc20

90-9681
CIP

In memory of
Jean MacDonald Beer

Contents

Preface

Environmental planning must form the basis for all site development decisions if the natural environment is to be conserved and people's environmental needs met. The planning process that has been evolved to deal with this is termed site planning.

This text is intended as an introduction to the basics of site planning. It indicates how a thorough understanding of a wide range of environmental factors is required to produce a site development plan. It has been devised for beginners in all the disciplines which include site planning as part of their vocational training.

It is suitable for use by first and second year undergraduates following courses in town and regional planning, landscape architecture, architecture, civil engineering, environmental planning, building, land management, amenity horticulture and parks management.

It should also be of use to postgraduates taking conversion courses in town and regional planning, landscape architecture, landscape management, recreation planning, and parks and leisure management, and to a lesser extent housing management or estate management.

It can be used by students studying alone or as part of the back-up material for a supervised site planning project. The latter situation is preferable, as the student who works through the text using a real site as a case study will learn the basic principles of the site planning process more quickly.

It can be used as a distance learning refresher course by those practising in the professions which are involved with the built environment.

More advanced texts dealing with the art and science of site planning and with environmental planning are available and many of these are listed in the references at the end of each chapter and referred to in the text.

The recommended text to use for further studies after completing this introduction is *Site Planning* by Kevin Lynch (MIT, Cambridge) (several editions, the latest being in 1985 and written together with Gary Hack).

Those interested in the philosophical issues relating to site planning, in particular as they relate to protecting the environment, should go on to read some or all of these books:

1. *Design with Nature* by Ian McHarg (1969) (Natural History Press, New York).
2. *City Form and Natural Process* by Michael Hough (1983) (Croom Helm, London).
3. *The Granite Garden* by Anne Spirn (1984) (Basic books, New York).
4. *Landuse Planning – from Global to Local Challenge* by Julius Fabos (1985) (Dowden and Culver, New York).

In addition to those books, each of the specialisms involved in the site planning process has produced an extensive literature on the site planning concerns of their particular discipline. This text is no substitute for those more detailed studies of the subject or its various aspects; the author has not intended or attempted to cover the information in the same depth as that more advanced literature.

This book is an introduction only, aiming to indicate to the students how their particular expertise fits into the total scope of site planning.

Site planning is not the prerogative of any particular profession or discipline – anybody involved with making decisions about what should go where on any area of land is involved in site planning. It is of essence a multi-disciplinary activity involving the expertise of many people if it is to be successful.

This text is particularly concerned with the external environment. It does not deal in any detail with the site planning considerations that relate to the layout of buildings; such matters are well dealt with in the architectural literature. It is, however, concerned with:

1. the environment immediately around buildings;
2. any open areas within the built environment, whatever the land use;
3. those areas of the countryside which are opened up for recreation purposes or other non-agricultural land use.

Site planning is described here as landscape architects have developed it over the past century. It is at the core of landscape architecture and all landscape architects are trained as site planners as part of their course of study, but even they – who see themselves as the specialists in the detailed planning and design of the external environment – must almost always work with others in multi-disciplinary teams if fully informed site planning decisions are to be taken.

Site planning is presented here as a linear process. This results more from the need to present the process in book form than the reality of planning a site. Of essence site planning consists of a series of loops, with those involved always having to refer back to and collect additional information about the earlier stages as the full complexities of the site come to be understood.

Site planning is a means of identifying and understanding problems that arise from the interrelationship between man and the land. Once problems are understood we are half way to solving them or avoiding them.

What you will learn by working through this book

1. How to decide the best location for each land-use and each activity on a site.
2. The information that you need to gather about the physical characteristics of any area of land and how to assess this, so that you can decide the best location for each activity.
3. A way of working out who is likely to use the land, what activities they are likely to want to do there and what sort of environment is required if they are to get a high level of satisfaction out of participating in a particular activity.
4. How to use your assessment of the physical characteristics together with your analysis of the environment required by each activity, to decide which parts of the site can stay the same, which parts will need to be changed and what those changes should aim to achieve.
5. How to influence the appearance of your site by developing appropriate landscape types and using suitable landscape management methods.
6. You will learn this best by carrying out a practical exercise for a site you are already working on or that you know well and producing a plan for the future development of that site.

Acknowledgements

The author wishes to thank everybody who has assisted with the preparation of this book: Mady van der Knaap for her support and encouragement, Geoffrey Beer for reading and commenting on the first draft and Penny Draper for the many hours spent editing the drafts, without her assistance and unstinting help the work would have taken many months longer.

The ideas presented here owe much to discussion with the students and staff of the department of landscape architecture at Sheffield University with whom I have enjoyed working.

Part One

Site Planning

This part defines what is meant by site planning and outlines the process involved in producing a site plan. The first chapter indicates the scope of environmental planning for site development, shows it to be a multi-disciplinary activity and lists in summary form the work to be undertaken by environmental planners. The second chapter outlines some fundamental principles of environmental planning as they relate to the type of problem tackled by those involved in site planning.

What is site planning? 1

This chapter shows that making decisions about what goes where on an area of land is a very common activity but one that has to be undertaken with care, if the results of the decision-making process are not to be to the detriment of the environment. It explains the advantages of a systematic approach to planning a site and indicates the vast range of environmental, social and economic factors which should have a bearing on the decision-making process in relation to site planning. It indicates the range of professional expertise available to tackle the problem-identification and problem-solving required by the site planning process.

What does site planning entail?

THE OVERALL LAND-USE PLANNING PROCESS

Site planning is an integral part of the land-use planning process; it determines the detailed layout of an area of land so that it functions effectively in relation to a given range of land-uses on the site and others around it. It occurs directly before or is part of the detailed design process, depending on the complexity and scale of the site.

In the overall planning process site planning occurs after the strategic planning has taken place and after the land-use has been decided in relation to social, economic and environmental needs.

Site planning is about working out the detail of what should happen on a given area of land, how it should happen and what it will cost to implement and manage the project on that area of land.

WHEN IS IT NECESSARY TO PRODUCE A SITE PLAN?

A site plan is needed:

1. whenever it is proposed to change the use of an area of land or build on all or part of it;
2. whenever it is proposed to change the way in which an area of land and its associated landscapes is managed and maintained.

Site plans are required for all developments involving the construction of buildings or other engineering structures:

- housing developments
- industrial developments
- commercial developments
- recreational developments
- communications developments.

Site plans are not only required when building operations are proposed; they are needed when it is planned that any part of the external environment should be used in a different way or for a different purpose, or that the land is to be managed differently. This includes:

- housing rehabilitation
- industrial rehabilitation
- commercial area rehabilitation
- reclamation of derelict land
- afforestation
- additional or improved parks and open spaces
- changing landscape management practices.

WHO NEEDS TO KNOW ABOUT SITE PLANNING?

Anybody involved in making decisions about land-use change on specific sites and involved in considering such change in relation to environmental, social and economic factors needs to understand how the physical and natural environment constrains what man can do on an area of land. Not everybody needs to know about it in the same depth, but the more that those involved understand the principles underlying the site planning process, the more likely it is that nature can be respected when making proposals to develop areas of land.

The process of site planning and its basic principles is relevant to land-use planning and environmental design in every continent and culture. It is only the detail that will be different. The process described here has developed out of experience of site planning in the English-speaking world, but there is no reason why the fundamental principles cannot be adapted by a reader to other situations, provided that the locally prevailing culture/nature relationship is thoroughly studied.

In Britain, it is the site planning process which provides the basic information needed by an applicant in order to obtain permission to develop through the development control system. As all development on, under, or above an area of land in Britain can only happen with official approval, this means that some form of site planning has to be initiated for large numbers of sites each year. Anyone involved with changing the use of an area of land and spending money to develop a site, even developers who see no need to employ professional advisers to guide their projects, will be involved in at least a rudimentary form of site planning because of the development control system. Such developers might not term their operation 'site planning', but even if their work is restricted only to a concern for the financial viability or profitability of the proposed development and to obtaining just enough information for the planning process, it is still site planning.

To carry out a proper financial appraisal, developers must collate and assess information about the site, its environment and the people who will ultimately live, work, or play on the land. For this reason the site planning process should not be seen as an unnecessarily expensive extra. It is, in fact, a part of the process which all public and private developers have to go through to assess the financial viability of a scheme.

The site planning process aims to be more consistent in its cover of the environmental issues which should determine the detailed layout and design of a site, than the relatively random approach so often taken by landowners and developers. The process also differs from the developers' approach to decision-making in that it attempts to look at site planning in relation to the interests of society as a whole as well as those of the developer, when determining what should and should not happen on the land.

Site planning is not a process devised to 'stop development happening' or to 'slow it down', as some politicians are wont to believe. On the contrary it aims to enable a development to happen, but with the least possible adverse effects on the environment as a whole. Only when the environmental or social impacts are totally negative does the process enable the developer and the planners to reach an informed decision that the project should not be allowed to take place for environmental reasons.

The emphasis of site planning is on environmental issues, but any consideration of environmental factors is also linked to other factors, involving as it does economic and social issues. However, site planners have to be pragmatic and recognize that it is often these other factors which hold most sway with the developers and politicians involved with the land-use development programmes. Very often their main interest is in meeting certain financial targets. Despite the increased awareness of the importance of the natural environment, factors such as fear of wasting money or not making enough to please shareholders can still determine the developer's final decision about a project more readily than environmental concerns. Encouraging developers and politicians to realize that economic disadvantage to individuals and society can result from a failure to take proper account of the physical and natural environment is, therefore, an important part of the site planner's task. Explaining this to developers and politicians can cause a radical change in attitude towards site planning.

Site planning can make money for a developer by ensuring that un-necessarily expensive development solutions are not chosen. For instance, developers who fail to have a thorough survey of the physical conditions of a site can inadvertently position buildings in locations where the soil bearing capacity is low and allocate areas of good bearing capacity as public open space – resulting in an unnecessary need for expensive pile driven supports for the buildings. Or, because of the lack of a proper site assessment, they can fail to recognize that the existing landscape could become a high-quality recreational environment with only slight modifi-cation and instead spend vast sums developing a new landscape.

It is not just the direct costs of development that site planning can help to reduce; it can also help to reduce the long-term management costs associated with operating on a site. For instance, the development of the site using a particular layout could result in very high energy consump-tion to keep the buildings warm in winter, whereas if the development were carried out differently, based on understanding the link between the local climate of the site, its landform and the distribution of vegetation, it would be possible to minimize those running costs.

SITE PLANNING AND THE COST OF DEVELOPMENT

Calculating the costs is an important part of the site planning process both in terms of actual cost to the developer of alternative solutions and the costs to society which result from the proposed development. Costs to society are incurred, for instance, through:

1. the need to provide an adequate infrastructure;
2. the extra work which has to be carried out to protect adjacent natural resources;
3. the need to create new landscapes because of damage to the visual resources caused by the development;
4. the loss of cultural resources;
5. the need to relocate people whose lives are disturbed by an unacceptable land-use change, for instance one which increases the local noise level.

SITE PLANNING CAN SAVE MONEY

Properly conducted, the site planning process can often indicate that more effective and cheaper approaches to site layout and design are possible and, therefore, it can be used as a way of increasing the profitability of individual projects or even making them possible where previously they had seemed uneconomic. The process is of particular value when it incorporates consideration of the long-term management cost of different layout and design solutions, for these too have an important impact on the financial viability of any project for the financier.

The development of any site entails capital costs for site preparation and the implementation of the project, maintenance costs and site management costs. For most sites the viability of development can be judged only if all these financial aspects are considered, not just initial capital costs.

WHY A SPECIAL PLANNING PROCESS?

If site planning is deciding what should happen where on an area of land, why was there any need to develop a special site planning process? The reason was that specialists in land-use and landscape planning came to realize that a process was needed which would allow all concerned to think systematically through the whole range of issues that relate to deciding what should happen on an area of land. Without such a system there was a danger that the problem would only be understood from the particular viewpoint of the person charged with producing the site plan.

The site planning process allows us to think through all the problems likely to be associated with developing a site or changing its use. It is the complexity of the man/environment relationship which creates the need to look at the interactions systematically. The land itself is complex, each area of land having developed to its present state through natural environmental change and, more recently, through modification by man's past and present actions. People are complex in the way they use land, with each different culture behaving in a way which results in a different relationship between people and the land.

It has taken until recent decades to recognize that people cannot exist without nature; that our activities are inextricably a part of nature. We now know that we are capable through our land-use and land management actions of irreparably ruining man's habitat and we have begun to recognize that all our land-use developments must be carried out within the constraints set by the physical and natural environment, if we are to avoid further damage to it. We have also begun to recognize that we can intervene to put right at least some of our past environmental mistakes.

If the fundamental relationship between man and nature is ignored by landowners and land planners and managers it results in:

- at best: costs to society to put right mistakes
- at worst: major environmental and/or economic disasters which may have long-term effects.

Since every change on the surface of the land has an impact, however small, on the environment, every change has to be thought through carefully by the proposer, the developer and those charged with land-use planning. To fail to do so can result in unnecessary economic loss as well as environmental and social problems.

It is to reduce the apparently haphazard occurrence of environmental problems and to guide us on how to repair past damage that the site planning process has been developed. It aims to act as a check by identifying possible problems with new developments and by indicating the way in which the potential of a site can be developed without undue cost to society (costs of counteracting environmental damage) and to the individual (costs associated with poor or mistaken use of the local features and resources).

Site planning goes beyond the stage normally identified by the term 'Environmental Impact Assessment' in that it aims to come up with the Site Use and Layout Plan and is inextricably related to the design of the site. Any site plan produced by the process will be based on the intention of doing least damage to the physical and natural environment, while providing adequate environmental settings for the people who will be affected by the new development. It can and does also provide the basic information for any Environmental Impact Assessment and for drawing up the documents necessary to apply for planning permission.

Why site planning is multi-disciplinary

TYPES OF SITE WHICH NEED A SITE PLAN

Site plans are produced for all types and sizes of site, from individual site plans for areas as small as a house and garden, to large housing and industrial estates or recreational areas covering several hundred hectares. The principles are the same – the level of work and detail are not.

In many circumstances the production of a site plan is inextricably linked with the detailed design of a site, but the more complex a site the more likely that the site planning and site design stage will be separated and even carried out by different people.

Each site plan will be different as it involves a different emphasis. The skill of the site planner or the site planning team lies partly in speedily identifying the particular problems of an individual site and concentrating on them. However, before reaching the stage of becoming a professional expert the student must learn the whole process and apply it in a wide variety of circumstances. Only then will the expertise which allows the short cuts to be spotted be acquired.

SOLVING SITE PLANNING PROBLEMS

Making decisions about how best to plan the layout of any area of land involves thinking about aspects of the physical, natural and social environment; it involves also aspects of economics, law and politics. Except in rare cases, when very small or simple sites are involved, no individual can hope to be sufficiently expert to understand the implications of, and interactions of, all the factors which have to be considered. For that reason, the most effective site planning is done by multi-disciplinary teams working under the leadership of someone trained to co-ordinate the information from different experts and develop it into policies to govern the planning of the site.

Students using this book will come from many different backgrounds and many will already have some expertise related to an aspect of site planning. It is inevitable, therefore, that some readers will probably already feel more expert in certain aspects of the site planning process than this introductory book expects them to become. This does not mean that learning about the site planning process is a waste of time. The intention is to alert all those involved to the full range of factors to be considered and problems to be tackled by the site planning process. It aims also to show how an individual's specific expertise interacts with that of people from other disciplines.

INITIATING A SITE PLAN

The owner of an area of land, or a person or organization with an interest in the land, normally initiates the site planning procedure. However, as has already been explained, unless they employ professional planners, architects or landscape architects, those involved are not always aware that they are initiating the process termed site planning. They may describe their decisions as 'deciding how to use or make money out of the land' – but that is exactly what site planning is.

It is important that the professionals have a clear understanding of the financial and other advantages to the developer of rigorously following the site planning procedure. Without that, few of the developers who do not presently use the process are likely to be won over to its benefits. It is particularly important that land-use planners and those officials in charge of controlling development understand what needs to be done to produce a site plan and can advise a developer where to find the necessary assistance and which short cuts can be taken for individual sites.

THE SCOPE OF SITE PLANNING AND THE NEED FOR TEAM WORK

The site planning team

Ideally site plans should be developed for every area of land on which changes are to take place. Such plans should be developed out of the fullest possible understanding of the interactions that occur on each site between man's use of the land, nature and the land itself.

Any proposals for a site should grow out of an understanding of:

1. the manner in which people's actions are constrained and limited by the physical environment;
2. the intent to conserve what remains of the plants, animals, insects, etc. that make up the natural world;
3. the need to provide for people's primary needs such as shelter, food and economic activity;
4. the intent to encourage the development of environments which people experience as satisfactory places in which to live, work or play.

Having to consider all these factors implies the need for the site planning process to be different, if only slightly, for every site. It also implies that different types of expertise will be needed in different circumstances.

There will be circumstances where the process involves little more than working through a check-list, to make sure that no major environmental or social problems exist or are likely to arise; in such cases the work can be done by the owner, the developer or a professional person briefly employed for their expertise.

There will be circumstances, at the other extreme, where the site is so complicated and the environmental problems so diverse that large teams of experts have to be appointed to work on the problems posed by developing a site; in such cases an overall co-ordinator will have to be appointed to link the work done by people from different disciplines.

The scale of the problem can also have an impact on whether the site planning process is separated from, or part of the site design process. Ideally the two should not be divorced, but on larger and more complex sites it may become necessary for the two to be separated for economic reasons. Whenever possible those who will be responsible for the detailed design of a site should be part of the site planning team and in particular involved in drawing up the site plan and the design brief. Failure to involve the designers in the planning process can mean that their solutions do not fully match with the intentions of the site planning proposals.

APPOINTING A SITE PLANNING TEAM

It is the developer's responsibility to appoint a site planner or a planning team. In most circumstances the developer will be a private individual, a private organization, a corporation or a public body. Large organizations will commonly appoint site planning teams even if they are just composed of financial experts and these teams are often able to co-opt the necessary expertise to allow them to do their task effectively. Small private organizations and individuals are less likely to think that site planning is an important part of the process of developing their site, but their attitude will depend on their past experiences.

In Britain the role of the development control officers and the local planners is crucial in persuading developers of the importance of appointing site planning teams with a proper range of expertise, if site plans are to be produced on the basis of a proper understanding of environmental requirements. Local planners have to be as expert in the aspects of the physical and natural environment which impinge on planning decisions as they are on the social and economic problems of their area. They can then advise the developers of the sorts of problems that might occur should they fail to carry out a proper site planning procedure; they also need to be sufficiently expert in site planning to be able to advise the developer of the appropriate short cuts that their site planners might investigate. The role of the local planners and development control officers in stimulating the initiation of the site planning process is so important because many of the developments proposed each year are carried out by people doing one-off schemes; they cannot be expected to have sufficient expertise to recognize that developing a site has any problems other than those involved with finance (Beer and Booth, 1983).

The developer who appoints a site planner becomes the client of the appointee. Even when the site planners are appointed as a team within a local authority they still have a client for whom they are operating. From now on the developer is usually referred to in this text as the client.

A wide range of people are involved in the site planning team. The team should not just be composed of technical experts. The client will always be involved in the decision-making and the users too, if they can be identified, as well as the local community and the local authority. The composition of the team will change as each stage of the site planning process is completed, but it is essential that there is a co-ordinator who is fully versed in site planning and capable of bringing together the contributions of experts from many different disciplines and applying them to the production of an assessment of the potential of the site for development and ultimately the site plan.

In the site planning team many people are involved in making site planning decisions – not just the owner of the land and professional advisers:

1. The client: the developer, the builder, the financier.
2. The technical team: landscape architects, planners, architects, engineers, surveyors.

3. The community: the local community, the future users, the local councillors and the council officers.

Site planning is rarely satisfactory without the involvement of all the above people.

Many people from different professions can be co-opted as part of a site planning team. The actual membership of the team depends on the site characteristics and the particular development problem to be solved.

Some of the major differences between sites which influence the composition of the site planning team are:

- it has different physical problems
- it has different natural environmental problems
- people use it for different activities
- each group using it has different needs
- it is owned by different people
- it is being paid for by differing means
- it is maintained in different ways.

The professions and disciplines most likely to be involved in the technical team are listed below. The expertise provided by the landscape architects is almost always required, as they are trained to conserve as well as plan, design and manage the external environment. To enable landscape architects to do this their training teaches them to base their decision-making on their best understanding of the interactions between nature and man that happen on any site.

The landscape architect can operate alone as a site planner, but more commonly must work with others with their special expertise in for instance building, engineering, recreation. All the work carried out by the site planning team even at the preliminary stages has to be within the constraints of the client's budget. The amount of time that can be spent on producing the preliminary ideas of how a project can be undertaken is normally limited by the budget allocated to undertake the required study. The ideas developed for the site also have to be within the financial constraints set by the client.

Professions and experts most likely to be involved in site planning are:

1. landscape architects, architects, urban designers, civil engineers;
2. environmental planners, town planners, land-use planners, economic planners, social planners;
3. building scientists, climatologists, geologists, geomorphologists, ecologists, hydrologists, pedologists, archaeologists;
4. estates managers, housing managers, recreation managers, open space managers;
5. public health, fire and safety staff;
6. built environment conservation staff, natural environment conservation staff, countryside management staff, site interpretation staff;
7. foresters, farmers.

THE SEQUENCE IN PRODUCING A SITE PLAN

Figure 1.1 summarizes the stages involved in the production of a site plan from the point when a developer (the client of the site planner) decides to develop a site to the production of design briefs.

So far this chapter has dealt with the first two stages of the process as shown in Figure 1.1: it is the client who determines the need for a site plan by deciding to develop a site; the complexity of the site and the problems involved are the determining factors in the composition of a site planning team.

Chapter 2 looks at the factors that have to be considered to establish the key issues. It also deals with the need to examine alternative sites and

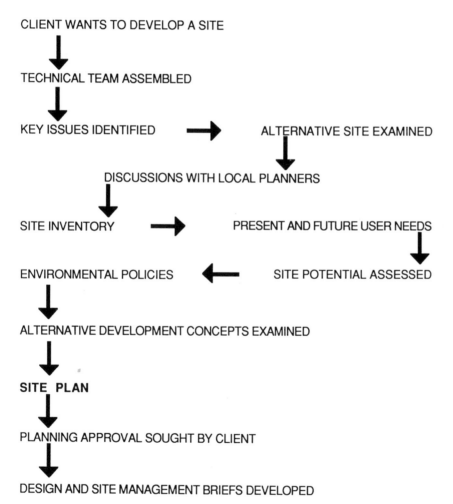

Figure 1.1   Production of a site plan.

to discuss the development of a particular area of land with the local planners, before too many resources are committed to the site planning process.

Points 1–6 below outline the work that has to be undertaken by the site planning team to draw up a site plan. This work will be explained stage by stage in Chapters 3–10 with particular emphasis on the work that the technical members of a site planning team would be expected to undertake.

The site planning process can be outlined as follows:

1. A thorough assessment of the natural environment and the associated physical characteristics of the site and its surroundings.
2. A detailed analysis of the users and their requirements in terms of facilities for each activity and the sort of environment needed to enable the activity to take place with the maximum possible user satisfaction.
3. An assessment of the potential of the site, based on the relationship between the physical characteristics of the site and the user requirements.
4. An assessment of possibilities for changing the physical characteristics of the site to make a better match between the users and the site.
5. Assessing the impact on the natural and visual environments of any changes to the physical aspects of the site.
6. Proposing a plan for the site which is a balance between man's requirements and the need to ensure the conservation and enhancement of the natural environment.

Part Five contains a summary of the whole process; the section is designed to be used as a check list of the work to be undertaken. The work that needs to be done under each of the stages indicated above is summarized below.

THE SITE INVENTORY

The physical environment
    geology and geomorphology
    topography
    water
    local climate
The natural environment
    soils
    vegetation
    wildlife
    air quality

ecological value
The social environment
    land-use
    built environment
    rural environment
    population
    historical development
    land ownership
    views and scenery
    landscape types
    landscape character
    unique areas and features
The user requirements
    functioning of the site
    the activities in buildings
    the activities outside
    diversity of environmental settings

SITE POTENTIAL

The client's brief developed
    client's requirements
    project goals and objectives
    major and minor users' needs
    facilities to be provided
    environmental settings to be created
Assessment of site potential
    site assets
    site liabilities
    constraints and opportunities

THE SITE PLAN

Strategies for development
    land-use and management
    natural environment
    visual environment
Objectives for development
    the built environment
    conservation
    experiential attributes
    financial
    operational

Environmental guidelines for the site
  appearance
  experiential characteristics
  financial
  operational
Site development concept and alternatives examined
  develop a proposed concept
  develop alternative proposals
  evaluate alternatives
Site plan and the landscape plan
  develop a site plan
  identify environmental problems
Site management plan
  develop a site management plan
  phase work
Design briefs
  prepare design briefs for each area.

Whenever possible the designer should be part of the site planning team. It is only then that it is possible to ensure that the design develops from a full understanding of all the factors considered in drawing up a site plan.

On small schemes it is often the designer who is asked by the developer to draw up the site plan. In such cases the site designer is responsible for making contact with people who have the necessary expertise to advise on the problems posed by the site.

Those who will be responsible for managing the site in the long term should also be part of the site planning team. The site plan and site design must either be worked out within the constraints of the maintenance regimes that can be operated, or the site managers have to be aware how their maintenance procedures must change. Whenever possible the site managers should work closely with the site designers.

Before proceeding to deal with these stages in more detail it is necessary to set the scene by looking at what could be termed some of the philosophical principles behind site planning. This is not the place to go into such a subject in any depth and other books are readily available, dealing with the development of the ideas behind land-use planning (Cullingworth, 1972). However, it is important for everybody involved in site planning to understand the principles and assumptions that are likely to be behind the development of a site plan proposal. These are summarized in Chapter 2.

To summarize, site planning is based on the assumption that there is an interaction between the social needs of users (space required for different users, as well as their physical comfort and psychological well-being) and the physical and natural environmental characteristics of each site (slope, aspect, sunshine, soil, vegetation and fauna).

However, it has to be acknowledged by all involved in site planning that knowledge about human behaviour, about the land, as well as the interactions of all the different facets of nature, is far from complete. Therefore, much decision-taking about site planning has to be done on the basis of assumptions and not scientific fact. Site planners must recognize the limitations of the information that they use and state which of their decisions are based on verifiable facts and which are based on assumptions and best guesses. It is only then that the public, or those elected to make decisions for the public, can decide whether they consider these an acceptable basis for making decisions about a particular site.

References

Beer, A.R. and Booth, P. (1983) Development control and design quality, Parts one and two, *Town Planning Review*, **54**, 3 and 4.
Cullingworth, J.B. (1972) *Town and Country Planning in Britain*, revised 4th edn, Allen and Unwin, London.

2 Environmental planning related to site planning

This chapter will:

1. outline some of the fundamental principles on which the need for site planning is based;
2. give some guidance on the historical development of ideas about site planning;
3. list some of the major concepts which can influence decision-making about the physical, natural and social environmental factors related to site planning;
4. indicate some of the work that needs to be done before the detailed site planning process is initiated in order to identify the key issues.

Fundamental principles

Four fundamental principles can be identified which establish the need for environmental planning for site development.

CONSERVING AN ENVIRONMENT CAPABLE OF SUPPORTING HUMAN LIFE

This is a basic requirement for all land-use planning. The need for food, clean water, clean air and shelter is fundamental to human survival. In operating as site planners we are rarely likely to be concerned with such issues, since they have to be sorted out at the strategic planning level if they are to be dealt with effectively. However, there are some basic considerations arising from these fundamental human requirements, which can and do have an impact at the site planning level.

The first stems from the need to grow food. This develops into a basic land-use planning assumption that, wherever possible, high-grade agricultural land should be retained as a natural resource of the highest long-term value to society. Even when present demand for food does not necessitate its retention this remains a basic assumption, as we cannot predict what the future can hold in relation to food supplies and population growth.

The second stems from the need for clean, uncontaminated water. This means that water supplies everywhere should be protected as a scarce resource vital to human life.

The third stems from the need for clean air if people are not to have high levels of ill health. This means that not only must we control emissions of contaminants, but we must also use any mechanisms available for naturally reducing air pollution and cleaning the air, such as dense vegetation.

The fourth stems from the need to build shelter – homes for people – which, as the human population grows, means that we have to attempt to house everybody in environments which will support their way of life. In the modern world such measures are inevitably linked to the need to provide economic and social support for those being housed and, therefore, imply a land-use as well as social and economic planning mechanism, to ensure that decisions can be taken on the best way to meet peoples' needs.

BASIC PHYSICAL REQUIREMENTS

Fertile soils

The first consideration can lead the site planners, working on large sites where the development densities proposed by the strategic and local planning system permit, to suggest building on the less fertile parts of a site, keeping the best land open to allow for the future possibility of cropping the land for food.

Site planners, particularly those operating in the fast expanding cities of the developing countries, might find Michael Hough's analysis of this issue useful (Hough, 1983) . He deals among other factors with how, even in the densest of modern cities, it would be possible and would make social, economic and environmental sense to keep some land for growing food. Such areas of land within the city would improve the whole quality of city life – its air , its water as well as its social qualities.

In the western world our planning processes tend to assume that no food is grown in cities, but this is a distorted picture, just as it would be in the cities of the developing world. For instance, a look at any British city shows that food, albeit in small quantities, is grown within the cities in gardens and allotments, with the capacity to grow substantially more if it were ever necessary. This illustrates how the development of land and its declaration as urban land does not necessarily rule out its use for growing food, provided the whole surface is not sealed off by structures.

Site planners recognize that most soils take centuries to develop the characteristics that make them fertile. Therefore, they classify good-quality soil as a scarce resource and one to be conserved with the utmost care wherever possible. Even on the smallest sites they will be involved in proposing soil conservation measures and on larger sites will also be involved in developing measures to limit the soil erosion problems so often associated with development schemes.

Clean water
The site planner must check local underground as well as surface water supplies, to ensure that any effluent produced on the site or chemical applied, or stored on the site, will not contaminate the surface water or the underground water.

The natural resources of the soil and water must be safeguarded for the benefit of present and future generations. The capacity of the land to produce renewable resources of food and water should be maintained and a reduction in capacity should only be accepted in exceptional circumstances when alternative supplies can be assured.

Clean air
There are many factors influencing air quality, not least emissions from factories, cars, heating and cooling systems. The air mass is perpetually moving and this to some extent acts as a cleaning mechanism, but local climatic patterns linked to local landforms can make this mechanism less or more effective. The site planner has to understand these factors and be able to predict where problems might occur and take measures to ensure the free flow of air through a site. Vegetation too can help to clean the air. At a time when air pollution seems to be once more on the increase, it could be that site planning has a role to play in ensuring no further deterioration.

Shelter
There are few areas of the world where man can survive without shelter from the elements and nature. The construction of shelters in the form of homes is a major concern of site planning and the issues related to this are outlined in the following paragraphs.

HUMAN WELL-BEING

Human well-being is a primary concern of all land-use planning. Our concern for the quality of the environment and the preservation or conservation of nature stems from that. Most humans are only concerned about that part of the environment with which they are most familiar, because it is that environment which has an immediate impact on their lives and supports their daily activities. It is, therefore, the planner's role to think more widely about how environments can be maintained or created which ensure human well-being, and to do so within the constraints of the local environmental, economic and social characteristics.

Planners need to translate the concerns of the individual for their immediate habitat into strategies and policies to guide the planning process. These have an impact on decisions made about individual sites. All sites are developed within the context of a wider area and the implications of the strategies and policies developed for that wider area have to be worked out by the site planner for each site. The site planner has to take national, regional and local policies into account when working on the detailed development of an area of land; the site planner cannot operate satisfactorily in isolation.

Almost every part of the land is now somebody's habitat and used by people for something, even if only very occasionally. Therefore, the need for strategic, local and site planning arises everywhere. For each site, we have to work out how we can ensure the maintenance or enhancement of environmental quality within this wider land-use planning framework.

CULTURAL DIVERSITY

Cultural diversity should be maintained while aiming to provide people with the environments that support their way of life.

People from different cultures have differing ideas about what constitutes a satisfactory environment. However, it has been shown by behavioural psychologists and others studying the residential environment in western cities (Cooper Marcus and Sarkissian, 1985) that it is probably a cross-cultural phenomenon of the modern city for people to care about and want to feel satisfied with and proud of the quality of their immediate environment. Recent studies of cities in developing countries have shown similar concerns about modern high-density housing schemes to those in the developed countries (Al Noori, 1988). However, because of economic pressures, as yet only the more affluent in these rapidly growing cities have the resources to live in an environment which they think adequately supports their way of life. The hardships suffered by the poor in such cities, with many struggling just to survive, mean that the majority have concerns other than the qualities of their environment uppermost in their minds.

In fast growing cities, it is again the planner's role to be concerned with the environment and to be aware of the long-term costs to society of not caring for it. Throughout history poor social conditions have gone hand in hand with a lack of care for the environment. The Victorian industrial city in Britain, often with appalling living conditions, was associated with a very degraded environment and the high death rates experienced in those cities were a prime example of what can happen if rapid urban growth goes unchecked (Briggs, 1963; Hoskins,

1955). It was only when the conditions in such cities deteriorated so that the more affluent feared for their health and lives (Hoskins, 1955), that the government recognized the need for intervention and the need to have some control over the profit-making activities of the developer. In Britain the Public Health Acts of 1848 and 1872 were the first national attempts to control the environmental conditions of the industrial city and from that time a series of legislative enactments have led directly to the present planning and development control system in Britain (Cullingworth, 1972).

The British planning system has as its basis the assumption that society, through the agencies of its local and national government, has a right to ensure that any development meets certain minimum environmental standards. It also assumes that society has a right to ask a developer to produce an environment fit to support the activities of those who will use an area of land. The amount of restriction on profit-making experienced by the developer changes from time to time, depending on political whim, but the basic right of everybody affected to have a say in the development process remains in theory the ultimate check on environmental quality. The British process has not always worked and even in recent decades some new housing environments have been constructed which have alienated the users. In some cases this alienation has been to such an extent that the housing areas have rapidly become almost uninhabitable. Other factors than the built environment determine whether people accept a particular environment or reject it, but the environment itself does play a part in determining the level of satisfaction they experience (Cooper Marcus and Sarkissian, 1985).

How people define the quality of their immediate environment must be expected to differ and to change with time and economic and social circumstances. Part of the site planner's task is, therefore, to establish what is required to satisfy the people who will live on or use the site. The site planner recognizes that satisfaction will be judged basically by the extent to which the environment supports and does not cause undue difficulties for the local people's or other users' way of life. The site planner has the difficult problem that the site itself can influence people's expectations and, therefore, help on how people might react in new environments is often only available by studying similar sites elsewhere.

A detailed understanding of how people react to environments is needed by site planners if they are to avoid causing unnecessary costs to society by unintentionally producing environments that alienate people. Cooper Marcus and Sarkissian (1985) have gathered useful examples of the problems and the costs to society that can arise if developments are not perceived as satisfactory environments by the users. Their examples are from western experience, but have lessons for all societies where cities are presently undergoing expansion.

The diverse human habitat

It is a useful concept for site planners to think of man's environment as the human habitat. However, unlike that of many animals, our habitat can have a wide range of differing characteristics and still be found acceptable.

As site planners we may wish for a clear picture of what constitutes a satisfactory human habitat, so that we can attempt to reproduce it on the sites. However, we have to recognize that it is the very diversity of human habitats which contributes so much to the quality of human experience and so allow for that diversity in our plans. It is the delight that comes from experiencing the diversity of place and people that we find so rewarding; this is at least part of the reason for the present-day popularity of tourism. As site planners we must attempt to find the means to conserve the diversity of experience and enhance it where it has been obliterated by unsympathetic planning decisions, through sensitive site layout and design.

The very diversity of what humans perceive as satisfactory settings for daily life makes developing ideas about what might constitute good site planning difficult. An essential ingredient must be to allow for cultural and social diversity, perpetuating and not obliterating the diversity of human life patterns.

THE EARTH'S NON-RENEWABLE RESOURCES

The earth's non-renewable resources must only be exploited with great care. Non-renewable resources are the soils and minerals and certain specific habitats. Soils have to be conserved as the medium for growing food; minerals, because once extracted they are gone and habitats because once lost they cannot always be recreated. Habitats, such as those found in tropical rain forests and presently under threat of felling in many countries in which they occur, are impossible to recreate because of their complexity and because once an area is cleared, the soil rapidly changes so that the same range of plants and associated animal life cannot be re-established. It is not just habitats which are lost; individual plants and animals and, even human ways of life can be eradicated by unthinking land-use or land management techniques. The relatively recent rediscovery by 'modern, scientific man' of the irreplaceable worth of many tropical plants as a source of medicinal drugs, as well as the more important realization of the role of those forests in the world's climatic system should have made the preservation of this a social and economic imperative; yet the exploitation of this resource for very short-term economic gain and political expediency continues virtually unchecked.

Of the non-renewable resources, some can be defined as scarce and others abundant. The scarce resources in particular need to be identified so that they can be conserved for future use. Such resources should only be exploited with great care and only after full assessment of the long-term impact of using the resource has been attempted – albeit that such assessment is restricted by the limitations of present scientific knowledge. It is not the site planner's role to become involved in such issues, which must be decided at a strategic planning level. However, it can be the site planner's role to identify any scarce resources on a particular site and work to meet the strategic planning objectives, by maintaining the possibility of access to the resource if it is mineral, and conserving it if it is a living resource. It can also be the site planner's role, when the resource is to be exploited, to indicate how this could occur with minimal damage to the environment.

It is a basic assumption of site planning that non-renewable resources must be used only with great care, and then only when a full assessment of the environmental impacts of their use has been attempted.

All the above concerns are beyond the role of the site planner to solve, but they have to be recognized as part of the basis from which the work of the site planner has developed. Even in the present complex world where food grown in one area supports people living in another, we have to recognize the importance of preserving land capable of high yields of crops. We have to understand that we damage a very scarce natural resource whenever we develop such land. Land, once built over, cannot be returned to high-quality agricultural land for many centuries and has to be accepted as a lost natural resource.

The evolution of site planning

Site planning has evolved as a process to guide the development of land in relation to natural resources and human requirements.

Over the past 150 years, landscape architects and planners have gradually developed a systematic approach to site planning. Landscape architects in particular have been concerned to develop ideas on how to integrate peoples' needs for certain forms and types of development with the existing natural environment and the desire to conserve things natural. As part of coping with people's needs, landscape architects have seen it as vital to conserve and enhance the visual attributes of the environment and to some this has seemed the main point of their site planning role. However, the good landscape architect is as much concerned with the totality of the human experience in relation to the environment and the conservation of nature as with things visual. As Nan Fairbrother (1970) one of the most influential writers about the quality of the environment and the role of the landscape architect, put it:

LANDSCAPE = NATURAL HABITAT + MAN

LANDSCAPE AS MAN'S HABITAT

Before proceeding further to investigate the development of the site planning process by the landscape profession in particular, it is necessary to understand the difference between what the landscape profession understand by the word 'landscape' and the commonly held view of the public, as well as many other professions.

Outside the landscape profession the word 'landscape' tends to be used only for things visual and then mainly to do with vegetation, specific designed spaces and gardens in towns and country estates, or to describe the total impression of a rural view. In contrast, landscape architects do not only think of the medium with which they work – the landscape – as that which is seen; more important, they think of it as that in which we all live – the totality of our environment. Indeed, in some contexts they take it as almost synonymous with the word environment. It is in this latter broad sense that the word will be used here as its use explains the landscape architect's attempt to develop an all-encompassing approach to site planning.

Frederick Law Olmstead coined the term 'landscape architect' in 1858. From that time he began to define the role of the landscape profession and by the end of the nineteenth century landscape architects were involved in city and site planning throughout the USA (Fabos *et al.*, 1968). His perception of the role of the landscape architect was of a profession concerned for the quality of the environment and able to plan and design the detail of city and countryside developments.

The American Society of Landscape Architects was founded in 1899 and the first course was established at Harvard in 1901. The town planning profession in the USA emerged out of landscape architecture in 1907 and soon after this split, landscape architects went through a period of being less involved in planning and more active in the detailed design of parks, estates and gardens. It was only later, in the second half of the twentieth century, after re-examination of the effectiveness of the town and regional planning system in relation to natural and physical environmental factors by landscape architects such as McHarg, that landscape architects came back to the realization that they had a vital part to play in the planning process if they were to design effectively on individual sites. It was recognized that decisions made at the planning stage without due regard to the physical and natural environment could run counter to the needs of good site planning and design. McHarg showed how landscape architects could make a special contribution to the planning process by interpreting such matters. McHarg (1968), Simmonds (1978), Fabos (1985) and others from the landscape profession emphasized that it had to develop an expertise in interpreting the way in which the physical and natural environment should influence overall regional and town planning, as well as site planning.

The landscape profession in Britain started in the 1920s and 1930s, through an involvement in site planning and detailed design. Only since the 1940s has it become more involved in larger-scale planning. The first time that British landscape architects made a real impact at the larger-scale was through the landscape plans which they produced for the new towns. Since then their role in determining the detailed form and layout of many of the new towns has been crucial (Turner, 1987). Landscape architects are now employed in many local authority planning departments, working alongside planners and developing strategies and plans for counties and cities, as well as working in their more conventional role of site designers.

FREDERICK LAW OLMSTEAD

The role of Frederick Law Olmstead in defining the work of the landscape profession was crucial to its development. Olmstead visited England in 1850 and was impressed with the planning and construction of natural-looking parks in the rapidly growing industrial cities (in particular the large town park being made at that time in Birkenhead fascinated him). As a result of this experience he began to develop his ideas; first about the place of naturalistic landscapes in cities and then about city planning in general. This, together with his growing awareness of social conditions in the rapidly expanding industrial areas in the USA, was to form the foundation for his ideas and writings about landscape architecture and city planning. He was a farmer by initial training, but his writings show an acute awareness of the link between culture and economics, between politics and social conditions, and between all those aspects and the environment in which people live.

Olmstead's social convictions led him to believe that city life could be improved if more care was taken of the environment by developers and if proper recreational facilities could be provided for the mass of people in the form of open spaces.

Olmstead wanted urban developers and city authorities to understand that they could create better environments for people's daily life if, instead of obliterating nature as the towns grew, they respected it and tried to integrate it into the urban fabric. He also wanted them to understand that they could improve the older parts of the cities by making parks and squares and planting trees. Together with Charles Elliot he produced the plan for a park system in Boston, showing how his ideas worked in practice.

He was also noted for the development of the concept of nature conservation as a concern of government. He took the lead in initiating the conservation of Yosemite Valley, California, in 1865 and as a result of his efforts the land was set aside for the public to enjoy in its natural state.

THE BASIC CONCEPTS SUMMARIZED

The basic concepts which influence site planning decisions* are summarized below.

Physical environment
1. Rare and unique geological and geomorphological features should be preserved.
2. Surface features such as rock faces, steep slopes and screes, which result from geological or geomorphological processes, should be incorporated wherever possible into the planned development of a site to add to its special sense of place.

Flora and Fauna
1. Rare and unique plants, plant communities and habitats for animals and other wildlife should be conserved, as should any areas that appear to be an original natural habitat unaltered by man.
2. Natural and semi-natural plant groupings which act as habitats for wildlife should be conserved wherever possible and disturbed as little as possible. Variety of local habitats should be maintained where it exists and introduced where possible and appropriate.
3. Where plants and wildlife which were native to an area have disappeared, they should be re-introduced, if possible by creating naturalistic plant communities which eventually form suitable habitats for locally native wildlife.

Soils
1. Very fertile soils should be conserved for future use.
2. Fertile soil should be used with care and where damage from development is inevitable, measures should be taken to store topsoil safely for use in the near future.

Water
1. Clean surface and underground water resources should be protected from any damage caused by development.
2. Efforts should be made to purify any surface water and to eliminate contamination of underground supplies.
3. Any foul water produced on a site should be properly cleaned before returning it to the natural environment. This includes water contaminated by flowing over the hard surfaces of a developed site.
4. Ground-water levels should only be altered up or down when there is a full understanding of the repercussions for wildlife and plants.

---

* The reader is also referred to the Nature Conservancy Council's statements on the principles for nature conservation in towns and cities.

5. Hydroseres of both still water and running water should be recognized for the unique habitats they create, and preserved and maintained accordingly. Damage from flash flooding or unnecessary tidying of banks should be avoided.

Climate and air quality

1. The link between site features and local climatic characteristics should be utilized to maximize human comfort outdoors.
2. The site features and local climatic characteristics should be exploited to minimize energy consumption in buildings during extremes of cold and heat.
3. New sources of air pollution should be avoided.
4. Existing sources of air pollution should be removed and where this is not possible, measures introduced to reduce the worst effects.

Human safety

1. Areas hazardous for human occupation should be excluded from consideration for development if they cannot be made safe without irreparable damage to the environment.
2. Areas liable to be made hazardous by the action of future users should also be excluded from development, unless measures can be introduced and applied to keep environmental damage to a minimum.
3. As well as applying the above concepts, to make the best use of the natural and physical environmental resources, the site planner aims to maintain and create environments which support and enhance the quality of human life through providing a range of appropriate experiences.

Diversity of human experience and the human habitat

1. Where new land-uses are introduced into an area of land, a study of the activities that people might wish to undertake should form the basis of developing ideas on the appropriate environmental settings. Whenever possible, the existing environmental features of the site should be utilized to provide suitable settings for activities.
2. Unique historic areas and features should be conserved, as they reflect the way in which the human race has developed and changed its attitudes and practices.
3. Areas and features of historic interest should be incorporated into site plans to add to the special sense of place. Where necessary site interpretation schemes should be developed so that people can understand the significance of the features.
4. Landmarks should be conserved for the role that they play in adding to the special sense of a place.
5. New landmarks should be developed to help people to identify

places and where they are in a space or sequence of spaces. Other unique and rare visual resources should be conserved: natural views, pleasing groupings of objects in the landscape or specifically designed landscapes.

6. The best features of the local landscape character should be reflected where possible and appropriate in the development of the site.
7. Where there is no characteristic local landscape worthy of reflecting in the new landscape, the landscapes of an even wider area should be examined in an attempt to gather ideas on an locally appropriate style to adopt for landscape enhancement.

PROJECT INITIATION

Identifying key issues

Figure 1.1 indicated the stages of the site planning process. The first two were dealt with as part of Chapter 1. Here we deal with the identification of the key issues, the examination of alternative sites and the first contacts with the local planning authority or others in charge of making land-use planning decisions.

EXAMINATION OF ALTERNATIVE SITES

Once they have been appointed to the site planning team by the client, the technical members have a responsibility to carry out a rapid check of the key issues, the problems likely to be posed by the development of a particular place for a use envisaged by the client.

The first essential is to establish what the problem is and if any key decisions have already been taken. The site planning process is always best begun when no key decisions have yet been taken regarding a site, the development programme or the market, although all too often that is not the case and the possibilities are constrained by irreversible decisions. In most cases clients have already fixed upon a site and it is impossible to get them to change this for financial or ownership reasons.

It is at this key issues stage that the site planner or the planning team establish the initial brief. This will later be developed into a more detailed site planning brief as more is learnt about the site and its users, then further expanded by the site planning process into a detailed designer's and site manager's brief.

THE INITIAL BRIEF

Once the degree of flexibility of the project has been established, the initial brief has to be developed so that it states concisely what the developer wants to do and the degree of latitude about where and when it can happen. It is often difficult to define the problem in these early stages. If possible, information is needed on:

1. what the developer wants to do;
2. who will use the development that is to be produced;
3. what they will use it for;
4. when they need to be able to use it;
5. how much the client is willing to spend on the development;
6. what profit the client expects;
7. what are the client and/or future users expected to contribute in terms of maintenance activities.

As each problem is different, the questions that will need to be asked to develop the initial brief cannot be defined fully here. It is part of the expertise of the site planner that comes with experience, to know the questions to ask. The above are just a starting point.

As the site planner begins to develop the brief, it may be found that the client's ideas about what should happen are at odds with the site planner's knowledge of what has been possible on similar sites elsewhere, where the users have behaved in a different manner from that expected by the client. This is where the development of the site brief becomes a circular process, with the client involved as final arbiter and the site planner involved as the professional giving advice on how the brief could be improved. The client is the person or organization whose firmly held opinions will need to be altered by convincing arguments by the site planner. It is the site planner's responsibility to ensure that any scheme will be properly organized and financed and that a site large enough for the proposed development is available. If the client is unwilling to commit sufficient resources, then there is no point in producing a site plan. The professional site planner has to be sure it is ethical to proceed.

CHOICE OF SITE

Once the initial brief has been set down, the next step is to move some way toward developing it in relation to a particular site. Ideally, at this stage, several sites should be inspected.

Using both the definition of what the client wants to do and a list of basic concepts, the site planner should check each possible site. The aim is to find the site that best suits the client's requirements within the limitations of the basic concepts of site planning. It is, however, rare for clients to involve professional site planners at a sufficiently early stage for them to be instrumental in assessing alternative sites. This is a pity, as one of the main functions of site planning, which allows decisions to be taken within the constraints of the local environmental factors, is often neglected in the initial decision-making by the client. This can lead to unnecessary damage to the environment, unnecessary costs to society of putting right such damage and often unnecessary additional costs for the client, who may have chosen a site which is not the cheapest to develop.

Whether there are several sites to be considered, or one has already been fixed, it is vital that the site planner visits the area of land and becomes familiar with it. This can only be carried out satisfactorily by walking over the land and experiencing it as a place. Good site planning cannot be done by anyone who does not have a clear picture in their mind of the site and its surroundings. It is this first site visit which helps the experienced site planner to develop ideas about the short cuts that can be taken through the site planning process. As the experienced site planner walks a site, getting to know its features and the lie of the land, it is usual also to be thinking fairly systematically about the environmental issues and what the land tells us about how best to develop it. The concerns are similar to those outlined in the basic concept list set out in this chapter, but modified by any knowledge of the special local situation.

MEETING THE LOCAL PLANNERS

Site planning almost never takes place in a vacuum. Either something is happening on the adjacent land, which has to be taken into account, or the planners have developed special strategies or objectives for the land-use and environment of the area within which the site is situated. In either case the site planner should proceed no further without establishing the requirements of the planning authority or other body controlling the development of land.

BEGINNING THE DETAILED PLANNING EXERCISE

Once the client's brief has been understood, the site visited and the requirements of the land-use planners checked, the main part of the site planning procedure can begin.

The next section indicates the information that needs to be collected about the site.

Al Noori, W. (1988) *The environment outside the dwelling*, Department of Landscape, University of Sheffield, Sheffield.

Hough, M. (1984) *City Form and Natural Process*, Croom Helm, London.

References

Cooper Marcus, C. and Sarkissian, W. (1985) *Housing as if people mattered*, University of California Press, Berkeley.

Briggs, A. (1963) *The Victorian City, Odhams*, London.

Cullingworth, J.B. (1972) *Town and Country Planning in Britain*, revised 4th edition), Allen and Unwin, London.

Fabos, J.G. (1985) *Landuse Planning – from Global to Local Challenge*, Chapman and Hall, London.

Fabos, J.G., Milde, G.T., and Weinmayer, M. (1968) *Frederic Law Olmsead, Founder of Landscape Architecture in America*, University of Massachusetts Press, Amherst.

Fairbrother, N. (1970) *New Lives New Landscapes*, Architectural Press, London.

Hoskins, W.G. (1955) *Making of the English Landscape*, Hodder and Stoughton, London.

McHarg, I. (1968) *Design with Nature Natural*, History Press, New York.

Simonds, J.O. (1978) *Earthscape: a Manual of Environmental Planning*, McGraw Hill, New York.

Turner, T. (1987) *Landscape Planning*, Hutchinson, London.

Part Two

The Site Inventory

This part outlines the main categories of information the site planner has to gather before making any decisions about what should happen on a site. It defines the information that needs to be collected about the existing situation, about the physical and natural environment and about the people who live on and near the site at present. This part gives guidance on the main ways in which the information might influence decisions about how to plan an area of land, as well as on the level of detail required about each item. It is linked to Steps 1–8 set out in Part Five. Those steps form a check-list of the information that the site planner should collect and assess.

Rarely will the site planner need to gather all the data listed here in the same level of detail, as each project and site is different. Part of the skills which site planners learn through practising site planning techniques is to recognize early on in a project where the main effort should be concentrated and which factors are unlikely to have a major impact on the particular site under consideration. In some countries the local planning system is based on such a detailed analysis of the local situation that reference to the local planners will provide sufficient information on which to base a site plan; in others the site planner will have to collect almost all the information. It is impossible, therefore, to predict how long it will take to make a site inventory for a particular site.

Each area of land is different, as is each proposed use, so each inventory will be different in its content and emphasis. It is, however, important to make a systematic check of all the factors before drawing up a site plan; it is only whether the information obtained is relevant to a particular situation which is in question.

Each item on the physical and natural environment check-list (see Part Five) needs to be considered for relevance in relation to each site, if only very briefly when it appears to have no bearing on the problem of planning a particular site. After the information on the physical and natural environment has been gathered, the needs of the present users living on and near the site have to be identified, keeping in mind the proposed future use of the site. It is these two operations which create the data base – the site inventory.

All the chapters in Part Two deal with the site inventory. The aim of this information gathering is to ensure that those involved in site planning understand how the present landscape or townscape has developed, the way in which the intrinsic physical characteristics of the area determine its natural environmental characteristics and the way in which the land has been and could be used.

An introduction to 3
making a site inventory

This chapter gives some basic information for beginners about the limitations of data gathering. Chapter 4 outlines the information to be gathered about the physical environment. Chapter 5 comprises the information about the natural (the living) environment and Chapter 6 covers aspects of the social environment – that is people's present use of the site and the adjacent land and how this affects the landscape.

Solving local land-use planning problems

Part One dealt in general terms with the purpose and scope of site planning, but to summarize for those who have started reading here at the 'how to make a site inventory' part, it is a working procedure which has been developed by Landscape Architects, Planners and Architects to tackle the problems associated with planning how a site should be laid out and designed. Site planning is a straightforward approach to land-use planning problems. It can be used for very small or very large areas of land – anywhere that it is proposed to alter the land use by building or making something new, or renovating something that exists. It links the need to conserve and enhance environmental qualities with the need for people to develop areas of land to meet their land-use requirements.

Essentially site planning is about getting the right thing in the right place and so being able to draw up detailed briefs to guide the designer and site manager; it is the first stage of the site design process and almost always leads to a site being changed in some way. The designer's brief and the land management brief are the end product of the site planning process and should be seen as part of the site plan. These briefs set the objectives for the designer for each part of the site and ensure that the whole site is designed and managed to achieve common environmental objectives within the constraints of the site and available resources.

Site planning almost always works best when the detailed design work is done by a person or group who have been involved in the production of the site plan. However, on larger sites the site planning and design function are often separated. Because of this separation, site design and site management often happen independently to the detriment of the development process. This is one of the reasons that clear site plans are needed, so that the design details are developed within the constraints set by the proposed long-term management of the site.

THE BEST METHOD OF LEARNING THE PROCESS

The best way to learn about site planning is to be involved in doing a project. Chapters 4, 5 and 6 present the background to making a data base for such a project and Part Five lists the information to be gathered by the site planner. The system illustrated in Part Five will work, whether the project is done independently for the individual's own benefit, or as part of a course requirement. Using it will ensure that any decisions taken about how to plan or design a site are based on a full understanding of the local environment and its inhabitants and not on arbitrary assumptions, as has too often been the case.

By carrying out a real project, those involved will learn not just the importance of gathering information, but the importance of assessing the meaning of that information for proposed land use and land management changes.

As each site is different, it will not always be appropriate or necessary to carry out the full survey procedure described here. However, it is important when using this book for the first time to read through and understand the total procedure, even if initially large parts of the process do not seem relevant to the particular problem on which work is being done.

Information gathering

The information that needs to be gathered about a site relates both to the area within the site boundary and to the area of land surrounding it. A site cannot be planned in isolation; unless it is an island it is always part of a larger landscape. Information, therefore, is collected about what is termed the site context area as well as about the site.

THE SITE CONTEXT AREA

Failing to look at any site in relation to the larger landscape of which it is a part, may result in making inappropriate decisions about its future development. Often it will also be found that much of the information that can be gathered from published data relates to an area larger than a project site; that data has to be interpreted in relation to the project area.

A site context boundary of up to 500 m from the edge of the site is suggested for any learning exercise undertaken while using this book. Thereafter, or if a 'real' project is being undertaken, the area to study will differ, depending on the complexity of the problem and its location. Many other factors can influence what should happen on a site and for many real projects it is necessary to look at a much larger area, particularly when major developments are involved.

THE PROJECT AREA

For the remainder of this book the site for which a site plan is to be produced will be termed either the project area or the site.

Anyone using this book to guide them through their first site planning exercise should choose a small example site, otherwise it may be difficult to cope with all the problems and issues that emerge. Unless they are on an architectural studies course, it is suggested that beginners might find it easiest to start on a site with no or few buildings. Perhaps an area of land which could be developed as a public open space might be the best starting point to test out the process.

INTERPRETATION OF DATA

The basic data gathered about a site and its surrounding area is rarely sufficient by itself. The information almost always needs to be interpreted before it can be used to decide what should happen on a site. It is knowing how to interpret it, and which experts to ask for help, which comprises much of the skill of the site planner. The interpretation of the information is the most difficult part of the site planning process and, perhaps because of this, is too often neglected. Beware of the trap of 'survey for survey's sake': if the information that you collect is not or cannot be assessed for its relevance to the site, then it is a waste of time to collect it. Without proper assessment of the survey data a site may neither meet peoples' needs nor be designed to ensure the conservation of natural features. The question should always be 'what does this fact mean in relation to this site and the people who will use this site'?

The first site planning project will soon illustrate that the interpretation of the facts about the physical environment in relation to how people want to use a site, is often difficult. The interpretation of the facts often produces what seem to be conflicting requirements for the future planning, and that in turn means that these conflicting needs have to be sorted out by the site planner before proposing a final site plan. Resolving such conflicts is the essence of site planning.

Inevitably there will be a difference between how definite one can be about some facts as opposed to others. The site planner should always state how any conclusions have been arrived at. Is the conclusion based on factual information or on a subjective assessment?

Factual information

Factual information is that which can be verified by others, either from published sources or by examining the site.

For instance: If the geological information shows that there is running sand under part of the site, then the site planner can be definite in saying that no large buildings can be built there without additional costs for more expensive foundations.

If the hydrological information (that which relates to surface and ground water) shows that an area is regularly subject to flash flooding, then the site planner can say definitely that the main access road should not be located there, unless the agency funding the development of the site can find extra money for flood prevention.

Subjective assessment

Subjective assessment on the other hand is based on the individual's or group's own best judgement. It is perfectly valid to use this sort of assessment to help make decisions, but it is important to explain fully how the interpretation of the basic information was arrived at, so that others can judge for themselves whether they would have come to the same conclusion. It is not possible to carry out the site planning process on the basis of factual information alone – we just do not know enough about nature and man to enable us to do that.

For instance: If the vegetation survey shows trees and shrubs over most of the site, and the site planner has to decide which to fell so that new recreational facilities can be constructed, a subjective decision will have to be made. It is possible to say definitely what the trees and shrubs are, where they are, probably how old they are and in what condition they are, but only a fairly subjective opinion on the relative ecological value of the mix of plants on each area of the site in relation to its ability to support wildlife can be given.

Or if the survey shows that good views are available in two directions from the site, the site planner has to decide which is the more attractive if the proposed development can only allow the view in one direction to remain open. Again a subjective judgement of the quality of the view has to be made before making your recommendation.

Carrying out the project work

You should read the whole of Part Two before completing the programme of survey work described in Part Five, beginning with Step 1. Remember that every site is different, so it will be up to you to decide which information is relevant to collect for the particular project with which you are presently involved.

The following chapters aim to show that decisions about future developments on any area of land should be based on a thorough assessment of the environmental problems and potential of a site and an assessment of the needs of the people who are likely to use it. It is a process which aims to make decisions about site layout understandable to the layman, to de-mystify the planning and design process by showing it is based on a logical sequence of decisions. At its best it should be a process which enables the client and the public to become fully involved in what should happen on a site.

4 The physical environment

The first stage of the site planning process is to assess the relative importance of the factors that make up the local physical environment. This chapter deals with why it is important to gather information about geology, geomorphology and surface water. It also describes the information that should be gathered about landform before indicating the type of information that can be usefully gathered about the local climate.

Geology, geomorphology and site planning

The first information that is needed about a site relates to the land surface on which the site is located. It is necessary to understand why the land is the shape it is. It should be established if the site is underlain by any geological structures which might cause difficulties as the site is developed. Details about the shape of the surface and its slopes also need to be recorded, so that it can be worked out where it is likely to be relatively cheap or expensive to place structures.

People are influenced in their use of land by what lies underneath. However, they can also influence what happens under the surface, although only on a very small scale and in localized areas. For instance:

- the building of heavy structures can cause shifting of the layers below the surface;
- the mining of coal and other minerals leaves tunnels and caverns which can collapse causing the surface layers to shift (Coates, 1981);
- the withdrawal of fluid hydrocarbons (for oil and liquid gas production) can cause surface areas to subside (Gregory and Walling, 1981);
- the withdrawal of water from aquifers (the underground water reservoirs) has been shown to cause subsidence at the surface (Coates,1981);
- the clearing of steep slopes for building purposes or the building of roads along such slopes of unconsolidated rock can lead to landslips (Coates,1981 and Betz, 1975).

It may be considered that a project site is so small that the geological factors are irrelevant, but it is still important to check.

There are certain indications which a non-expert can use to establish whether the underlying geology is likely to pose the type of problem which influences development. The two main ways in which geology influences the site planning decision making process are through:

1. the bearing capacity limiting what can be built on the site; and
2. the presence of geological features which restrict the options for development because they are associated with varying degrees of hazard to life.

The following list cannot cover all eventualities but does suggest some of the factors limiting site development decisions.

The material which forms the base on which structures are built is sometimes solid rock, sometimes weathered and fragmented rock and sometimes deposited material (windblown, waterborne or of glacial origin). Each material has different implications for site development. The surface is normally a layer of loose material of various origins which is referred to as soil. For the purpose of this site planning text soils are divided simply into topsoil, which is discussed in a later chapter as the medium supporting plant-life, and sub-soil which is considered here along with rock as part of the way that geology can have a direct impact on site planning and development.

To establish whether there are geological problems in relation to a site, it is best to gather preliminary information by working with geological maps and then on site. The information from the published geological maps is unlikely to contain sufficient detail in itself. If there are any features which cause doubt as to their impact on the development potential of a site, expert geologists or structural engineers must be consulted.

BEARING CAPACITY

The bearing capacity can be defined as the ability of the surface and sub-surface materials to carry the weight of structures. The reason that the information about bearing capacity needs to be assessed so carefully is that the weight of buildings can produce settlement, which in time damages those buildings. When the structures are improperly engineered in relation to the substrates, this can cause costly problems for the owners of the buildings and other structures.* Buildings, dams and roadways have all been known to produce subsidence in the underlying materials and this is almost always followed by structural damage (Coates, 1981). At the extreme, the introduction of large engineering structures such as reservoirs in areas of unsuitable geology, has been known to have catastrophic results.

Building in loosely consolidated materials can cause problems too, unless proper precautions are taken by rafting. In some towns, where developers have persisted in building on sand without proper foundations, inevitably subsidence has occurred. The present Building Regulations in Britain were developed in part to ensure that such problems were overcome by the developer putting in appropriate foundations.

In any area which has been subject to glaciation, unexpected problems can be found beneath the surface soils. These are mainly due to the random deposition of boulders of a variety of sizes, as well as pockets of sand and other materials. Wherever such conditions occur, the site planner must assess the additional costs of preparing the site for development. For instance, the need to remove subsoil containing many large boulders can greatly increase development costs. Sometimes the boulders can be easily shifted by earth-moving equipment, but sometimes they are more difficult and costly to move and depending on the type of project their presence might dictate the form of the development. Sand is always a problem but it too can be overcome, for instance by pile driving into lower, more stable layers, although this adds to site development costs.

In some cases bearing capacity is not dictated by the surface layers but is related to subsidence caused by the possible collapse of underground caverns. Whether caverns are natural or are man made, they can pose problems for buildings on the surface. The problems with subsidence experienced in coal mining areas are the best examples of the difficulties for development posed by this factor.

The presence of solid rock very near the surface is not always an advantage as it can make the provision of the necessary infrastructure† expensive.

On large development projects, which involve erecting structures, civil engineers are normally employed to assess bearing capacity. For such schemes material extracted from boreholes or pits has to be inspected by experts. It is important that the data about the materials which underlie

---

* The Building Regulations as applied by the local planning authority in Britain give strict guidance on foundations. The standards relate amongst other things to the materials being built on.

† The word 'infrastructure' is used here to define the support system needed by any development – the sewerage, the energy supply pipelines and the other underground and overhead wires, the roads and footpaths, the parking areas and anything else needed to allow the main function of the site to run smoothly.

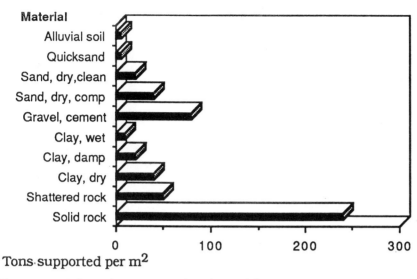

Tons·supported per m^2

Figure 4.1   Relative bearing capacity of materials.

the site is gathered systematically, so the necessary boreholes are normally made on a regular grid.

On small development projects, in particular schemes which involve few or small scale buildings, or on large projects involving no structures, it is rare for expert geologists or civil engineers to be employed. Instead the person charged with the site planning study has to decide whether detailed surveys are necessary. It is the sites with low density use, but including some structures, where the most benefit can be gained from a full survey of the ground conditions. Such a survey will establish where it is most economical to build and, therefore, can save the client money. If a site is to be developed for low density recreation, with no require-ment for buildings, then it is normally unnecessary to do more than record surface conditions so that the most economical positions to build roadways and other tracks can be identified.

Before the meaning of the observations on geology and subsoil made by the experts can be assessed, the clearest possible information on the type and scale of structures that might be placed on the site has to be obtained from the client by the site planning team. Only then can struc-tural engineers decide whether there is an adequate bearing capacity for the size and type of structure proposed.

Figures 4.1* and 4.2 give some guidance on the relative bearing capacity of different materials. If large or heavy structures are involved,

* Figure 4.1 has been developed from information in *Time-saver standards for site planning* by De Chiara and Koppelman (1984). Other useful information on soil bearing capacity, and when piles are needed to support buildings and on the depth of foundations, can be found in that book. The figures cannot be exact and should be taken as a rough guide only.

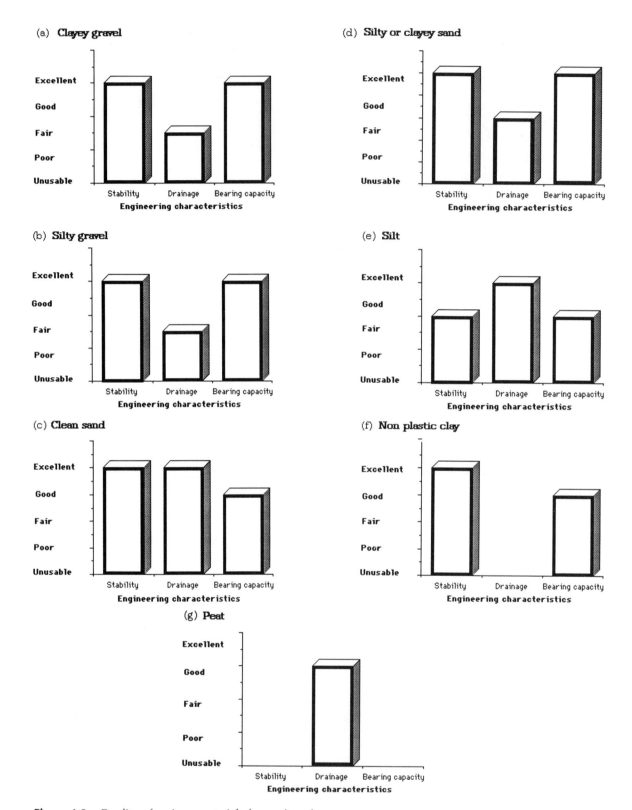

Figure 4.2 Quality of various materials for engineering purposes.

expert advise from engineers and architects is required for an interpretation of site data.

Although factors relating to bearing capacity are the most easily identifiable way in which geology influences site planning, a great variety of other geological considerations can have an impact on the site planning process. Some of these factors are discussed briefly here but to understand the implications fully the site planner needs to take the advice of geologists.

GEOLOGICAL FAULTS

It is very important to establish whether there are geological faults running through the site (Figure 4.3). Faults are lines of weakness caused by previous movements of the earth's crust and always have a potential for further movement. If the geological maps seem to indicate the presence of a geological fault, it is normally advisable to seek geological advice before any building takes place.

Faults are more liable to movement than the area around them and sometimes that movement can cause damage to structures. For this reason, if building is to take place in areas susceptible to earthquakes, special precautions have to be taken to enable the buildings and structures to withstand movement. These will add substantially to site development costs.

OUTCROPS OF ROCK

Outcrops of rock on the site can be seen both as problems and assets, depending on the purpose for which the site is to be developed. If the intention is to develop the full leisure potential of an area of land and

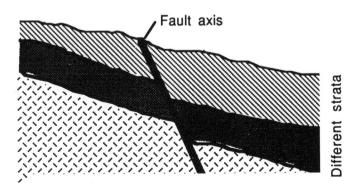

Figure 4.3 Simplified diagram of a geological fault.

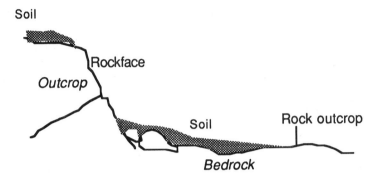

Figure 4.4   Diagram to illustrate rock outcrops.

there are rock faces which can be used for climbing on the site, this could add to its attractiveness for recreation. Another attraction might be if a rock face turns out to contain fossils, for many people enjoy searching for fossils (they should, however, be discouraged from removing fossils from the site). As rockfaces often become habitats for relatively rare plants, it is always important to check what is growing there, as that too can be part of the recreational potential. There is an educational and scientific value attached to sites with exposed rockfaces which needs to be recognized by the site planners.

However, if a project site is to be developed for housing, the presence of a rock face can become a problem because of the safety aspects. Then there is often a tendency to attempt to bury it by dumping against it. This sort of solution, to deal with a site planning problem by hiding it, can be an over-reaction. Careful site planning can often make use of such a feature to the benefit of the development, rather than by obliterating it.

If hard rock occurs on or near the surface of the site, this can also cause problems. The expense of excavating channels into it for underground services can be considerable, as can the expense of levelling it if the site plan does not make allowance for its presence.

AQUIFERS

An aquifer is an underground 'reservoir' of water. The water is not usually held in open ponds of water but in the pores between the individual particles which make up the rock, or in the fissures in the rock. It is the water tapped when drilling artesian wells. It can have been deposited gradually in past millennia or can be water which is still regularly being topped up by percolation from the surface.

Much of the water supply in lowland Britain is extracted from aquifers, so even in a country of heavy rainfall they perform a vital function in relation to water supply. In drier climates they are often the only reliable source of drinking water. Wherever they occur aquifers must be recognized as a scarce and valuable resource to be conserved with care. They are a resource to which long term damage can be done both by over-exploitation and by pollution.

When working on a small site, worrying about distant and unseen aquifers might seem unnecessary, but if the land use is likely to cause any chemical contamination of the land, what happens on a site could adversely affect water quality in any aquifer into which ground water from a site ultimately percolates. Therefore, it will be necessary to take the advice of a geologist wherever ground contamination is likely to be a problem.

Aquifers can be contaminated by apparently minor events. For instance, the oily wash from the areas where cars stand or are serviced can trickle into an aquifer and contaminate it, as can the fertilizers and pesticides used in gardens and open spaces. In the vast areas of the world where cesspits are still the most common means of disposing of waste from homes, there is an even greater risk of ground-water supplies being contaminated from badly engineered or maintained systems.

Although the site planner will always have to take expert advice about the impact of pollution on ground water it is perhaps useful to be aware

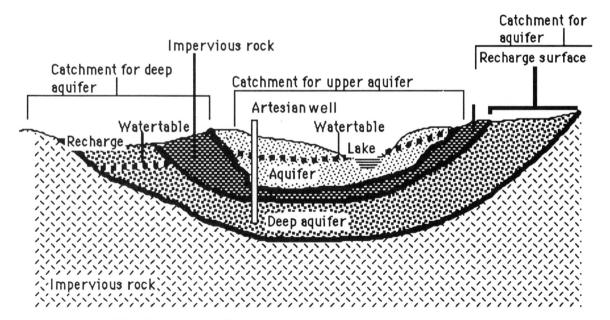

Figure 4.5 Simplified diagram of aquifers.

of some of the issues involved in assessing the extent of the problem. For instance:

The amount of pollution entering an aquifer is related to the type of material through which the water percolates and the distance it has percolated before reaching the aquifer. Some rocks act as better filters than others. Aquifers can be at any depth under the surface to which water percolates and in general the deeper they are the less likely contamination is a problem.

The over-exploitation of aquifers has in some cases led to the pollution of the high-quality drinking water by seawater contamination. This can make the water from even the deep wells unusable and it may take decades before the water is again usable. Other wells have dried up totally, sometimes because the recharge has been cut by building over and otherwise diverting water from the recharge surface. Figure 4.5 illustrates how each aquifer has its own recharge surfaces.

Shallow ground-water storage areas can be fed from the area of land directly above them, whereas deep aquifers can be fed by water from a surface level at some distance. If a project site is immediately underlain by porous rock, the surface water will percolate down into the water table below. That water table may be the top of a surface level water storage area, in which case the water will probably surface somewhere locally in springs, lakes, ponds, streams or shallow wells. Alternatively the porous rocks immediately under a site could be the top end of an inclined strata of rock which ultimately, although not always directly, leads to a deep aquifer. In either case any polluting of the surface will mean that the contaminants eventually reach the water storage systems. The passage of polluting materials through the soil and rocks can in some instances be very slow. For instance the fertilizers that were added to some British farmland since the 1960s are only in the 1980s beginning to contaminate water supplies.

As a general rule every attempt should be made to keep land open over recharge areas and to ensure that no or as few pollutants as possible enter the soil. If it is necessary to locate places for storing waste or disposing of refuse, then the better location is one away from areas of land which act as recharge surfaces for aquifers and also away from land which, although underlain by impervious materials, has a surface flow which finishes up in the recharge surface area. So even if the water from a site does not percolate directly into an aquifer, it is the responsibility of the site planner to find out where it will be disposed of, if it is polluted in any way.

HIGH AND FLUCTUATING WATER TABLE

Gathering information about the water table under a project area is important, as is seeking evidence on the extent to which it normally fluctuates. This is because high and fluctuating water tables can cause problems for development. The latter is a particular problem when associated with heavy clay because of the way in which clay shrinks when wet. It can cause structural damage if foundations are inadequate. High water tables can indicate that the land is liable to flood.

High water tables can easily be identified by digging a hole of up to 2 m deep and seeing if it fills with water. To find out about fluctuating water tables help is needed from soil scientists who can examine subsoil samples for evidence (local people living on or near a site can help to establish if fluctuations are likely to be a problem). Special foundations are needed on waterlogged sites and this can add to the cost of development. See the section on surface water for more detail.

IMPERMEABILITY

If it is found that a site is underlain by an impermeable material such as clay, ironpan or impervious rock, the costs associated with attempting to drain it will have to be incorporated in the financing of the project. Alternatively a site plan is required which allocates appropriate activities to the more easily drained areas and the wetter areas, so avoiding the need to change the site.

Areas of land which have impermeable layers are an advantage if the land is to be used for certain sorts of fill or refuse disposal.

UNCONSOLIDATED MATERIAL

Any areas of sand on a site should be noted as a possible constraint on building or track making. Freely moving sand below the surface creates difficult and, therefore, expensive conditions for constructing foundations for buildings, roadways and paths.

Sometimes the site survey reveals unconsolidated dumped material, as found in a waste disposal site. This too can cause problems for buildings, partly because of the presence of chemical effluent and partly because of the subsidence problems which occur as the material rots, and perhaps more important because of the accumulations of methane gas which can sometimes lead to structural damage through explosions and so in the worst circumstances to direct danger to human life. Old waste tips can also be associated with dangerous chemicals which, through capillary action, can eventually find their way to the surface. This can be a problem, almost no matter how well the surface is sealed by capping the refuse with clay .

Wherever survey work identifies old refuse tips on a site, the client should be informed that expert environmental scientists ought to be employed to assess the danger to human life associated with developing the site. They must also be employed to advise on the measures necessary to make the site safe, if it is to be developed. In cases where the client is unwilling to carry the extra expense involved, the professionals involved would be well advised to withdraw their services.

OLD MINE WORKINGS AND QUARRIES

It is important to establish if the project area, or the area around it, has been worked over or under for mining or quarrying. Are there any old mine shafts, capped or uncapped, on the site?

Through what is known about adjacent sites with similar geology, is there any danger that old shafts could exist and their location have been forgotten? Are there any waste heaps from mining operations on the site and are these likely to contain toxic waste?

Anything that is known about mineral extraction should be recorded. If evidence of mining, extraction, or the deposition of mining waste is found, it is advisable for the site planners to contact the local geologists. The aim is to establish the extent of the problem and the development limitations posed by them.

POTHOLES

If the area is underlain by limestone, the site planner needs to determine if there is any likelihood of potholes being found under the site. In some cases the potholes can be used as a recreation facility, although one that can only be exploited by specialist groups, in others they form a local hazard which restricts the use of the site. Not all limestone is associated with the hazard of potholes but it can be linked with other geological features which develop in a karst* landscape and inhibit certain types of development.

MINERAL RESERVES

The site planner needs to establish if the rocks, gravel deposits or sands underlying the project area are of any economic value. If so, are they likely to be needed in the foreseeable future or are they part of the long-term national reserves? Different countries have different laws with regard to minerals: in some countries all minerals belong to the state, in others only some minerals and in others the owner is the landowner.

---

* Karst landscapes are frequently waterless at surface levels and where the limestone is at the surface in dry conditions they can form deserts of rock.

Ownership may be the key to the likelihood of exploitation and determine the economic value as far as the client is concerned. It is the site planner's job to advise the client to employ experts to assess whether any minerals underlying the project area could be exploited in the future. Information from mining and quarrying experts can also help in assessing the impact that exploitation might have on the proposed use for the site.

Geomorphological factors and the development of a site: some indicators

Geomorphology is the study of the processes that have shaped the earth. The shape of every area of the earth is constantly changing, although the very slow speed of change can make it appear that the processes involved in the change have halted.

GEOMORPHOLOGICAL PROCESSES WHICH INFLUENCE LAND USE

The geomorphological processes which interest site planners are those which have an impact on the land over a relatively short time scale and, in particular, those which might have left the surface unstable and difficult to develop. That is processes such as:

- erosion and deposition along rivers; these processes can result in rivers changing their course and making it ill advised to develop near them, or less spectacularly in the slow removal of the land along parts of the river, while along other parts the silt is slowly deposited;
- erosion of cliffs by the sea which can reduce the area of safely developable land;
- rocks breaking away from mountain sides because of frost action on the joints, which can in some circumstances make it dangerous to build on the mountain sides;
- landslips occurring where surface materials are not yet at a stable angle in relation to the local geological structure, their composition and the angle of slope; areas with a high tendency to slip are unsafe for construction or even recreational use.

The information on most geological maps is very general and not specific enough to be of much use in relation to the geomorphology of individual sites. If there is any indication of erosion or deposition on or near the site the site planner needs to involve someone who has studied the local geomorphology. It is the geomorphological processes operating within and immediately around a site and which could have an impact on a project which concerns the site planner, not a general examination of the processes and theories.

An exact boundary within which to restrict the search for geomorphological data cannot be defined, as each site is different. In many cases it is not necessary to look outside the site itself, but in mountainous areas and in the vicinity of rivers and cliffs it is normally advisable to do so.

EROSION AND DEPOSITION

It is useful for the site planning process if it is known where erosion or deposition by natural processes is taking place or likely to take place. What this information means in terms of the way in which the site could be developed then has to be assessed. This can only be done by determining the relative speed of the erosion process and whether it is likely to have any adverse effects on the site within the likely lifetime of the proposed development. It would be inadvisable for instance to build at the top of a deeply incised valley slope if it were composed of comparatively unconsolidated material and rapidly undercut by water at the foot of the slope. Similarly it would be inadvisable to spend money on building a riverside footpath where a river bank is being eroded actively, or in any location where the river frequently changes its course.

The rate of erosion by a river depends on the flow of the water and the material in suspension as well as the hardness of the material over which the water flows. If the material is loosely consolidated, change in the shape of the landform can happen rapidly (Figure 4.6).

WATER EROSION

Figure 4.7 shows a simplified version of how a change in the material over which a stream flows can have an immediate and rapid impact on the shape of a valley and the rate of erosion associated with a stream and, therefore, the land available for development. (The diagram illustrates a stage in the process of river valley development. In this case it shows what happens if a river erodes through a capping of clay and hits loosely consolidated material.)

Streams where the erosion process is still very active often have V-shapes. In Figure 4.7 a stream, which in the top diagram is illustrated as having the valley cross section of a mature stream, is shown to have worn through an impermeable clay layer which caps sandstone. Once the stream runs over the more easily eroded sandstone, it rapidly wears it away and becomes incised to form a valley with a V-shaped cross

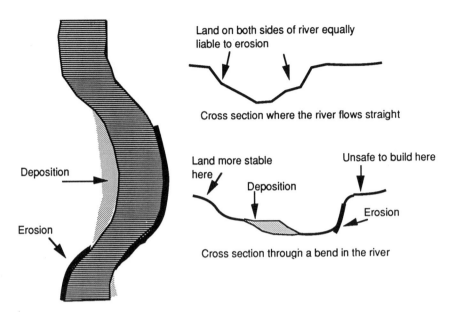

Figure 4.6   Erosion and deposition along a river.

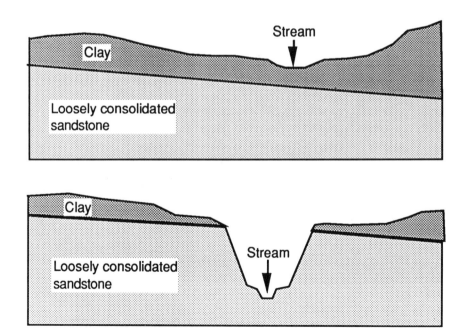

Figure 4.7   Valley cross sections.

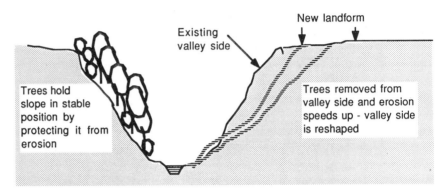

Figure 4.8 An example of how a landslip problem can develop along a V-shaped valley.

section.* For site planners these two different conditions – the 'mature' stream valley and the 'young' valley – pose different problems. With a steep sided V-shaped valley the problems relate mainly to landslip; with the mature valley the problems relate to the erosion caused by the stream as it meanders across the valley floor and to floods.

Running water erodes, carries and deposits material. The rate of erosion along a stream being determined by the material over which it flows, the volume of water and what is transported by the water. In simple terms it can be taken that ultimately all streams are attempting to wear the land down to sea level, taking millions of years. Because of the time scale the process is, therefore, frequently interrupted by climatic change.

Figure 4.8 illustrates how man's actions could accelerate a natural geomorphological process. In the case illustrated trees have been removed from the side of a deeply incised valley, in a location where that valley is running through soft rock and unconsolidated material. The removal of the trees allows the action of rainfall and water wash to erode the valley side faster, so rapidly reducing the area of developable land at the top of the valley slope. It is this sort of incident, where geomorphological processes can be inadvertently accelerated by land management change or land use change, that the site planner has to attempt to identify. It is the site planner's role to ensure that no proposals are made which lead to unnecessary loss of developable land, unnecessary expense in connection with site engineering, or danger to human life.

* This is a very simplified version of the processes involved in valley formation by streams to illustrate the relevance to site planning. Readers needing to understand the processes are advised to refer to any advanced geomorphological text for a detailed explanation of the processes.

Figure 4.9 illustrates another form of erosion, in this case of cliff-faces where resistant strata are interspersed with a material such as shale which erodes easily. In the circumstances illustrated in Figure 4.9a it is unwise to build near the cliff-top; in those shown in Figure 4.9b it is safer provided no other factors are involved.

LANDSLIPS

The diagrams in Figure 4.9 only indicate some of the factors that might account for land-slippage occurring. The site planner needs to be aware that, although many factors can be involved, it is possible for geologists to predict which areas of land might slip (Leighton, 1966). Proper studies should be undertaken when there is any steep land on or near a development site. Geologists base their predictions on the study of a complex series of geological interactions not just the factors illustrated above.

A slope may seem perfectly stable, with a vegetation cover indicating

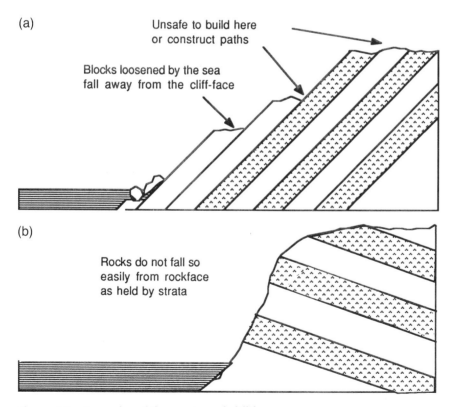

Figure 4.9   Examples of the erosion of cliff faces.

that it has not moved for decades, if not hundreds of years. However, as soon as the vegetation is removed, for instance to allow the building operations to take place, or to add to the area of cropland, the unconsolidated material beneath can suddenly become mobile again. It is no longer bound together by roots and covered by a dense mat of vegetation and so is no longer protected from the effects of water erosion (Figure 4.10).

Wherever unconsolidated material is combined with a slope there is a potential for landslip. When this is combined with high levels of ground water the problem is exacerbated. How dangerous this is depends on various factors, not least the length of the slope. Where the problem is minor, for instance where a short slope of unconsolidated material is held by vegetation, the site planner has the option of producing a site plan which avoids stripping the area of vegetation, or of ensuring that the scheme is costed to allow for the necessary stabilization works. Where the problem is major, for instance where rapid coastal erosion cannot be checked and will bite into the project area eventually, the site planner should inform the client of the inadvisability of carrying out the proposed scheme because of hazard to human life and property.

Figure 4.11 shows an example of how land can slip, in this case because the limestone is underlain by a clay band which becomes wet and allows slippage to occur. Site development practices which add water to the clay layer can trigger such rock-slides.

Site planners must be constantly aware that development projects can accelerate erosion of sites that left alone would be relatively stable. The problems associated with accelerated rates of erosion can cost the developer dearly. For instance, problems can occur when excess water enters the ground because of new patterns in surface drainage associated

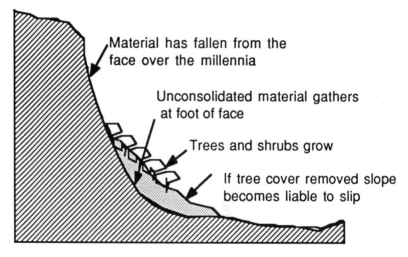

Figure 4.10   Unconsolidated material is particularly liable to slip.

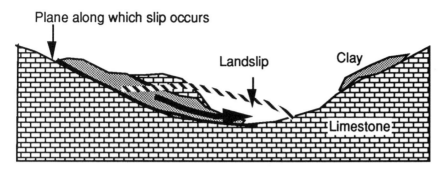

Figure 4.11   An example of a landslip due to the characteristics of the underlying geology.

with development. In some locations this can cause the sub-soil or weathered rock to become unstable.

Excess water can enter the soil because of badly designed storm sewers or even excessive irrigation. The chance of erosion can be reduced by the way in which the site is laid out. For instance, it is possible to plant any areas vulnerable to soil slip, so holding the ground. This uses bio-engineering techniques to reduce an environmental hazard.

The geomorphological processes which are of most interest to site planners are those operating on soils or weak rock. While geomorphologists need to be expert in the weathering processes that result in weathered rock and soils, these are not the concern of site planners. However, geomorphologists are well placed to advise on the likely constraints on development that arise from geomorphological processes and site planners should approach them for assistance.* Slope stability investigations are expensive, but carrying out repair work is more so, and if there is reason to be concerned about local soil conditions as they might affect building, then the client must be informed that additional surveys by experts are required and that additional costs will be involved in developing the site.

Surface water is inextricably linked with geology and geomorphology and developing an understanding of the lie of the land. This too is dealt with separately for the convenience of gathering information for the site planning process.

Surface water and site planning

Water is one of the major determinants of the shape of the land. It erodes, it removes the weathered material from parts of the surface and deposits it elsewhere. Rivers are important in the shaping of many

* For further information on slopes and weathering and their impact on development see Gregory and Walling (1981), Chapter 6 (Bird, E.C.) and Chapter 7 (Selby, M.J.).

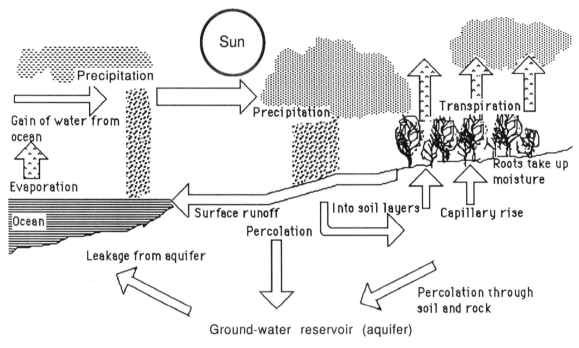

Figure 4.12   A simplified diagram of the hydrological cycle.

landscapes throughout the world, particularly in wetter climates.* The site planner needs to understand something of the processes involved.

The simplified hydrological cycle shown in Figure 4.12 illustrates how water arrives on the land and how it drains back to the sea, a process vital to the survival of most forms of life on the earth. The land where water does not fall in the form of rain or snow, or where no water flows through in rivers is desert. Without water soil does not form and there is no life.

Surface water channels distribute the rain and allow some of the water to return directly to the sea. They are also involved in transporting water to the recharge areas that fill the aquifers. The importance of ground water reserves was indicated in the section on geology. The need to conserve them, through controlling the type of development that happens in recharge areas and in any areas from which water drains into recharge areas, has an important impact on site planning. This section only looks at water running over or held on the surface and what this means for site planning; it does not consider water in general. It shows also how important water can be as a determinant of the form of development. It indicates the detailed information which the site planner needs on water

---

* In Britain in particular the landscape owes many of its distinctive features to running water. Together with glaciation it has determined the shape of many of the valleys.

– the quantity and quality and flow characteristics of water in streams and rivers, the danger of flooding, the usefulness as drinking water or as a recreational resource.

THE RIVER BASIN

The streams that drain the land link together to form drainage basins. Each drainage basin is surrounded by a watershed. These basic geographic units are frequently used by landscape planners developing ideas for integrating a concern for landscape and environmental matters into regional and sub-regional planning.

The watershed and its associated river/stream basins can also be useful concepts when site plans are being produced which cover substantial areas. For instance, when new settlements are to be planned the watersheds indicate basic natural zones. Each zone can be dealt with differently and yet nature is still reflected in the plans (McHarg, 1969).

The river basin is important to site planning in that it indicates the area from which water is gathered to fill streams and rivers. Streams in or near a project area can be prone to flooding because of what is happening elsewhere in the river basin, or they can lack the normal flow of water because of drainage schemes elsewhere in the river basin. Changes in the vegetation cover, or development of land for urbanization upstream, can make streams and rivers and adjacent areas of land liable to flash flooding. The development potential of a site can, therefore, be influenced by land use and land management change which takes place at some distance from the project site. Such changes upstream can also influence water quality by the flash flooding having a devastating impact on the biota which help to maintain the water quality, or by reducing water flows to a level where there is insufficient water to ensure that the natural processes which keep water clean can operate.

As with the other factors identified as influencing the site planning process, expert help is often required to assess the problems related to surface water. If the preliminary surveys identify any likely problems, then the site planner should approach hydrologists or water engineers for information about the flow of water and water quality. In addition, botanists/ecologists can give advice on using the natural processes to cleanse water.

The site planner needs to prepare a base map of the site context area showing the total surface drainage system and, with the aid of maps covering a larger area, to identify the water catchment area that feeds any local surface water. This preliminary plan should indicate the position of all the water courses containing running water (rivers, streams, ditches) within the site context area and within the project site as well as any dry valleys.* Samples should be taken to establish water quality and the ability of the stream to cope with pollution.

The amount of foreign material held in suspension in the water – soil, bits of vegetation, dirt, influences a water body's ability to cope with pollution and remain self-cleansing. The impact of contaminants is also influenced by whether the water is slow and sluggish or fast and bubbling over rocks and pebbles. In the latter situation additional oxygen is incorporated into the water and this makes a substantial difference to a stream's ability to remain self-cleansing.

WATER QUALITY

In Britain and many other countries detailed information is kept on water quality by government departments and local government agencies.† While such water quality information rarely includes the smaller streams, it does provide a wealth of data on how clean the water is and how safe for a variety of uses.

When a project site has running water within or on the edge of it, water quality information should be collected, to ensure that the development of the site plan is based on a full understanding of any problems associated with water quality. For instance, where water is found to be contaminated, it would be foolish to suggest the development of a scheme involving use of the water for recreation and the client should be advised of the additional costs involved in providing clean water. There are other health hazards than chemical contamination (organic or inorganic) of water: bacteria and other organisms can live in water which endanger health and life. It is important to check for their presence, prior to the use of water for any form of recreation.

Contaminated water often has an offensive smell and if it is not within the control of the developer to eliminate the contamination, this can greatly reduce the potential of the site for development. Remember that temperature and water availability conditions can vary and these natural fluctuations will affect the likelihood of smells being a problem.

Streams that are only slightly polluted can become highly polluted and a smell problem as well as a health hazard, even if there is no increase in the level of contamination entering the water. This can happen as a direct result of the development process. For instance, when the flow of clean water into the stream is reduced so that the natural cleansing processes can no longer operate. Water flow can often be reduced by

---

* That is a valley with no stream in it at present (either because the water has disappeared underground or because the local surface water system has changed). Such valleys can suffer from flash flooding or develop streams along the bottom in wet weather.

† In Britain, the Water Boards produce maps showing all the rivers and larger streams in their area and the relative water quality. They can also advise on sewerage.

development operations which divert the surface water into alternative storm water systems. It can also be reduced by irrigation schemes and by flood control measures as well as the building of reservoirs upstream. Since all these factors can have an impact on water quality and quantity within a given site, it is important to gather information for the wider area and not just the site itself.

Water pollution problems can also be reduced by the site planning process by increasing the flow of clean water into a stream. This, however, must be done in such a way that there is no danger of flash flooding disturbing the biota in the stream, for the latter have a vital role in maintaining water quality. It is possible to build water retention areas (often termed balancing lakes) when development takes place and to some extent these can replace lost natural water retention areas. They have the added advantage of giving water which has been washed off developed land time to settle, so that the water entering the natural drainage system has less particles held in suspension. Oxygenation of the water by introducing small weirs can also help the natural cleansing processes work more efficiently – a form of bio-engineering.

FLOOD PROBLEMS

Information on the likelihood of flooding is required so that the areas potentially hazardous to human life are identified.

If there is a flood problem, it is often possible to solve it locally by building flood defences, but beware of the implications of these for other existing and new developments downstream. If the site plan for the project area restricts the area of floodable land and, therefore, the water retention capacity of a valley, this can have disastrous consequences downstream. In such a situation there could be claims against a client if it could be proven that the development of a project site caused environmental hazards elsewhere.

Where a project area is liable to flood it is essential to establish how regularly such floods occur in the local river system and the area of land commonly inundated. In some countries, water boards have plans showing the likely extent and frequency of flooding. Any flood control measures that could have an impact on the project should be identified.

If no other information is available and the project site seems in a vulnerable position, then hydrologists will need to be co-opted into the site planning team to calculate the likely occurrence of floods. They do this on the basis of information about the water catchment area and rainfall patterns within the watershed basin.

On a small project site where the risk of flood problems seems low, talking to the local people about the occurrence of floods can be an acceptable substitute for expert help (Figure 4.13). If people have lived

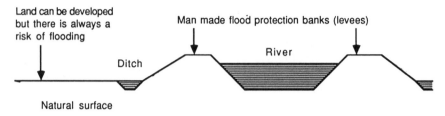

Figure 4.13   Diagram of flood protection measures.

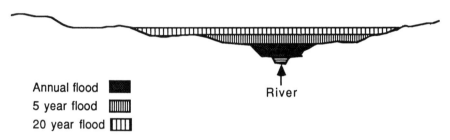

Figure 4.14   Valley cross section indicating the flood plain.

in an area long enough, they will know which roads, paths and areas of land regularly flood, which fields most often get covered with standing water and for how long this lasts. They will also know which, if any, houses have been inundated in the recent past. All this information can give a pointer as to whether to call in expert help.

Hydrologists can calculate the likelihood of flooding in great detail by studying the catchment area and the local weather patterns. They can estimate the likelihood of flooding happening in five, ten, twenty, thirty, forty, fifty or more yearly intervals (Figure 4.14). The client has to decide what the reasonable risk is in relation to a particular project, but the site planner should advise on the risks.

CANALS, PONDS, LAKES AND WETLANDS

It is also important for site planning purposes to know where all the still water is. The location of the ponds, lakes, wells and wetlands (including bogs and marshland) that are within the project area and in the site context area need to be recorded (both natural and man-made water features). Detailed information needs to be gathered on their water quality, wildlife value, recreational value, permanence and also on the condition of their edges. The latter is often crucial to their conservation value.

Throughout the world some of the most interesting and scarce wildlife

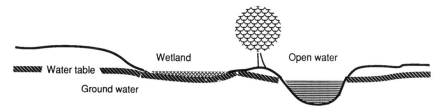

Figure 4.15   Wetlands.

habitats are associated with water. So recording the location of wet areas, near as well as within the project site, may help later with the development of a plan for nature conservation within the site. It will also help in making decisions about which areas should be drained and which retained as water bodies.

There are many possible ways of treating still water and wetland, ranging from drainage to conservation. The site planner should assess the range of possibilities.

Many areas of still water are man-made: ponds, lakes, canals. It is important to distinguish these from natural water systems and to establish how water is held in each and how the supply is replenished. Many old man-made water features exist in towns as well as the countryside. They may have been built to breed fish, as with the medieval fish ponds associated with many abbeys in Europe, to provide water power for mills and early factories, or as part of an agricultural system.* In addition, some lakes and ponds of substantial size have been made purely for recreation or leisure purposes, for instance, in large gardens and parks. Such water areas, properly maintained, make attractive and interesting features within development sites and are often seen as an asset by site planners.

Remember that an area of natural open water or wetland normally indicates the top of an area of ground-water (Figure 4.15) and all the issues related to causing no further pollution of ground-water supplies by decisions taken during the site planning process hold good (see the section on geology and site planning).

SEA

If the project site is near the sea, it is important to gather information on where it is safe to build houses. To do this information needs to be gathered on the local results of 'surges' (exceptionally high water caused

---

* For instance, many of the marl pits of the Midlands of England which now appear as natural water features, but initially developed where the farmers took nutrient rich soil from lower layers to spread on the surface to act in the same way as fertilizers.

by a combination of air pressure and high tide and storm conditions). When combined, such conditions can damage the structure of houses or other buildings constructed on the edge of the sea. If there is to be substantial development on the coast it is important to involve the skills of marine engineers in the site planning team, particularly when erosion is likely to be a problem. The building of marinas in particular needs to involve those with a thorough and long-term understanding of local sea conditions.

Coastal sand-dunes are very vulnerable geological features which can be easily eroded by over-use. They are often important components of the coastal protection system. Any development in their vicinity needs to be undertaken with great care and on the basis of the best possible understanding of the long-term implications of disturbing the system.

The pollution of sea water is an increasing problem and care has to be taken that existing pollution will not inhibit the proposed project. The site planner also has to ensure that the project causes no additional pollution of the sea.

Recording the topography

Topographic plans such as the British Ordnance Survey plans are usually sufficient to indicate the general shape of the land, but are not so useful in relation to the detailed ground-form within the project area. This section concentrates, therefore, at the detailed level, and in particular on how a more accurate idea of the landform within a project area may be obtained.

Many site plans are prepared as project feasibility studies. In these circumstances some developers are unwilling to go to the expense of a detailed topographic survey, until they decide to proceed. Much site planning is done, therefore, on best available information about the topography rather than absolutely accurate plans (Untermann, 1973). Indeed many projects, particularly those not involving the building of structures, never need totally accurate information about level changes.

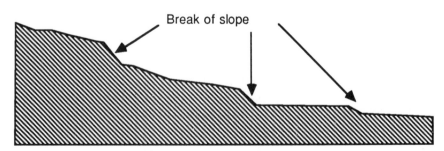

Figure 4.16   Break of slope.

It is part of the site planner's task to advise the client on the suitable level of information so as not to lead to unnecessary expenditure.

Even when details about the topography are available, it is essential to walk over the site with a copy of the base plan and check that it records all the breaks of slope. A break of slope occurs when the land is suddenly steeper between two planes (Figure 4.16). The location of these changes of level can be particularly important in developing ideas for planning sites.

SLOPE ANALYSIS

It is useful for making decisions about the distribution of land use to have a plan showing the location of the vertical and near-vertical banks, the very steep land, the steep land, the moderately sloping land, the gently sloping land and the flat land.

Different angles of slope have different implications for development. Table 4.1 gives some rough guidance on the link between angle of slope and development potential. Such information can be used to decide which angles of slope are important in relation to a particular site planning problem.

If the project area is to be used for buildings, the angle of slope can have severe repercussions on building costs. It costs money to flatten sites or to terrace them for development. Earth shifting can do considerable environmental damage, often to areas much larger than that covered by a building, so a slope analysis that is produced to ensure the minimal area of disturbance is, therefore, a vital piece of information for the site planning process.

Table 4.1   Slopes and land uses

Type of land use	Permitted angle of slope			
	Maximum		Minimum	
Streets and drives	8%	1:12	1%	1:100
Parking areas	5%	1:20	1%	1:100
Main footpaths – bitumen	8%	1:12	5%	1:20
Main ramp on footpath – short	14%	1:7	—	
Entrance areas	4%	1:25	1%	1:100
Minor footpaths	14%	1:7	5%	1:20
Terraces – paved	2%	1:50	1%	1:100
Lawns	5%	1:20	1%	1:100
Mown grass banks	33%	1:3	—	
Planted slopes	50%	1:2	—	

Local climate and the development of a site

By careful site planning and design it is possible to create very local climates where people can be screened from the worst extremes of an area's climate.* The possibility of manipulating local climate can be used to encourage people to use the outdoor areas associated with buildings.

For the past hundred years increasing amounts of energy have been used to produce internal climates which are more comfortable to humans than those prevailing outside. In cold climates houses, factories and shopping centres are heated. In hot climates they are cooled by air conditioning. Too often massive quantities of energy have to be used to compensate for thoughtless site planning and design. Many of the building forms favoured today are not the most efficient in terms of the internal climate they produce. Building scientists and architects have become increasingly aware of this and some have shown that such energy expensive schemes are unnecessary. If careful consideration is given to site planning, the structure and form of the building and to the external environment abutting the buildings, even in the more extreme climates energy consumption can be kept down.

Site planners have to be aware of the link between energy consumption and the local climate, particularly if they are to keep to a minimum the cost to the user of any proposals. For instance, in northern latitudes putting housing on a steep north facing slope inevitably means a higher demand for energy or extra expenditure on insulation materials, whilst in hot sunny climates placing a house on a slope facing the full sun with no shading of its roof or walls adds substantially to the cost of cooling it artificially. In any climate, even the most moderate such as prevails in much of lowland Britain, the site planner can be well rewarded for time spent studying and understanding the local climate.†

The site planner's aim is to develop more comfortable conditions for human life both indoors and outdoors in the built environment; when working in rural areas it is to improve the conditions for crop growth, livestock and recreation. The possibility of controlling the climate locally is of crucial importance to achieving these aims. Information is needed which will allow an assessment to be made of the restraint imposed on planning the site by the local climate. The information should be gathered in such a way that it also allows a consideration of the best means of modifying that climate. For instance, by increasing protection from the wind in cold areas, by ensuring a free flow of air in hot areas, by eliminating frost hollows, by creating shady or sunny areas. Through

---

* There is also evidence that man's activities have resulted in climatic change over large areas although such issues are not dealt with in this book. See Chapter 4, Man modified climates by Rouse, W.R. in Gregory and Walling (1981).

† An excellent primer for site planners on the subject of climate and site planning is the book edited by McPherson (1984) *Energy-conserving Site Design*.

these and other means a site planner and designer can do a great deal to ameliorate the worst effects of the local climate and make the 'outdoors' more usable. Site planners have to understand which built forms are the most cost effective of energy consumption, in relation to each different area on which they work. They have to be able to work with the architects to produce a scheme which considers the interaction of the indoor and outdoor climates.

GATHERING INFORMATION

The first stage is to gather all the information available about the local climate so that the limits within which the scheme must be developed are established. As far as site planning is concerned the local climate makes a substantial difference to the way the site is best laid out as well as to the detailed design of any structures. Usually, a moderate climate with limited fluctuations imposes less limitations than a climate of extremes between winter and summer.

In most countries general information can be obtained from the government meteorological service and they will advise on where to obtain detailed records for a range of weather stations.*

The range of information that is available from local weather records:

- the average temperatures for each month of the year.
- the average number of hours of sunshine in each month.
- the average rainfall for each month.
- the average number of days when frost occurs.
- the average number of days when fog occurs.
- the average number of days when snow lies, and the expected depth.
- the average number of days of drought.
- the lowest and highest temperatures experienced.
- the humidity level throughout the year.
- the wind direction and strength.
- the diurnal range (only needed in hot/dry countries).

The information available on wind can be used to construct a monthly or annual wind graph. In certain climates such information can determine the form of the development. Figure 4.17 shows a wind rose for one month. Wind information has to be linked to the air temperature and humidity information before the site planner decides whether it is necessary to develop sheltered locations for buildings and people.

If the weather station from which the local climate data is accumulated

---

* In Britain virtually every town has detailed information, which has been collected often by amateurs (contact the geographers at the local schools to find out if any really local information is available).

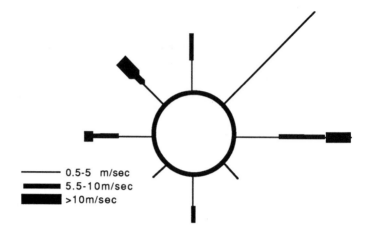

0.5-5 m/sec
5.5-10m/sec
>10m/sec

Figure 4.17 An example of a monthly wind-rose.

is some distance away, it is important to find out how the different location might be expected to affect the climatic statistics by talking with expert climatologists or meteorologists. Even over short distances climate can change, particularly in mountainous areas.

The major factors that can normally be expected to cause variations in weather are:

- height above sea level;
- the type of topography between the weather station and the project site;
- the direction and steadiness of the winds, and their moisture content;
- the temperature and the distance over the land mass that the air flows before it hits the site.

These factors and the distance between the weather station and the site can give some idea of the likelihood of the statistics being directly applicable. If their relevance seems doubtful, it is necessary to rely on local investigations. Investigations on and around the project site are anyway going to be important for site planning, as local aspect and exposure can have a substantial impact on the way people experience the extremes of the local climate.

Climatologists can use climate statistics for an area and by looking at the landform and its shape, height above sea level and ground cover create a fairly clear picture of the problems that might be expected in relation to a particular site. Whenever possible their expert advice should be sought. Building scientists too have developed expertise in this field, in particular on the interaction between local climate and buildings. If no information is available from official sources, the best source of information is often local farmers. Because of the problems involved in growing food they will know a great deal about the local situation and, while not able to provide statistics on temperature and rain, will often be able to interpret the site in a way that is useful for site planning.

The following is a summary of some of the factors which can affect human comfort in the local climate. It is by no means complete and it is stressed that whenever possible experts on the local climate should be consulted before decisions are made on detailed layout.

HUMAN COMFORT

Various authors have different opinions on the temperatures at which humans feel comfortable. The range is from 58° which has been suggested as the lowest acceptable in Britain (Brooks, 1950) to 80° which has been suggested as the maximum comfortable temperature by authors in the USA (Robinette, 1972).

In indoor environments the temperature can be controlled. In outdoor areas only very limited control is possible, but if usable outdoor environments are to be created, it is necessary to use whatever means are available. Figure 4.18 shows the main factors determining our perception of the temperature.

Site planners have to attempt to produce outdoor environments which people will find pleasant. If they are to do this they must understand something about human body temperature.

The deep body temperature has to be maintained at a temperature of between 35°C and 40°C (normally about 37°C) for survival. Skin temperature has to be lower than deep body temperature, and to allow

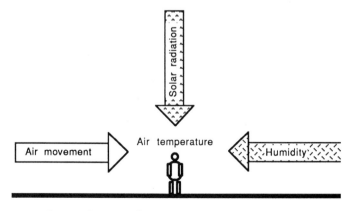

Figure 4.18 Climatic factors influencing human comfort.

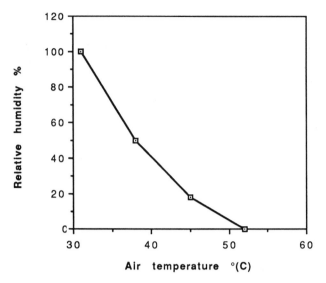

Figure 4.19   Human comfort and the relationship between relative humidity and air temperature.

cooling to take place, the immediately surrounding air temperature has to be lower than skin temperature. Heat from the skin has to dissipate, although it is possible for humans to survive much higher temperatures for periods of time, given the right environmental conditions. The range of temperatures between which heat dissipation takes place at satisfactory levels is termed the human comfort zone.*

The actual air temperature is not the only factor in our perception of human comfort. Of particular importance is the relationship between the humidity of the air and the actual temperature. This, added to the speed at which the wind blows, can make us feel substantially cooler or hotter than the air temperature by itself would suggest.

Figure 4.19 relates to wind still conditions. Relative humidity affects the rate of evaporation of moisture from the skin. Evaporation happens more quickly in dry than humid conditions. At high temperatures evaporation is the main way that the body controls human temperature. For instance at 100% relative humidity no evaporation can take place and, therefore, conditions are extremely uncomfortable and people cannot survive high temperatures long. When the relative humidity is below 20% the mucous membranes dry out, also causing discomfort. In cold conditions very dry air increases the feeling of cold as perspiration is evaporated rapidly from the skin and this adds to the sensation of cold.

* To understand more about these issues see Szokolay (1980).

Above 60% relative humidity the air temperature begins to feel warmer than it really is.

Air movement accelerates evaporation and, therefore, makes conditions feel more comfortable at the higher relative humidity and air temperature levels, but less comfortable in cold air.

The individual, through the clothes being worn, has a strong influence on how the comfort level is perceived. Therefore, the site planner needs to have some idea how site users might dress as they move between buildings and across the site before any judgement can be made of the need for creating special micro-climates outside the buildings.*

When the air is dry air temperatures of over 40°C (over 110°F) can be tolerated, but when the air is moisture laden a temperature of 30°C (85°F) can feel unbearable. In different climates people find different temperatures more or less tolerable depending on what they are used to. Szokolay has suggested that in the UK the comfort zone, when the relative humidity is between 30%–50%, is 16–22°C, whereas he suggests that at the same relative humidity in the USA, at the latitude 40°, it is 20–26°C and in hot climates 23–30°C. The preferable zone for relative humidity is 30–60% but extensions to 18% on the low end and 77% on the high side have been found to be acceptable (Szokolay, 1980).

Once the air temperature is below about 22°C (70°F) sun is needed for it to feel warm enough to sit outside. If the sun is really bright and clear in Britain, it is even possible to sit outside in winter and feel warm, provided there is shelter from the wind. Once the air temperature is below the high fifties and it is cloudy, it is only pleasant to be outside when working hard enough to keep warm. In winter, if cold air is heavily laden with moisture and the wind blows strongly, the wind chill factor operates and our bodies find the air unbearably cold.

The task of the site planner is in part to ensure that the outdoor temperatures are as pleasant as possible within the limitations imposed by the climate of the area.

SOLAR RADIATION

Only about one-fifth of the solar radiation reaching the earth hits the surface. People feel warm in the sun because of direct radiation which is registered as heat, but also because of the reflected radiation which bounces back from vertical and horizontal surfaces. Site planners have

---

* Such factors are much more important in the internal design of buildings. For instance, where an entrance hall and an adjoining office in a cool climate are heated to the same temperature, this can mean that one is perceived as unbearably hot, because of people wearing outdoor clothes, and the other as too cool, because people would normally expect to take off their overcoats.

some limited control over how much direct and reflected radiation people experience when they are outside. For instance, they can reduce the direct heat by creating canopies of plant material or some form of roofed structure, or can cause shade to fall in a particular spot by planting vegetation, building walls or changing the landform.

Figure 4.20 illustrates very simply the complicated process by which the sun warms the surface of the earth. The process is complicated by the fact that different surfaces reflect solar radiation to different levels. This means that by altering the surface, the level of warmth people experience in a place can be adjusted by careful site planning. Plants in particular help to cool the air as they reflect less heat than hard surfaces. The difference in reflective properties is referred to as the albedo rate of various surfaces.

Robinette (1972) has collated data on albedo rates of interest to site planners and designers. The albedo of snow is between 75% and 95% (that is why people get so brown when skiing – because of the radiation bouncing off the surface), for light sand it is between 30% and 60%, for grass meadows between 12% and 30%, for densely built up areas between 15% and 25%, for woods between 5% and 20%, for dark soil between 7% and 10% and for the sea between 3% and 10%.

For site planners these differences in albedo can be important, as can the ability of some materials to hold heat longer than others. For

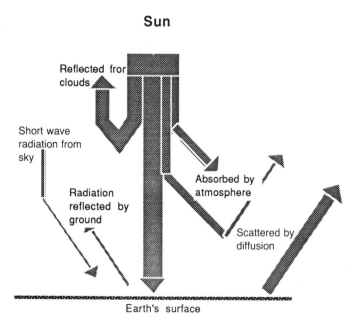

Figure 4.20   How solar radiation warms the surface (Szokolay, 1980).

instance, in high latitudes site planners might want to trap heat so that a corner of the site will be warm enough to linger in and sit in. In such cases the information on albedo and heat-holding capacity allows us to choose a material that will absorb and hold the sun's heat and only gradually give it back – so warming the sitting area after the sun's strength has waned. If on the other hand the interior of a building should not be too warm, surfaces that reflect the sun's heat can be used, so helping to keep it cool.

Shade

In hot climates, even tropical ones, an area is more pleasant to walk through if it is well treed. This helps limit the unpleasantness of extremely high temperatures by making an area feel relatively cooler. This latter effect results partly from the plants shading the ground from direct solar radiation and partly because plants have the type of albedo which absorbs and does not reflect heat. Even a single tree can have a major impact, even if only very locally (Figure 4.21).

Deciduous trees can be particularly useful in areas with strong seasonal differences. The leaves create shade in the summer when the most radiation strikes the ground and the leafless trees let the warmth through in winter. Particularly in North America this feature has been used in the positioning of shade trees to screen the afternoon sun (the hottest) from the roof and walls (Robinette, 1972). Choosing the right-

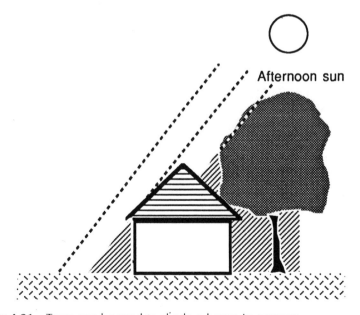

Figure 4.21   Trees can be used to shade a house in summer.

shaped tree can become important, as crown density and tree form produce different shadows.*

Shade is a common tool used by site planners to control microclimate. It is important to get it right for the local circumstances. In high latitudes, such as in Britain, the last thing a site user wants in winter is the sunlight to be shaded out from rooms or external spaces. The amount of sunlight in winter, spring and autumn in such latitudes can be limited and people want as much in their homes as possible. Therefore, any tall trees must be positioned at sufficient distance to prevent shade in winter when the sun is low; in these circumstances the place for large trees is the sunless side of the building or at some distance from it.

The site planner must be able to calculate the position of the shady areas on the project site. Both those that exist before the development commences and those that will develop as it progresses are important in the decision making process. The angle of the sun varies with latitude and time of year and the exact situation can be calculated for every site. In the higher latitudes there can be significant differences in shadow area between winter and summer and autumn/spring. It is, therefore, very useful to show plans for at least three periods in the year. The nearer a site is to the equator the less important it is to do seasonal plots and the site planner has to decide from local knowledge what is appropriate.

The higher the sun is in the sky, the more radiation is available to hit the ground.† In the summer at higher latitudes the sun is visible for longer and this too increases the opportunities for warming the surface and air (Figure 4.22). These considerations, together with local information on average cloud cover, allow the site planner to estimate the amount of sunshine and spread of it through the year for an individual site.

Tables of the direction and altitude of the sun for particular latitudes are available. Architects and building scientists can often provide the information in a readily usable form. However, if it is not available it can be calculated by the site planner (Lynch and Hack, 1984, Appendix E). For instance at latitude 42° the sun's altitude is 71.5° at noon in midsummer, 48° at the equinoxes and 24.5° at midwinter. It is, however, important to work out not just the difference in shadows between the summer and winter, but also between morning, midday and evening as these can all affect how a site is ultimately used.

Local factors influencing solar radiation
At the level of individual sites, solar radiation levels can be influenced

---

* For information on tree shapes see De Chiara and Koppelman (1984) Section 6.
† On 21 June the sun is at the zenith for northern latitudes, it is perceived as directly overhead at the Tropic of Cancer (23.5N). On 21 March and 23 September it is directly overhead at the Equator and on 21 December overhead at the Tropic of Capricorn.

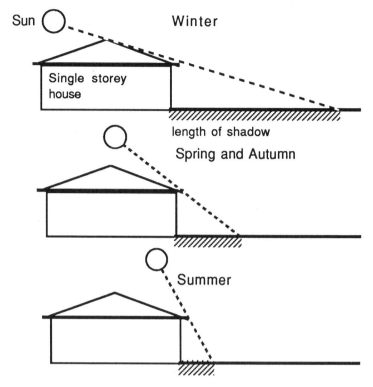

Shadows at noon calculated for Sheffield (latitude 53°22' North)
Sun's altitude at noon at equinox is 37°
Sun's altitude at noon at midsummer is 60°
Sun's altitude at noon at midwinter is 14°

Figure 4.22   Shadows as a factor in site planning.

by the direction of slope of the landform, the shadows from plants, structures or nearby hills and the level of air pollution.

In higher latitudes, such as those of Britain, landform can have a particularly strong impact on the amount of solar radiation at ground level (Figure 4.23). This influence is accentuated by aspect, that is the direction in which the slope faces, whether away from or towards the sun (Figure 4.24).

Identifying the warmer and cooler slopes in northern latitudes:

warmer:

- the south and south-west facing slopes are warmest and any hollows facing those directions will be particularly warm;
- the south-east and west facing slopes are the next warmest and again any hollows, or any sun-trap areas surrounded by walls or vegeta-

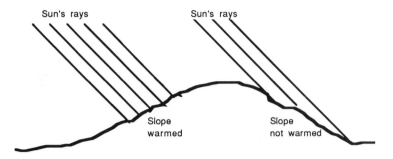

Figure 4.23 A diagram indicating the influence of the angle and direction of slope on solar radiation at ground level.

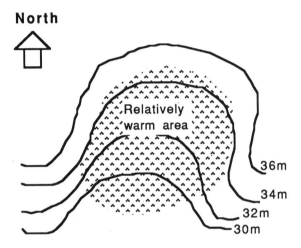

Figure 4.24 Warmth can be trapped by landform.

tion, have particularly pleasant sheltered micro-climates warmed by the sun to temperatures well above those of the surrounding land;

cooler:

● the north-west facing slopes tend to be colder than average;
● the north, north-east and east facing slopes are the coldest areas.

In winter in Britain, the low temperatures experienced on the north, north-east and east-facing slopes are exacerbated as they bear the brunt of the cold winter winds, which in certain conditions blow straight off the Arctic. Such slopes do not make the best crop land. They are the least attractive for development, because of the additional energy costs involved in heating buildings in such locations. They are also the places where it is always going to be more difficult to establish plants and so involve a client in additional development costs where planting is required. However, even in the cooler areas any pockets of sheltered land that are orientated towards the afternoon sun will be relatively warm.

In Britain, where our concern is in the main to have an external environment in summer in which it is warm enough to sit out, site planners attempt to identify the warmest areas as sitting-out spaces. Areas protected from the wind by trees, landform or structures and yet facing the mid-day or afternoon sun are best for warmth. Such places are ideal for sitting areas, parks or lunchtime picnic spots. Where they do not exist the site planner attempts to create them.

The situation described above for Britain would hold true for most of the higher latitudes in the northern hemisphere, but the directions would be reversed for the same latitudes in the southern hemisphere.

The need to cool the air in hot climates

Over much of the earth the problem in summer is not so much one of trying to find the warm areas but trying to locate the cool places, the shady places through which breezes blow so that the temperature is kept at a bearable level. When no such places exist, modern man is driven indoors to expensively air-conditioned buildings. Air conditioning and cooling is not only expensive in terms of the capital required to build the cooling systems and the power needed to run them, but also in terms of the air pollution created by the system.

Before modern times other systems of cooling were developed throughout the world, which worked without great use of energy. Site planners working in environments where extremes of temperature are experienced can learn much by studying how life was made bearable in the past.

Some of the best examples of man adapting to a local climate are the different forms of housing developed in different parts of the world, for instance:

- the igloo designed to give minimum surface for largest volume and with few openings to the wind;
- the old houses with openings only on the side facing the sun found in much of northern Europe;
- the courtyard house of the hot dry climates designed to have a cooler shaded open area at its core, often with a pool or fountain to humidify the air;
- the apparently flimsily constructed houses of the wet tropics designed to give the cross-ventilation so necessary to make such climates bearable.*

* For further information on climate and form of development see Szokolay (1980).

Air pollution and solar radiation

Another factor influencing the amount of solar radiation reaching the ground is the amount of air pollution: dirt, smoke and dust. These act in the same way as clouds and reduce the amount of solar radiation reaching the surface. In cities where air pollution controls do not operate, this can be a problem. The problems associated with the chemical reactions in the air that occur at higher temperatures in sunlight are not dealt with here: with the exception of controlling emissions within the project area, there is little that the site planner can do to limit this. However, the site planner can help to clean the air locally by ensuring a sufficient density of vegetation so that the leaves trap some of the dust and dirt and allow a free flow of air through the site to carry pollution away.

Manipulating the micro-climate

This can be done by making small pockets which will have temperatures differing from the surrounding areas. While the shading of buildings and open spaces by deliberately positioning trees or other buildings to cast shadows is an important tool for site planners attempting to manipulate the local climate in hot countries, in cool countries it is the trapping of the sun's warmth which is important.

In higher latitudes sheltered amphitheatres or valleys facing towards the sun are normally warmer than the surrounding land. Figure 4.24

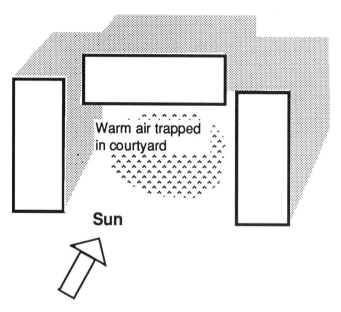

Figure 4.25   In cool climates buildings can be arranged to trap warm air in courtyards.

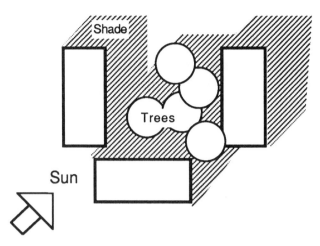

Figure 4.26 In warm climates buildings and trees can be arranged to cast shadows on outdoor spaces.

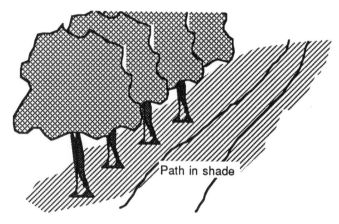

Figure 4.27 The shadow cast by trees creates a different micro-climate in open spaces and gardens.

illustrates how warmth can be trapped by landform in northern latitudes.

Warmth can also be trapped by walls and buildings as shown in Figure 4.25, just as temperatures can be reduced by creating shady areas as in Figure 4.26. These factors are important to the site planner as ideas are developed on where different activities might occur outside buildings.

The site planner does not just consider the micro-climate around the buildings, but uses the 'warm' and 'cool' pockets that occur on every site to develop a site plan which makes best use of them (Figure 4.27).

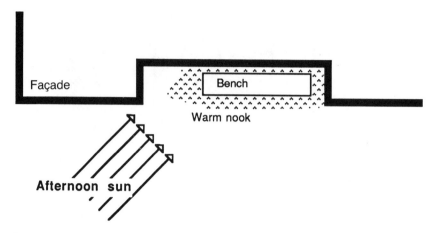

Figure 4.28 Even small recesses in the façade can form pockets where the air is relatively warm.

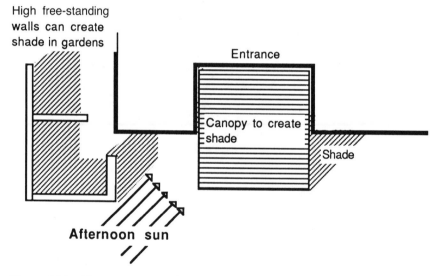

Figure 4.29 The positioning of walls and buildings can create cooler areas by casting shade.

The detailed design of the facade of a building can be used to create very local effects of cooling or warming (Figures 4.28 and 4.29). In cool climates this type of space, with its special micro-climate, can increase the likelihood of people sitting outside or lingering there, even in the cooler seasons. In hot climates shade around entrances cast by canopies or walls is welcome, in particular when waiting to meet others or to be let into a building.

Vegetation and temperature control

As mentioned in relation to albedo, temperatures over different surfaces can vary substantially and this can be important in creating pockets where the microclimate is different. For instance, in sunlight the temperature over grass is 10°–14° cooler than over exposed soil and the air under the canopy of trees and shrubs is always cooler than on the top surface (Waterhouse, 1955). This means that vegetation can be a useful means of lowering the temperature where necessary.

Shrubs and trees are also useful at night as they retain warmth under the canopy because the leaves restrict the outflow of radiation at night. Robinette (1972) has suggested that climbing plants and shrubs growing against buildings act as insulators, so that the building surface is cooler than it would otherwise be in daytime and warmer at night. Planting climbing plants such as vines over pergola structures, so that they form a canopy, is a common device in many sunny countries to create cooler spaces immediately adjacent to the house.

Frost

Frost occurs when the temperature drops below 0°C (32°F). There are two types of frost – air frost and ground frost. Ground frost occurs when the micro-climate at the surface is cooled more rapidly than the surrounding air and there is a very shallow layer with freezing conditions. Its occurrence can cause problems for vehicles, as road surfaces can become slippery and it can create unsatisfactory growing conditions for crops. Such areas need to be identified, otherwise ground frost causes few problems. The real problems occur when there is air frost, as this can cause extensive icing of structures, including roads, and severely affect plant growth.

The occurrence of frost may seem to be something that the site planner can do little about. This is true in the areas of the earth which experience severe frost for long periods of the year. However, in mild climates like that of Britain, where ground frost as well as air frost are common, the site planner has a role to play in ensuring that no unnecessary frost pockets develop. In particular, the site planner can ensure that such pockets do not adversely affect road driving conditions or crops.

Frost pockets

Frost pockets occur because cold air drains down hills to the lowest point, exactly like water would. At the lowest point it is ponded by whatever obstruction causes the draining to stop. Even small road embankments can act rather like a weir would for water, holding the cold air back until it reaches the top of the embankment, at which stage it spills over the road embankment and continues draining downhill. In wet conditions this causes ice to form on the road surface.

Buildings, dense planting, walls, fences and embankments can all act as the barriers which result in cold air ponds. They can even pond the air flow at any position on a slope, provided that the barrier is angled to trap the air as it flows downhill.

In areas where mild frosts are common, the site planner is advised to check the present conditions and predict what might happen if the development takes place. There are rare occasions such as when the site planner is looking for a position for an outdoor skating area when frost pockets are deliberately created, but in most site planning the intention is normally to eliminate them.

Hard prolonged frost

In areas where hard frost is common, there are also associated site planning problems. This is particularly so where frost enters the soil to a depth sufficient to cause the soil to heave in the freeze/thaw process. In such conditions, and especially where permafrost occurs, special measures have to be taken during construction which add considerably to the cost of developing a site. Expert advice is needed to decide what can be done to allow building and associated infrastructure development in any such areas. Even constructing roads can be difficult.

WIND

Air is perpetually moving in great masses around the world, driven by thermal factors and the Coriolis Force (the effect of inertia on air particles which deflects them east or west). These broad patterns are modified locally by pressure variations and topography, so that the ground wind may differ from the general movement of the air mass. Precipitation is linked to movement of the air masses; rain is most likely to fall when the air mass is rising and impossible when it is sinking. It is this latter air movement which is linked to the location of deserts. In warmer latitudes these areas of sinking air coincide with the sub-tropical high-pressure zones.

Wind speed and site planning

Wind can be important for site planning, not just for the way in which it makes us experience the air temperature as more extreme than it really is, although this latter factor results in our attempts to control wind speed and so keep the sensible temperature bearable. In addition to that, wind can make it difficult to move around easily and problems associated with this can be accentuated as it eddies around and between buildings. High wind speeds also make it difficult to establish and grow plants satisfactorily, partly because high winds blow them over and more important because they desiccate plants and soil. For centuries

Table 4.2 The effects of wind

Wind speed (m/sec)	Effect	Beaufort wind force
0.5	Smoke rises vertically	0
1.7	Smoke slightly inclined	1
2	Wind felt on face	
3.3	Slight breeze, leaves rustle	2
4	Papers blow about, dust lifts, hair messed	
5.2	Twigs move, water ripples	3
6	Noticeable effect on walking	
7.4	Moderate wind, small branches move	4
8	Progress slowed when walking	
9.8	Strong wind, branches move, white wave crests	5
10	Umbrella difficult to use	
12	Walking unsteady, noise in ears	
12.4	Very strong wind, leaves torn off	6
14	Totter in wind from behind	
15.2	Storm, small trees bend, twigs torn off	7
18	Grab supports when walking	
18.2	Strong storm, large branches torn down	8
20	Blown over often	
21.5	Very strong storm, light building damage	9
22	Cannot stand	
25.1	Gale, building damage, trees uprooted	10
29	Gale, buildings destroyed, woods uprooted	11
>29	Very severe	12

farmers have planned their farms in relation to the need to have shelter from the wind – planting shelter belts for their houses, their cattle and their crops. This latter is an example of the instinctive understanding of site planning which seems to have been more common before the use of high levels of energy to heat or cool buildings.

For the site planner it is important to understand how wind turbulence and speed might affect the use of the site, how wind is a factor in the growth and survival of plants and how it affects the sensible temperature* for humans and animals and, therefore, leads to the need for shelter.

Lynch and Hack (1984) have drawn up information about the effect of wind speed on people and this, added to information about the effect of wind on vegetation and buildings, provides a useful starting point for site planners (Table 4.2). One of the problems with using such informa-

---

* The sensible temperature is that which we feel the air temperature to be, not that which it is according to the thermometer.

tion is that wind at ground level rarely blows steadily, it more often gusts and this can increase its nuisance value for people using a site. This in part is caused by local ground conditions and position of buildings and in part by the overall landform. Even at sea winds come in gusts. This is due to localized weather conditions relating to pressure distribution and the position of fronts (the interface between air masses) with different characteristics.

Lynch and Hack have suggested that for comfort, when sitting outdoors, the wind speed should not exceed 4 metres per second (m/sec) for more than 20% of the time and for easy walking in streets and piazzas it should not exceed 12m/sec more than 5% of the time. They have also suggested that the wind should not exceed 16m/sec for more than 10 hours per year on any area of land where people are likely to be outside.*

Wind around buildings

The problems involved in estimating the effects of gusting around tall buildings are such that building scientists, or architects specializing in such problems, have to be involved in the calculations for urban and high-value projects. However, even medium-sized buildings can cause problems and the site planner should advise the client of these, unless measures can be included in the site plan and design to eliminate the problem. A very useful tool for assessing what happens on the ground at present and what will probably happen when the form of the site is changed is the wind tunnel.[†]

Prevailing wind

The importance of the prevailing wind differs from place to place. Site planners in Britain often worry most about the prevailing winds, the westerlies.[‡] However, in Britain those winds are often the warmer winds, not the cold ones from which shelter is required. The winds

---

* Wind standards quoted here are given in terms of the 'equivalent speed'. Hack and Lynch suggest that for site planning we assume that the equivalent speed is 1.5 times the average speed.

† Block models of the buildings are constructed to scale and the landform is modelled, this model is then put in a wind tunnel and the 'ground' surface is painted with a special paint over which air is blown at a predetermined speed and from a predetermined direction to simulate wind. This process is repeated to show the effects of wind from a variety of directions and at a variety of speeds, the choice being based on local conditions. The result is that the special paint is marked by the 'gusts of wind' and the site planners get a clear picture of how the wind will behave in the given circumstances. Alternatively and more cheaply plumes of smoke can be blown in the simulated wind. Watching and photographing how the winds from different directions and of different speeds behave allows a general picture to be built up of the localized wind patterns, which can be very useful in identifying the sheltered corners of the site and those that will need extra attention to solve problems with exposure or turbulence.

‡ For farmers in Britain, the westerlies are often a sign of wet conditions for working the ground. Perhaps this is the reason they are emphasized in the literature on climate.

which matter in the British climate are the bitterly cold northerlies and easterlies. They are the winds which site planners need to plan to exclude from areas in which people might want to linger in or sit. They need to exclude them as well from areas where the more delicate species of plants might be introduced. Ensuring that people have some shelter from these cold winds, increases the attractiveness of a site for outdoor use.

Wind near the sea

In seaside districts it is of course always important to consider the prevailing winds, particularly where planting is involved, as they can carry salt spray a distance and so damage plants.

Seaside winds are different from those inland and site planners have to take care to understand the particular situation. Seaside winds often run counter to the general air mass as light thermal breezes develop in the summer months.*

Wind in cities

Such localized air movements also happen in big cities, with air being drawn into the hot city centres in warm weather to rise upwards over the hottest point. Spirn (1984) has drawn attention to the great importance within the city of understanding the way air behaves, as it moves between buildings and along streets and into open areas. She indicates the importance of planning to increase ventilation in summer and to reduce it in winter because of the wind chill factor. This is not an easy task, as the two create conflicting design requirements in terms of the built form required to make them happen.

Wind and landform

The topography of the site context area and of the site will affect the behaviour of the wind. Climatologists can normally predict how the wind will behave when it comes from different directions. It will, for instance, be affected by ground temperature. Air rises over warmed ground and sinks over cooled and this causes localized air currents.

As winds tend to follow the line of least resistance near the ground, a local wind will be modified by a valley which can funnel it. This happens particularly if the wind is already blowing along the same alignment as the valley.

It is important to identify where these very local winds might occur, so

---

* This is because air is drawn from cool areas to hotter. Beside the sea the result is the morning breeze off the cooled land flows towards the sea and the exact opposite occurs in the afternoon and evening when the land is hotter than the sea. This can create very drafty conditions in some seaside locations in cool countries with the need for sheltered corners for people wanting to sit and enjoy the seaside atmosphere. In hot countries the breezes are a great relief and make the high air temperatures more tolerable particularly for those sitting beside the water.

that a site plan can allow for shelterbelts or other screening devices, to reduce any ill-effects, or to use the air currents to make conditions more pleasant. For instance, at the site planning stage it is possible to plan to reduce the chance of air pollution being trapped in part of a site, or to create the cooling breezes in hot climates.

Windbreaks

The importance of vegetation as a cooling agent was briefly touched on under the earlier section on solar radiation, but vegetation is also important as a local modifier of wind speed and direction. Foresters, farmers and landscape architects have studied planting design for wind control and a great deal of information is now available, which the site planner can use to develop schemes for reducing the worst effect of wind wherever it is possible to grow trees. Heisler (1984) has reviewed the literature available on windbreaks and identified ways in which they reduce wind speed.

Four of the ways in which windbreaks reduce wind speed horizontally:

- by absorbing some of the energy of the wind;
- by frictional drag as the air passes through and around the plants
- by deflecting some of the wind to higher levels; and
- by making the wind move in random patterns so that it becomes turbulent.

Different types of windbreak have been studied for their efficiency. In different circumstances the site planner will have to recommend different solutions: there is no standard solution. The information given here is very simplified and only aims to indicate the options open to the site planner. Expert help is needed to design windbreaks, as badly designed shelterbelts can be useless and even create the sort of turbulence not wanted on a site.

Normally a dense wind break is less effective than an open one. This is because it has many of the characteristics of a solid wall and causes the wind to move fast in a different direction, so increasing local disturbance.

The evidence on windbreaks indicates that narrow fairly open tree belts (Figure 4.30a), are more effective than major blocks of woodland in providing shelter. This is mainly because wind, after it has blown over a dense woodland, behaves similarly to wind which has hit a solid obstacle. The resultant turbulence means there is a smaller area of protected ground.*

Problems can occur with windbreaks when it is necessary to punch holes in them for roadways or overhead cables. The result of these holes is an acceleration of the wind-speed through the gap. The site planner has to

---

* Site planners working in Britain will find the work of J.M. Caborn (1957 and 1965) most helpful.

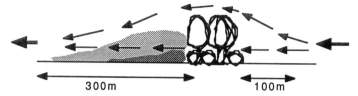

(a)A 10m high shelterbelt of trees and shrubs affects wind-speed for about 100m upwind and 300m downwind when it is not densely planted.

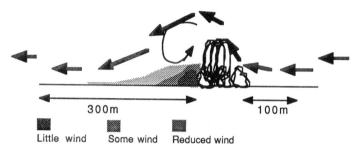

(b)A dense shelterbelt of trees and shrubs shelters less land and causes severe turbulence.

Figure 4.30   Influence of shelterbelts on wind-speed.

be aware of this potential effect when laying out shelterbelts, whether to protect agricultural areas or sites being developed for another use. Careful positioning of other small woodlands or plantations can do much to alleviate the problems.

There is increasing evidence that strategically positioned windbreaks are not just a benefit for agriculture* but that they can be effective in decreasing fuel consumption in residential and other built-up areas (McPherson, 1984). It appears that the cost of planting them and allocating land to them can be paid back in between 8 and 20 years, but this depends on the type of windbreak and the associated costs and the local land cost (Heisler, 1984).

Slowing wind speed in cities

The rougher the surface, the more the wind is slowed. Therefore, the site planner can use vegetation of different types, ages and sizes to help slow the local winds. Substantial areas of edge of city wooded parkland, like the Amsterdamse Bos near Amsterdam, can for this reason feel less exposed to the elements than the surrounding built-up areas of the city.

---

* Windbreaks in the form of woodland have the advantage of reducing desiccation of crops, reducing the problem of blowing soils and providing shelter for livestock. It is probable also that they could have the added advantage of providing a woodland edge habitat for the birds which feed on the aphids, so reducing the need to use pesticide on the crops.

Wind speed can be reduced by vegetation as it flows over and through the city.

It is possible through site planning to link the effects on the behaviour of wind of landform and vegetation to produce new, although only localized wind patterns. This can benefit the quality of the local environment. For instance, work in Stuttgart has shown how air quality in the inner city can be improved by allowing the cooler air, such as naturally occurs as the land on adjacent hill slopes cools at night or occurs during the day under woodland in warm weather, to drain down into the city through a valley system and expel the hot dirty air, which tends to gather in any city centre during the summer (Spirn, 1984).

Wind and structures
Just as a wind permeable tree belt is more efficient in creating a relatively large area of land with a lower wind speed, so an open fence is more efficient than a solid one. To create an area of very still air a solid fence or wall is necessary, but this only creates a very small space where people can feel protected from the wind when it blows from a particular direction. Such a solution is of little use for sheltering crops or cattle.

Wind and soils
Wind can be a major cause of erosion, particularly where soils are unprotected by vegetation. This aspect is dealt in the section on soils in Chapter 5.

PRECIPITATION

There is nothing a site planner can do directly about precipitation, since the mechanisms that cause rain or snow to fall operate over much larger areas than that with which the site planner is concerned. Part of the site planner's responsibility towards the environment, however, is to ensure that any site remains as well vegetated as is possible and appropriate in the local context.

At the site planning level the most important link between vegetation and precipitation of which the planner has to be aware, is the way in which the leaves and twigs intercept the rainfall. They ensure that it falls gently to the earth or trickles down the bark, reducing the risk of erosion.

Once vegetative cover is removed erosion begins. Then the steeper the slope the more effective rainwater is as an erosive agent. Removing forest cover on steep slopes, where the surface layers are unconsolidated, has led to major environmental disasters. It is not just the removal of vegetation which can cause erosion problems, the type of soil also affects the rate of erosion (Chapter 5).

The effects of different types of vegetation on the way in which rainfall reaches the ground and, therefore, the amount of water available to be absorbed locally, have been measured. If rainwater washes too quickly over bare soil, as it does when there are no leaves or twigs to slow it down, then there is a danger that insufficient rainwater can enter the soil to replenish the ground-water storage areas.

In particular the effectiveness of conifers versus hardwoods as a means of trapping rain for water supply collection has been investigated. The latter have proved more effective in slowly letting rainfall into the ground, although in light as opposed to heavy rain it is the other way round (Robinette, 1972).

Rainfall and drainage

Information on the normal annual rainfall is available for many areas. It can differ greatly over short distances depending on the local topography. The amount of rain that normally falls in a project area has a direct impact on the site planning, mainly through the need to provide a drainage system to cope with the maximum expected wash off or through the site.

The site planner has to work with engineers to assess the extent of the problem. Both have to be aware that changing the cover of the land, for instance by removing vegetation and laying a hard surface, will affect wash-off in a major way. Paving of any surface results in accelerated runoff, when compared with the same amount of water falling on bare soil or vegetation. The problems that arise when attempting to cope with the increased rate of runoff can be major determinants of a site plan, particularly when it proves necessary to build flash-flood holding lakes or extensive ditch systems for excess water.

Snow

Snow, like rain, is something over which the site planner has no control, although the likelihood of it occurring for more than a given number of days can have an important impact on a site plan or even the decision to build in the first place. Snow on steep slopes can quickly make them impassable for vehicles, drifting snow can block roads and footpaths as well as entrances to buildings. Information on the number of days on which snow can be expected to fall and lie is normally available in the local climate statistics.

A site planner needs to be aware of where snow might be expected to accumulate and either plan to avoid those areas or to layout the site elements in such a way that the problem is lessened. Plants, in particular, can be useful snow traps and strategically positioned can act as snow fences, so keeping the routeways clear. For this mixes of shrubs and trees can be particularly effective (Heisler, 1984). Carefully designed planting schemes, based on a full understanding of the site conditions, can reduce the cost of snow removal and so save the client, or future users, money.

Snowfall can be an important determinant of site planning in mountainous areas. Combined with unstable and steep slopes it can lead to potential avalanche situations, which eliminates the possibility of development in certain locations.

FOG AND MIST

Radiation fogs develop when the air is still, the sky is cloudless and an inversion forms, trapping the cold air at the surface. Such fogs can form over wide areas or very locally. It is only the local fogs that the site planner can in any way limit.

As cold air drains downhill, fog can begin to form once the pond of cooler air drops below the critical temperature. Therefore, if the cold air is ponded by any obstruction such as landform, buildings or even dense vegetation a local fog can form. It is useful for the site planners to be able to predict where fogs will form, as it can help in deciding the areas to avoid for road traffic and on a larger scale with the location of airfields. The location of local fog pockets is predicted in the same manner as for frost hollows, that is by looking for anything which will impede the free flow of air. Even minor elements in the landscape, such as small embankments or low walls, can act as dams for cooled air.

In mountainous areas clouds can often descend to ground level and this mist can envelop and disorientate any visitors. In some conditions such clouds come down on lowland too and make driving conditions hazardous, but this too is quite beyond the scope of site planning to influence.

The next chapter takes a look at the information the site planner needs to collect about the natural (the biological) environment. It starts with soil as a growing medium, then considers vegetation and wildlife.

Carrying out the project work

Once you have completed reading through this chapter you should follow the programme of survey work described in Step 2−5. Remember that every site is different, so it will be up to you to decide which information is relevant to collect for the particular project with which you are presently involved.

References   Betz, J. (1975) *Environmental Geology*, Dowden, Hutchinson and Ross, Stroudsberg, Pa.
Brooks, C.E.P. (1950) *Climate in Everyday Life*, Benn, London.

Caborn, J.M. (1957) *Shelterbelts and Microclimate*, HMSO Edinburgh.

Caborn, J.M. (1965) *Windbreaks and Shelterbelts*, London.

Coates, D.R. (ed.) (1981) *Environmental Geomorphology and Landscape Conservation*, (Vol 2, Urban Areas), Dowden, Hutchinson and Ross, Stroudsburg.

De Chiara, J. and Koppelman, L.E. (1984) *Time Saver Standards for Site Planning*, MacGraw Hill, New York.

Gregory, K.J. and Walling, D.E. (eds.) (1981) *Man and Environmental Processes*, Butterworths, London.

Heisler, G.M. (1984) Planting design for wind control, in *Energy-conserving Site Design*, (ed. E. Gregory McPherson), Landscape Architecture Foundation, American Society of Landscape Architects, Washington, DC.

Leighton, F.B. (1966) Landslides and hillside development. In (eds. R. Lung and R. Proctor) *Engineering Geology in Southern California*, Association of Engineering Geologists, Arcadia, Calif.

Lynch, K. and Hack, G. (1984) *Site Planning*, MIT, Cambridge.

McHarg, I.L. (1969) *Design with Nature*, Natural History Press, New York.

McPherson, E. Gregory (1984) *Energy-conserving Site Design*, Landscape Architecture Foundation, American Society of Landscape Architects, Washington, DC.

Robinette, G.O. (1972) *Plants, People and Environmental Quality*, American Society of Landscape Architects Foundation, American Society of Landscape Architects, Washington, DC.

Spirn, A. (1984) The *Granite Garden*, Basic Books, New York.

Szokolay, S.V. (1980) *Environmental Science Handbook*, The Construction Press Ltd, Lancaster, England.

Untermann, R.K. (1973) *Grade Easy, the Principles and Practice of Grading and Drainage*, Landscape Architecture Foundation, American Society of Landscape Architects, Washington, DC.

Waterhouse, F.L. (1955) *The Quarterly Journal of the Royal Meteorological Society*, **81**, 63–71.

5 The natural environment

The second stage of the site planning process is to gather information about the natural environment and to assess the meaning of that data. This chapter indicates the information that can usefully be collected in relation to plants and wildlife and how this data can form the basis of a preliminary assessment of the relative ecological worth of the different parts of the site and of the need for site conservation measures to be applied. However, before looking at the living elements it is necessary to consider soils in more detail than in the previous chapter. There, soils were considered in relation to their physical properties – to illustrate soil mechanics as a limitation on site development. Here, soil is considered as a growing medium which supports plants and, therefore, animals.

The natural environment and site planning

The site planner needs to understand how the natural environment can influence the site planning and design process and to identify when expert help must be co-opted into the site planning team. Ideally a site planning team would always contain an expert in one of the biological sciences, but it is not financially sensible to set up a full site planning team which includes members of all the related disciplines for any but the largest sites. A major part of the co-ordinating site planner's role is to identify which experts are needed and when. To do that, the co-ordinator needs to be familiar with the whole range of expertise, but not necessarily an expert on a particular topic.

Site planners need to be aware that without the expert help of those with specialist training, a proper assessment cannot be made of the influence which each natural environmental factor should have on local site planning. Soils scientists are the experts on soil, but if they are not available, then farmers and horticulturists are often helpful with information on the local soil. Botanists and ecologists are the best experts to approach for information on native plants and farmers and horticulturists on cultivated plants. To assess the ecological value of an area, it is best to approach an ecologist trained to work on the interactions that occur within larger areas, rather than the very minute detail of a single habitat which is most often the interest of expert ecologists.

However, site planners rarely work in ideal situations. Most site planners have had no training in ecology, although those who have trained as landscape architects will have had some. The problem that can face the non-expert is how to begin identifying whether the site contains something of importance. The methods of assessment indicated in this chapter aim only to enable the site planner to make a reasonably informed decision about the advisability of co-opting an expert ecologist or soil scientist into the site planning team. When in doubt, the client should always be advised to employ additional expert help by the site planner, particularly if at a first inspection the site would seem to be one likely to be rich in plants and wildlife, or one likely to contain rare or relatively rare habitats.

In Britain, Sites of Special Scientific Interest have been identified and lists are available from the Nature Conservancy Council. This list is helpful, but it has resulted in many planners believing they can have *carte blanche* on any areas of land not specifically designated as of 'special' ecological value.

At present many developers and site planners take a look at a site, particularly one which appears disturbed and a bit derelict, and assume that it has no particular ecological value. Such a simple judgement is not always appropriate and it is important that even sites which appear to have little of ecological interest are investigated.

This chapter investigates the natural environmental worth of the *ordinary* sites, those that have not been scheduled for conservation. If a project site has been designated for conservation, then the agency concerned must be contacted and it should be established if and how the land use or land management can be changed without falling foul of the law or damaging the natural environment.

The specialist ecologist, when involved in nature conservation, normally has to concentrate efforts on identifying the sites of special interest and then on developing strategies for preserving what already exists. The site planner's priority, however, is in improving the overall quality of the human environment; one of the factors involved in this is the natural environment, which at the basic level supports human life but also enhances its quality.

In addition to needing information about which habitats should be preserved for nature conservation reasons, the planner needs to know which might be enhanced easily and where new habitats could be created to support plants and animals of interest to people. The important role of the physical and natural environment in developing a sense of satisfaction with the environment has been shown by Mostyn (1979), and Harrison and Burgess (1988) in various studies of the role of nature in cities. From their work and that of others it is now recognized that a variety of wildlife habitats can play an important role in making many sites a more attractive place for people, both as a place in which to live and to visit.

The site planner needs an evaluation of the natural environmental attributes which shows the parameters within which change is possible and desirable, so that this information can be linked to any requirement to provide more diverse settings for people's activities as the site is developed.

The role of the natural environment as a factor in the quality of life as referred to above, relates specifically to the European context. In north-west Europe, with a relative paucity of wildlife, mostly harmless to humans, a very particular attitude towards the benefits of nature in cities has developed which does not easily transpose to all other cultures, least of all to those of the tropics. When certain habitats support wildlife dangerous to human life, it is inevitable that people are less keen to have nature on their doorstep. There different solutions from those being developed in Europe are needed. The site planner has to make decisions within the constraints of the local culture as well as the physical and natural environment.

Soils and plants   The proper use of soil resources has to be based on an understanding of how soil works and a knowledge of the capability of soil in relation to agricultural production. Any non-expert needing more detail about soils than can be included in this introductory text, is recommended to read a basic text on soils (Courtney and Trudgill, 1984). More advanced information is available in any of the books produced by the Soil Survey of England and Wales (Jarvis et al., 1984) which indicates how information about soils should influence our use of the land. Soil scientists have made a special study of the link between soils and planning (Davidson, 1980).

In a world with a growing population there is a never-ending demand for food and for this good soils are needed. However, the demand for building land is also insatiable in many parts of the world and somehow a balance has to be struck between this demand and the need to keep the most fertile land workable to feed present and future generations. Such issues relate to economics and politics and are not something with which the site planner can be asked to deal. However, when the site planner is working at lower development densities, and when not all the land is to be built over, it is possible to carry out site planning in such a way that the best land is kept open for future agricultural use, even if it is not at present required. This is particularly important in the developing countries, where it is still possible in many areas to plan to restrict the area where soil structure is damaged and fertility reduced, to the least fertile soils within any area affected by development.

The site planner should establish whether there is anything about the local soil which might inhibit, limit, or encourage plant growth and in rural areas information should be gathered on the relative fertility of the local soils and their suitability for food or other cash crops. Information on soil conditions helps to indicate to the farmer or the landscape architect the range of plants that can be considered for use on a site, particularly when the information is linked to a study of the local climate. In addition, man's activities, in terms of working the soil and adding organic and inorganic material to it as well as altering the moisture content, mean that the intrinsic qualities of soils cannot be considered the only factors influencing plant growth. Plants themselves also influence soils, particularly by changing the humus layer, structure and the pH (acidity) .

Soils: their influence on site planning

The information below relates to the soils of western Europe. For areas with totally different soil conditions, expert help should be sought. This is particularly so in areas where evaporation exceeds precipitation, where deeply weathered tropical soils predominate, or where excessive rainfall leads to leaching and podzolization. Courtney and Trudgill (1984) give some useful introductory information on soils and how they develop in different climatic conditions.

Soils can vary greatly even over relatively small areas and, therefore, the investigation of conditions even on a small site is worthwhile. Soils derive from rocks and those rocks are known as the parent material. The rocks may be igneous (rocks which have their source deep in the earth's crust) or sedimentary (rocks which have been formed from deposited weathered material), but in both cases they are changed into soil through the process of weathering. A soil may be one that has developed in situ from the gradual decay of the local rock; it may have been transported to the site by water (alluvial soils), wind (loess* and sand dunes), or glaciers (many of the soils in Britain and other countries in high latitudes have developed on glacial drift) (Figure 5.1). A soil can also develop from decayed vegetation(peat).

It is the movement of water through soil which governs the development of soil. Without the original involvement of water and air, soils cannot occur and without them soils cannot act as a growing medium. As the weathering process continues, the special characteristics of the soil develop and gradually change as plants and man interact with the soil.

---

* Loess is a windblown deposit from the glacial periods. Its occurrence normally indicates very fertile soils. Such soils are highly erodible.

Soil is the result of:

Weathering of rocks

However, all soil does not derive from local rocks.
It can derive from material deposited from distant
sources:

Glacial deposits
Wind blown deposits
Fluvial deposits

As well as being the result of deposition soil can
also derive from:

Decay of vegetation

Soil quality can, therefore, vary considerably within
small areas.

Figure 5.1 Development of soil.

LAND CAPABILITY AND SOIL CLASSIFICATION

The concept of land capability is important to site planning as it implies
that if a soil is not cultivated beyond its capability, then soil erosion can
be avoided and soil fertility and structure maintained so that yields do
not drop. In a world where the food distribution system frequently
cannot cope with localized shortages, particularly when they occur in
developing countries, it is important to maintain whatever land capability already exists for agriculture and to enhance that where possible.
The site planner takes it as axiomatic that, wherever the type of development allows, the quality of the soil as a growing medium should be
maintained.

The characteristics of the local soil work together with the local
climate and the angle of slope as well as the aspect of the slope to
determine the land capability.

Within the countries of the European Community where food surpluses have recently been a problem, it is easy to disregard the import-

ance of protecting high-quality fertile soils. Speculators demand more land for building in the countryside, because it is cheaper for them to develop new sites than redevelop old. Because of the food surpluses in Western Europe, it is difficult to argue against this use of agricultural land. The long-term advantage for society as a whole of allowing this to happen, when so much disused non-agricultural land could be made available to developers within city boundaries, albeit at a higher cost, remains doubtful. Such issues are political and the individual site planner cannot be expected to become involved in them except when able to advise a client on the advantages and disadvantages of a variety of sites.

There are many different systems for classifying soils and agricultural capability. Two that have been drawn up in Britain are:

UK soil survey (classes 1–7)

The seven classes are related to the wetness, soil type, gradient of slope, local climate and erosion risk all linked together to determine the classes:

1. very minor or no limitations
2. reduced choice of crops, some interference with cultivation
3. moderate restrictions on crops, careful management needed
4. severe limitations, very careful management needed
5. restricted to pasture, forestry, recreation
6. very severe limitations: rough grazing, pasture, forestry
7. land with very severe limitation which cannot be rectified.

UK agricultural classification

This is a very general classification of agricultural capability for England and Wales called the Agricultural Land Classification scheme. It was produced by MAFF (Ministry of Agriculture, Fisheries and Food) in 1974. The MAFF holds detailed information for large parts of rural Britain and their regional offices may be able to give advice.* In other countries you should contact the Ministry of Agriculture for any information.

The Agricultural Land Classification scheme classifies land under five grades:

1. no physical limitations
2. some minor limitations
3. land with moderate limitations
4. severe limitations
5. little agricultural value.

* In Britain too the local branch of the National Farmers Union can be helpful.

The system is particularly useful because it helps to identify the land that should be kept open for agriculture in the long term, even if it is not presently needed, and by a simple process of eliminating the best land, lets us identify where development will cause least problem.

When no land classification is available, the site planner has to work with local experts to arrive at one. The type of information listed in the remainder of this section should be gathered and assessed in conjunction with that already gathered on slopes and climate.

IDENTIFICATION OF SOIL TYPES

Mapped soil information is available for much of Britain but the information tends to be too general to be of much use at the detailed site planning level. However, it is useful for site selection and in giving some general guidance as to what can be expected in the site context area.

The importance of working with the local characteristics when planning and designing, and not imposing unnecessary alien solutions, is well understood.[*] It is, therefore, important to identify the link between local soils and native plant material. Landscape architects and ecologists have worked together to show that native vegetation often survives best on any development site where maintenance levels are low.[†]

All species are site specific to varying degrees, so it is possible to predict that in different soil conditions in given climates and continents particular ranges of native species of plants should be found. Each soil type is also capable of supporting given ranges of non-native species, always with the proviso that the local climate is appropriate to those species. As soils are such an important factor in determining the type of vegetation that can be selected to grow on a site, it is very important to have accurate information on soil type, soil depth and water content for the area covered by any site planning project. It is also important to locate any areas where alien material has been tipped, whether it is soil or subsoil from another site or a waste material.

Physical characteristics of soil are described by looking at:

- profile
- water content
- texture
- acidity
- fertility.

---

[*] See Laurie (1979) for discussions of such issues and the impact on planning and design.
[†] If any soil information is available for the area, the first task must be to plot it on a site context plan; it is unlikely that such information would be in sufficient detail to be worth recording on the project area base plan. To interpret the information, without access to a soil scientist's advice, it will probably be most useful to talk with the local farmers. If the context area is built over, talk to the people who work any local allotments or gardens.

SOIL PROFILE AND TOPSOIL

The study of soil horizons is complex (Figure 5.2). The expert can work out a great deal about a soil just from looking at its profile; each soil type has a characteristic soil profile (Courtney and Trudgill, 1984).

The best way to observe the soil profile on a site is to dig a hole at least 600 mm deep. The depth of the topsoil layer is often indicative of soil fertility and, therefore, of interest to the site planner needing to identify the more fertile land. The darker colour towards the top of a pit normally indicates the topsoil and from the point where it changes colour the soil is often, although not always, less fertile. The depth of the topsoil layer can be natural, or it may have been modified by man's farming or gardening activities, particularly in areas where deep ploughing or digging has taken place.

Topsoil is an unsuitable material to build into and should be removed wherever structures – roads, paths, buildings – are to be positioned. It is expensive to strip topsoil properly but if it is not done with care, the topsoil loses its special qualities as a good growing medium. When that happens a special natural resource that can take many centuries to develop is lost and wasted.

Topsoil is a very valuable commodity but unfortunately in urban situations it is frequently sold off development sites illicitly, too often without anyone in the site planning or design team realizing that something of value is disappearing. The site planner, therefore, needs to work out how to store any stripped topsoil so that it can be reused. Stored topsoil deteriorates very rapidly with age and in relation to the depth at which it is stored and the degree of compaction.

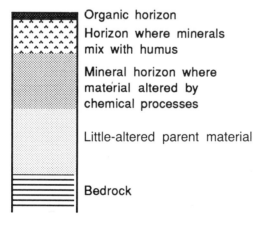

Organic horizon

Horizon where minerals mix with humus

Mineral horizon where material altered by chemical processes

Little-altered parent material

Bedrock

Figure 5.2 Simplified diagram of soil horizons.

IMPERMEABLE LAYERS

The qualities of the subsoil, the layer under the topsoil, have significant impact on site drainage conditions and soil water content. It is always important to understand the impact of drainage on any project site, as unidentified problems can lead to unnecessarily high site development costs.

The site planner should establish, therefore, whether any part of the site is underlain by an impermeable layer (a layer through which water cannot move). It can be rock, clay or in certain conditions iron pan.* If such a layer lies under a site it will be obvious in the soil pits. It will be darker and perhaps redder (because of the iron content) than the surrounding layers. Heavy clay under a site will be just as obvious in a soil pit, but impermeable rock will probably lie at a lower level and not be exposed when a pit is dug.

SOIL WATER CONTENT

Drainage conditions can vary across a site. To identify these there is no real substitute for knowing a site well. Walking over a site, in all sorts of weather conditions, best identifies localized drainage problems. Extremes in weather conditions also have an impact on growing conditions, sometimes as important an impact as the average soil moisture content on plant survival.

SOIL TEXTURE

The different particle components of soil texture work together to produce a soil of different properties. Soil texture can be described by describing the relative proportion of the different components:

Sand
Sand gives an open texture, so that the soil will normally drain freely, but it contributes little in the way of nutrients to the soil.

Silt
Silt is normally made up of very small sand particles; it also gives few nutrients to a soil, but it makes a soil very dense and often difficult to cultivate.

---

* Iron pan is an impermeable layer which has gradually formed over the centuries as the result of chemical processes linked with water movement through the certain soil types (podzolized soils).

Clay
Clay results in soils rich in nutrients although they too can be difficult to work.

Peat
Peat derives from vegetable matter.

Loams
Loams are the mixed soils; they are the easiest and most productive to work for agriculture.

The different components do much to determine the availability of the nutrients to plants.

Some of the construction problems associated with sandy soils and clay soils were mentioned in the previous chapter. They can be important in influencing site planning proposals. For instance, in some circumstances sand can be an unstable base and heavy clays can cause particular problems because of their characteristic of shrinking when dry and expanding when wet. Peat too can pose a major construction problem, particularly when it is deep.

SOIL ACIDITY

Soil acidity is important in determining the sorts of plants that will thrive on the site. Acidity derives directly from the material from which the soils developed, but it is also influenced by various chemical processes that happen in different types of soil in different climates. It is, therefore, necessary to test the local soil acidity. To test this accurately a good quality pH tester would be required, but for most site planning a soil-testing kit of the type used by the horticultural industry will suffice.

SOIL FERTILITY

Soil fertility is normally taken to be the capacity of a soil to produce a desired crop consistently. Soil fertility is influenced by the availability of nutrients from the soil which in turn is influenced by its structure, drainage and organic matter content. It is which of these factors that is at the minimum level of availability to the plants, that ultimately determines the way in which plants react to an individual soil. Man frequently intervenes through adding water or chemicals, so changing the soil structure and its composition. Soils can be defined, therefore, as having a natural inherent capacity for fertility and an actual fertility which results from the soil being manipulated by man. Experts are required to assess fertility.

Soil scientists can advise on the relative fertility of any soil and how it can be manipulated to increase yields of given crops.

SOIL EROSION

The problems associated with soil erosion are world wide, although in countries with a very moderate climate, it has sometimes been regarded as relatively unimportant. However, even in Britain, modern farming practices, which have included more use of mechanization, more use of inorganic fertilizers and the creation of larger fields, have made us aware that soil erosion can be a problem here too.

Soil erosion can mean the removal of the topsoil by wind or water, but it can also mean the erosion of soil quality by the progressive removal of nutrients as water moves through the soil. This latter type of erosion is the chemical erosion of soil which is associated with an intensification of nutrients in soil water. Any water bodies fed by that water can suffer eutrophication (excessive growth of plants in water caused by the excess of nutrients and resulting in a lack of oxygen in the water, which kills life).

Soil erosion and its prevention are part of site planning, for the erosion has to be prevented at the local level.

Wind erosion

Wind erosion is likely to occur where the soil is exposed over large areas. The finer particles in the soil are lifted into the air by the wind and can be blown varying distances. This depends on particle size and strength of the wind. Different soil types are more or less susceptible to wind blow, with those containing high levels of silt being the most likely to blow away. The best way of controlling such erosion is a mat of vegetation. However, when that is not possible shelterbelts must be used to limit the impact of wind. The site planner needs to establish whether local soils are likely to blow. If so proper shelter belts need to be incorporated in any scheme where the earth will be left bare at any time.

Surface wash erosion

Surface water erosion is the most rapid form of erosion. Any bare soil is likely to be eroded in heavy rain and by the associated surface wash, particularly if the land slopes. The only really effective measure against such erosion is a continuous mat of vegetation which allows the water to trickle down leaves, twigs and branches before it hits the soil. The site planner needs to establish the extent of this problem in relation to the project area and to introduce measures to control surface wash as necessary.

All soils move slowly in relation to slopes. On steeply sloping sites this natural down-slope movement of particles of soil is accelerated if the soil is cultivated. In addition to the influence of the angle of slope, different types of soil are more or less susceptible to erosion by water. Heavy rains falling over short periods cause the worst damage and when these are combined with a highly erodible soil type and relatively steep slopes, the results of the erosion can be catastrophic.

There are few areas of the world which have moderate climates and the site planner working outside such areas needs to be aware of the link between soil type, slope and the local climate and realize that this information can be used to predict the likelihood of erosion. Even on small sites, bare areas of earth combined with steep slopes can rapidly lead to erosion which undercuts structures and trees.

Many land management techniques have been developed to reduce the ill-effects of soil erosion by water, including terracing, drainage schemes and contour ploughing. The latter is the most effective means for large areas of land.

The terracing of mountainsides, as found in China, southern Europe and elsewhere, has developed over the centuries as a solution to the problems of holding soil on steep slopes and so allowing difficult land to be productive. In Europe many of the upper terraces have gone out of use in recent decades and a long-term problem is building up of how to control the movement of these slopes, now that they are no longer maintained by farmers. The terrace walls which held the soil are gradually crumbling, and in many of the steepest areas there is an increasing risk of landslip in periods of heavy rain. The only way to reduce the problems if the land is not returned to agricultural use, would seem to be the development of a sufficiently dense mat of vegetation by planting woodlands or forest.

The simplest means of avoiding the problems associated with soil erosion – loss of fertile soils and landslip – is to avoid disturbing the soil in the first place. The site planner should avoid producing proposals which leave steep slopes bare, as whatever benefit can be gained from doing so will rapidly be lost through the washing away of the soil. The problems of natural chemical erosion cannot be influenced by site planning, but the present-day problems that result from the long-term misuse of fertilizers can be corrected by education of the farmers and national policies.

TIPPED MATERIAL

If there is any possibility of water reaching a project site from any tip, it is essential to check on the composition of the waste that was deposited there. The local authorities in Britain all have departments that keep records of the location of recent tips and they will be a useful source of information. Otherwise it often needs a very vigilant site planner to spot where waste has been dumped.

There is always the danger that such tips might contain contaminants that could endanger life. If people are going to use the project area after it has been developed, then it is vital to identify and record the extent of such areas and have their content analysed by experts in chemical analysis. There is often much ignorance about the composition of many older tips and the site planner should always be a little suspicious about the problems tips may cause, as they can mean a site cannot be developed. The client should always be advised of any contamination problems and the scheme should proceed no further unless a solution can be identified to deal with the problem.

SOIL SALINITY

Soil salinity is normally only an issue for site planners working in arid and semi-arid lands, but there it has proved a very major limiting factor to plant growth. In such climates it is all too easy for man to destroy the natural balance and increase the areas of soil which are too saline to cultivate. Some plants such as the date palm, sugar beet, cotton and coconut have a fairly high tolerance of salinity, but others such as beans and citrus fruit have a very low tolerance. In all cases plants only accept a certain limit of salts and in areas of really high salinity nothing can grow. Soil salinity can be measured by experts and in a dry climate it is important to investigate the local situation.

In dry climates it is the use of irrigation which causes salinity and many mistakes have been made up to the recent past. Land that would otherwise have been fertile has become unusable for crops. In any area of the world where evapotranspiration exceeds precipitation, soil moisture is always inadequate for crops. Therefore, farmers welcome irrigation schemes as a means of increasing food production. The quality of the water, and in particular the presence of dissolved salts, together with the chemical characteristics of local soils determine whether irrigating the land will cause problems. Soil scientists now understand the processes that lead to soils becoming too saline and can advise on the appropriate type of irrigation. The key lies in ensuring that the water is of an appropriate quality and supplied only in quantities equivalent to the use of the water by the individual crop, plus the level of evaporation from any bare soil in which it is growing. Soil salinity can also be a problem when land is reclaimed from the sea or when it has been flooded.

Vegetation and site planning

PLANTS AND PEOPLE

The human race could not exist without plants, yet their importance is persistently ignored by governments, their officials, developers and individuals when they make decisions about what should happen on individual sites. It is not an overstatement to say that, if human life is to survive, every decision that is taken about the use and management of land must include a consideration of the impact on vegetation.

Plants are vital to human life because among other things they provide much of the oxygen we need to breathe; they provide the food we eat; they provide the habitats to support wildlife and domesticated animals; they protect the soil from erosion; they control the rate at which rain-water is made available to the soil and underground water supplies; they make soils fertile by providing humus and returning nutrients to the soil and influencing soil structure; they make the climate more moderate locally and they also have a major impact through the great forests on world and regional climates. Despite all these aspects and perhaps because they have always appeared to be self-regenerating, until recently plants have been ignored as an issue by the planning process.

Plants are fragile living organisms and if too many are removed it can lead in some areas to environmental catastrophies. We do not yet fully understand the links between plants and climate, as for example between tropical rain forest and the climate. Climatologists are aware of some links between vegetation distribution and climate, but the exact relationships are still being investigated. In our present state of ignorance of the exact repercussions, to continue to fell yet more of the world's forests would seem to many unwise in the extreme.

Until recently plants were given a low priority by those involved in site development. Now, it is at least partly recognized that the conservation of plants, where possible, should apply on all sites.

Particularly in cities it has been regarded as justified to eradicate plants totally from a site. Only recently have site planners and developers begun to understand that plants are more than decorative elements in cities, for they have too often only been seen as useful in improving the visual quality of the city. Now people are becoming aware that plants have an even greater influence over environmental health in the city than they have over the visual environment. They perform many functions which make life in the city more bearable. For instance they modify the microclimate, they reduce glare, they create shade, they influence the movement of air through the city and through its unbuilt areas, they remove dust particles and cleanse the air of other impurities and they increase the possibility of privacy. In addition, through the wildlife they support, plants provide signs of the link between man and nature which, as the Urban Wildlife movements of many European countries attest, is seen as of growing importance by city dwellers in the developed countries. Perhaps because in the modern industrial city populations are furthest removed from the ultimate man/nature interface of having to work the land for food, they seem to be seeking to renew the link with nature in a new way within the city.

PLANTS AND SITE PLANNING

Site planners must collect very detailed information about the plants that grow on and around the project area so that they can understand the role that plants do and could play in the site layout proposals.

The site planner has to understand the role of plants in the environment, that plants can never be neglected by any site planner intent on producing an environmentally sensitive layout. That plant selection can never be arbitrary because all plants are site specific in their requirements for growth and survival. There are sites where the use of plants is inappropriate but, to be able to identify where these are, the site planner has to understand how plants are used in a wider area than that covered by the project and, therefore, must always look beyond the immediate area of the project site.

The decision to preserve existing plants or to introduce new ones should never be arbitrary. It should relate to the area in which the site is located as well as to the character of the project. The positioning of the planted areas, the species used, whether the plants are native or exotic, will be determined by the site plan and design. The choice should be guided by the information about the site assessed in relation to the needs of the user.

PLANTS ARE LIVING THINGS

Within development projects plants have rarely been understood as living elements in the landscape. In particular the number of dying mature trees on sites developed within the last two decades attest to this attitude (Gilbert, 1989). Too often trees are regarded as sculptures, which will survive whatever happens around them. It appears probable that this lack of understanding of the tree, as a living element requiring certain conditions for survival, is a reason for the very high death rate among newly planted trees in recent development schemes. Planting is often carried out in totally unsuitable 'soils', with no proper preparation of the ground and with no aftercare. Perhaps due to the increasing public understanding of the natural environment, the way site planners and developers regard plants appears to be changing. Public and political attitudes, however, need to change faster, if the continued erosion of natural vegetation and particularly the decline in the number of mature trees is to be halted.

PLANT COMMUNITIES

To those unfamiliar with plants it often appears that plants grow haphazardly. This impression of randomness is emphasized in Britain

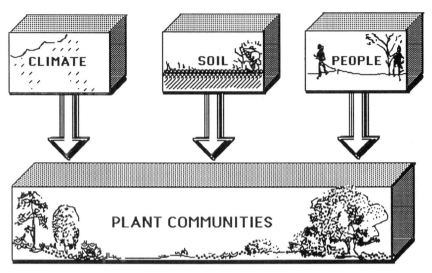

Figure 5.3 The major factors influencing the characteristics of plant communities.

where, because of the mild climate, plants from all over the world flourish in parks and gardens. It is generally only when, as site planners, we become concerned to conserve nature and the integrity of a landscape, or to keep the costs of landscape maintenance to a minimum that we realize the importance of using native and not exotic species.

Wherever it is the intention to conserve nature or produce a naturalistic landscape, it is necessary to work with natural plant communities. Native vegetation will support the greatest range of native wildlife. It also has the added advantage that it 'fits' the local landscape, it looks right – its form (shape) is characteristic of the local landscape, its colours blend with the local landscape. Therefore, when the aim is to conserve to local landscape, it is appropriate to use the native species of plants.*

In addition, native vegetation has the advantage of being more resistant than exotic species to the plant growth problems associated with local fungi, aphids and plant diseases. It is, therefore, sensible to use it where possible to minimize the long-term management costs associated with the care of all landscapes.

Certain species always seem to grow together in nature, some only in particular places, others almost everywhere. These groupings are often referred to as 'plant communities'. The major factors that influence the distribution of plant communities are indicated in Figure 5.3.

To understand the usefulness for site planning of identifying the

---

* The only exception might be when it is intended to recreate a particular historic style of landscape when exotic species might legitimately be used.

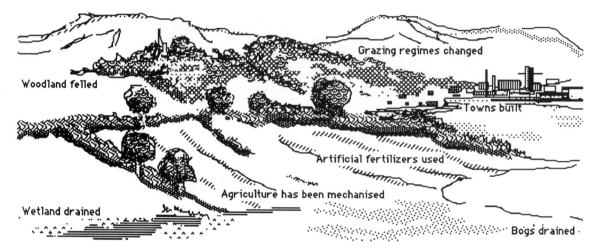

Figure 5.4   Plant communities are changed by the past and present actions of urban and rural populations.

locally appropriate native plant communities, try to remember a long journey undertaken recently. For instance, travelling from Northern Europe by car to the south of Spain several different landscapes are crossed and the changes in plants are noticeable as you move southwards. There is probably less difference in the plants seen in the formal parks and gardens, but in the countryside the changes will be obvious.

Even in a small country like Britain there are distinct vegetation changes in different parts of the countryside. These vegetation changes are because plants are only tolerant of a certain range of conditions, some a wide range, others a narrow range. Survival is determined by local climate and soil and influenced by the way in which people have tended the land in the past and present. Figure 5.4 illustrates some of the factors which have influenced changes in vegetation in Britain.

In particular, people's activities have determined how much is left of the natural vegetation and the local plant communities. In Britain, where almost every square inch of land is or has been managed in some way, there is very little that can truly be termed natural vegetation (Figure 5.4). Bogs have been drained, forests and woodlands felled, forests planted, grazing regimes changed, agriculture mechanized, towns built.

Over most of Britain forest would be the natural climax vegetation, with the composition in each part of the country determined by the local climate, which in turn is influenced by latitude, the proximity of the sea and height above sea level and soils. There are, however, quite substantial tracts of landscape where man's interference has been minimal for sometime, which now have many of the characteristics of natural landscapes and plant communities. *The History of the Countryside* by

Rackham (1986) is an excellent starting point for anybody interested in investigating this further or who has to work on a project in the countryside in Britain.

In order to produce natural-looking landscapes and to conserve the local wildlife, the site planner has to know the range of plants that are locally important and to understand how they can be grouped together in communities, to function as support for different types of wildlife. The site planner also needs to recognize the scarcity of natural and semi-natural vegetation in various parts of the world and to ensure that any areas worthy of retention as a scarce resource occurring within the project site are conserved. Advice will be required from ecologists on how best to do this.

It is also necessary for the site planner to consider the impact of development within the project area on any adjacent or nearby areas of rare vegetation or plant communities. For these reasons a detailed survey of the plants immediately around the site is required. This information also gives the site planner who is working on a plantless site an idea of which plants might be appropriate in relation to the local natural environment.

Plants: their influence on site planning

The following notes summarize some of the ways in which a knowledge of plants, and the range of roles they can play within a site, can influence the decisions the site planner must make. For convenience the factors are dealt with under four major headings – plants and wildlife, plants and physical environmental quality, plants and people, and bio-engineering. In reality all the factors overlap and interact.

PLANTS AND WILDLIFE

The link between plants and wildlife is usefully summarized in the diagram of the oak tree (Figure 5.5). Native plants, those which would naturally occur in an area of land without the interference of man, support a wide range of insects and animals. They also support other plant life.

Wildlife and plants are inextricably linked and many insects for instance can only survive if a particular plant is present.* Because of this strong link between plants, insects and other wildlife it is possible to

---

* Any site planner unfamiliar with the principles of ecology should read a basic text covering the subject, for instance Odum (1975).

Figure 5.5 An oak supports.

predict which wildlife is likely to thrive if a given range of plant species is growing together.

PLANTS AND PHYSICAL ENVIRONMENTAL QUALITY

Plants support most of the other life on earth by producing oxygen. They influence various aspects of the physical environment, in particular they are of major importance for the maintenance of air quality and can be used in microclimate control.

Air quality

Plants, through photosynthesis, remove carbon dioxide from the air and return oxygen to it, so cleansing the air and making it breathable by animals and man. However, plants also cleanse the air by trapping dirt and dust particles. It is the latter factor which is of particular relevance to site plannings in urban areas. Air pollution is a major problem throughout the world and the more that can be done to reduce its ill effects, the better for the quality of the environment. Plants cannot solve the air pollution problem, that can only be done by stringent controls on emissions, but the site planner can plan to make the air more pleasant to breathe locally.

Air pollution can be a major problem in cities, but so far few have attempted to tackle it through increasing the amount of vegetation in and around the city. Spirn (1984) has indicated the ways in which planners can improve air quality through manipulating urban form and working with the natural physical processes of the environment. It would appear from her studies that Stuttgart is the largest city to positively manipulate its environment in a successful attempt to clean its air. In Stuttgart a major factor in the success of the programme has been the forests and other vegetation within the city.

The developed nations have taken measures to clean up the air in cities with varying degrees of success. Most have used legislation to ban the production of the most obvious pollution, but few have attempted also to work with nature to further improve the air quality. For instance, until the 1950s Sheffield, England's fifth largest city, had what was perhaps the worst air in Europe. However, during the 1960s the level of air pollution was so reduced by measures introduced to control emissions of coal smoke from homes and various smokes and chemicals from factory chimneys, that it became a city with relatively clean air. The success of the Sheffield scheme was probably inadvertently helped by the many wooded valleys which channel the cooler air off the hills to the west through to the city centre and the industrial areas. However, the existence of those valleys and their woodlands had not been sufficient to solve the pollution problem before the smoke control orders were imposed, perhaps indicating that beyond a certain limit nature cannot cope with such pollution.

In general, in Britain and other northern European countries the sulphur dioxide levels produced by homes and some factories have been reduced by legal controls over air pollution. However, the level of other contaminants entering the air as a result of increased traffic and changed industrial processes has increased, so that in certain weather conditions air pollution can still be a cause for great concern. This also applies in many other developed countries, in that they are aware that they rely on the wind to remove their unwanted pollution and that this does not always work.

In some European cities, particularly those in the 'sunbelt', conditions in the hot sunny summer months can become intolerable because of the quality of the air. For instance, Athens is now one of the cities with a very major air pollution problem. In part, this problem has been caused by the emissions from factories, and by the use of air conditioners, but the major factor is thought to be fumes from vehicles. The whole problem is accentuated by the local climate and the local landform, which traps the dirty air between the hills.

Air pollution in many third world countries is increasing as industrialization spreads. An increase in the associated health problems is inevitable, unless local and national governments are willing to intervene. It has to be a political decision, as it is unfortunately cheaper for the industrialist to pollute the air than it is to take measures to clean the emissions before they escape into the air. Without the political will nothing can be done. Clean air programmes are so expensive that it is hardly surprising that the much poorer developing countries have such a growing air pollution problem. However, as air pollution is linked with the survival of plants and, therefore, human beings, it is a problem that will have to be faced by all nations. Air pollution is also thought to be a contributory factor in the 'greenhouse effect'.

The site planner needs to be aware that what happens on every site in relation to air pollution contributes to the whole. Site plans in urban areas should be developed in sympathy with any intention to improve air quality by controlling the form of development and the distribution of vegetation. For instance, cities can use a land-use planning system to restrict development in certain areas, so as to open up 'air channels' through the city, encouraging the free flow of clean air down from the hills at night.

Air pollution kills plants

The air may appear clear when we look sky-wards, but it always has particles in it. A good proportion of these occur naturally, but increasingly contaminants produced by industries have entered the air. It has been recognized for sometime that different plants are more or less tolerant of dirty city air, but the most recent concern has been the effects of acid rain on rural as well as on urban areas. Acid rain is thought to be the result of certain chemicals held and mixed together in the air and is now known to have a devastating effect on trees and forests, as illustrated by the devastation of parts of the forests in the Harz mountains. The damage appears to be spreading so quickly that we have no idea of the long-term impact of the present situation. In parts of southern England the effects have been described as more devastating than dutch elm disease or the 1987 hurricane. If that proves to be so, then it is perhaps already too late to save the very special landscape of that area which depends so much on large individual trees and copses of mature forest trees.

It has been known for sometime in the industrial areas that trees can die off rapidly if they are subjected to a continuous stream of pollution from a factory chimney. They can struggle for life with varying success depending on the composition of the fumes which hit them (Gilbert, 1989). Such disasters are less common today in western Europe, because of the stronger controls on emissions from factories, but in other areas of the world plants still die directly from heavy contamination by pollutants in the air.

The problems of visible and odorous pollution are not new, but in previous centuries the concern has been mainly for smoke produced from coal fires (as Spirn has pointed out, the earliest recorded law against the use of coal in cities was in London in 1273, when a short-lived law prohibited its use). This problem increased as factories grew in size through the industrial revolution. In the twentieth century many cities banned the use of open coal fires, so apparently instantly improving air quality. More recently the use of oil to produce energy has caused problems, although this is less easily recognized by the public as little smoke is visible. This, together with the increasing use of chemicals required by many modern industrial processes, has meant that contaminants are being allowed to enter the air without any full understanding of the damage they might do to the environment, particularly when mixed together randomly by the air.

Perhaps one of the reasons it took so long for governments to admit the problem of acid rain was that it could not be seen or smelled. Now that acid rain is more understood, it still seems beyond the will of many governments to take the necessary measures to clean the air. All possible measures involve spending taxpayer's money or reducing the profits available to industrialists, or both.

Plants help to clean the air

Plants act as air cleaners because much of the 'dirt' settles on their stems and leaves. It may be this very useful mechanism which makes them particularly vulnerable to acid rain. They cannot clean the air totally once it is polluted beyond a certain level, but they do improve air quality locally even in polluted conditions. The more trees there are in cities, the better the cities' environments will be in terms of air quality. In addition to the way in which plants make the air more pleasant to breathe in cities, trees and shrubs also have a particular use in relation to traffic, as they remove some of the carbon monoxide and other particles produced by it. Spirn has suggested that hardy, vigorously growing species should be selected for planting near roads. It seems that the type of vegetation which is most effective is that with dense branches, rough bark and twigs and hairy leaves. Work by Bernatzky (1966 and 1969) has indicated the effectiveness of trees in relation to their surface area. He has pointed out that the surface area of a tree can be enormous in relation to its size, suggesting that an 80 year old beech tree may have a total surface of leaves adding up to 1600 square metres. It is these large surface areas which make them such effective air purifiers in cities and along roads and in farmed landscapes.

Whenever a site planner is dealing with a project located in an area where the air tends to be naturally dusty or contaminated in some way, it is essential to keep as much of the existing mature vegetation as possible and to add more densely planted vegetation. The information given in the previous section on wind behaviour and shelterbelts applies here too, as the dirty air needs to blow gently through the leaves to be cleaned, rather than be pushed over the top as it would be by a dense area of planting.

Plants and wind control

The behaviour of wind in relation to vegetation was discussed in the climate section. Plants can be used to control air movement locally. The site planner needs two main pieces of information before deciding where to position a shelterbelt. The first is a very clear picture of air movements common at different times of the year. The second is a clear description of the desired amelioration of the very local wind pattern at different times of the year. If, for instance, in the winter the problem on the site is a piercingly cold north wind which causes very high fuel consumption within the building and makes conditions outside unbearable, then the solution might well be a windbreak of plants on the north side of the building; if the summer problem is heat with the wind from the afternoon sun side, in the northern hemisphere the south-westerly direction, then extension of and minor modifications to the same wind break can help catch the light breezes and funnel them towards the building.

In some situations with harsh climates it is useful to use vegetation as an insulator, using it to hold a layer of relatively still air against the building so that the plant and the still air act as an extra layer of protection against the cold wind. This can only work if the vegetation is very dense.* In positions where cold air will drain down a slope, cooling a site too much, dense vegetation can be used to divert the coolest air away from the area needing protection.

In some sites which are exposed to the elements, the problem is finding a place sheltered enough to enable plants to grow. The site planner has to refer to the experts to find the best plants for these circumstances. Clues can often be found about the best species by inspecting the local flora and seeing what is surviving at present. The site planner can also work with or modify the local landform to create conditions suitable for plant growth.

Plants and solar control

Some of the ways in which plants can be used to lower the temperature locally were mentioned in the section on climate. For instance, the fact that the air is always cooler under trees in sunlight and particularly in woodland and forest means that in hot climates it can be a relief to have dense vegetation. The shade under such vegetation is welcome, but so is the draught of air which builds because of the temperature difference between the area under the trees and the surrounding land unprotected from the sun.

The way in which deciduous trees have been traditionally used to protect houses from the strong summer sun in certain parts of the world, was also identified as an important contribution of trees to the local environment. In many countries with hot summers another way shade trees have been used is to create canopies over public open spaces.

In many sunny countries a major problem for those inside buildings looking out and for those passing through paved areas or over any light coloured surface, is the glare of light that bounces back up and hurts the

---

* Olgyay (1963) suggests Thuja or Picea as the best for this in higher latitudes.

eyes. Vegetation is important in controlling this, either by using it as a ground cover so that less light is reflected, or by using it to create shadow areas. The site planner can, therefore, manipulate local conditions.

Those working in the British climate have opposite concerns. In Britain the problem is one of making sure that no shade is cast in the areas that need to be warm enough to use for outdoor activities, or on the windows of rooms that need to be warmed. The other problem in colder countries is to create enough shelter or wind screens to keep out unwelcome cooling breezes.

Plants and noise

Robinette (1972) cites some evidence that plants in sufficient quantities reduce the level of sound, but it is normally accepted that for site planning purposes plants cannot reduce the level of noise sufficiently to be used alone as noise screens. Unfortunately a noisy road on the other side of a shelter belt of trees sounds just as noisy as without a belt of trees, particularly in winter when there are no leaves. The major usefulness of trees when there is a noise problem is psychological. People seem less aware of a noise source they cannot see. The only really effective method of reducing noise is a solid wall or earth mound and even that is only effective over a short distance because of the way in which sound waves travel.

Trees are at their most effective in decreasing perceived noise when the leaves are rustling in the wind. This increases the ambient noise level (the background noise which is almost always there in any indoor or outdoor environment) and overpowers the mechanical noises from traffic and industry. Just as with rushing water, rustling leaves appear to create a noise more acceptable to the human ear than traffic or factories.

PLANTS AND PEOPLE

Part Three deals in some detail with the influence which plants have on peoples' attitudes to the environment. In addition, many of the factors mentioned in this chapter in relation to plants also relate to their impact on the quality of peoples' lives. It is, however, useful to consider some of the aspects here in more detail.

Plants as a source of delight

Plants stimulate the senses. Their many different forms, habits of growth, colours and sizes create such diversity that no-one could know all the plants of the earth. Few people have not been enchanted by the beauty of flowers and plants. Even urban man, often cut off from contact with the land for many generations, seems drawn to plants. The more affluent build gardens and large numbers of the population make use of parks and other green spaces. It is very noticeable throughout Europe and North America how the richer urban populations prefer to live either in homes with gardens, or in flats with balconies well stocked with plants. It seems that for many people, when their income rises above the subsistence level, it is acceptable to spend at least part of the surplus to ensure some contact with plants.

Plants in the built environment give a welcome contrast to the harsh lines of buildings and other man made structures. They introduce different textures, patterns, shapes, colours. They can hide ugly buildings and views and they can be placed so as to enframe a particularly beautiful view of a building or scene. When it is appropriate landscape architects can use them as a painter would a palette to create a picture and so add special qualities to an urban or rural scene.

Plants are particularly important in urban areas for the sense of scale they impart. The human mind seems able to comprehend and adjust to the size of plants. Sometimes they dwarf the human form, but they are still of a size that our minds can understand. In modern cities where many structures are so immense that they make the human feel insignificant, it is often useful for the site planner and designer to be able to forestall any feeling of alienation by incorporating trees in the spaces between and around buildings.

For some, plants are part of the intellectually stimulating settings that they require to feel satisfied when pursuing a particular activity. This intellectual stimulation can come from association of the plants with things remembered from other places or the same place, from the fact that the way the plants are arranged agrees with that person's view of what constitutes beauty, from an interest in the insects and animals associated with a plant or group of plants.

Recent evidence from attitude surveys in London and Birmingham (Part Three) has shown that there is a very wide spread of interest in wildlife and nature throughout the income groups and throughout ethnic groups. These surveys seem to indicate that ensuring the presence of certain wildlife could add much to people's pleasure at being in various spaces within a city, let alone the countryside.*

The usefulness of plants as screens and delimiters of spaces should not be overlooked by site planners. The problems associated with the scale of spaces are dealt with in Part Three, but here it is important to recognize the role plants can play in screening. They allow the site planner and designer a relatively cheap way of determining how people view and experience a site and its surroundings. The importance of being able to provide people with privacy will be discussed later.

---

* This research is reported in more detail in Chapter 7 as it is of crucial importance to the way in which any site should be planned and designed if the users are to be satisfied with the external environments produced by the site plan.

Plants are also important to the site planner for the way they can be arranged to help unify the appearance of a site. Many modern buildings and their associated service areas, have little to commend them in terms of aesthetic value or spatial experience, but, when combined sympathetically with a well-organized structure planting scheme, a site can be knitted together by the planting. This allows the user a satisfactory experience of place (Part Three) (Relf, 1976).

BIO-ENGINEERING

In Europe, particularly in Austria, civil engineers have increasingly recognized that plants can play an important role in major engineering schemes (Stiles, 1988). This is especially because of their erosion control attributes. Bio-engineering is a new branch of engineering and landscape architecture and the growth in interest is partly because using plants to do the work of concrete and other hard materials can be cheaper and partly because it can be a more permanent solution to erosion problems.

Plants such as the willow (Salix species) have been used for centuries to hold river banks and prevent erosion. They and several other species are excellent for holding any steep slope of unconsolidated material. Hydroseeding is a process developed relatively recently which aims to stabilize slopes by spraying seeds mixed into a growth medium to ensure rapid establishment of the plants. The object is to obtain a total cover of plants as rapidly as possible.*

In traffic engineering schemes too plants have their uses, as they can create good screens between carriageways to prevent headlight glare and dense shrubby vegetation can act as an excellent 'catcher' for cars going out of control on bends or hills.

Ecological value and site planning

Non-experts need to be able to identify when to call in expert ecologists. Assessing the ecological value of any site is such a complicated task that it really has to be undertaken by a fully trained ecologist. However, to be able to convince the client that there is a problem needing special expertise, it is often necessary for the site planner to gather some basic data.

One way is to attempt to identify which areas of vegetation should not be disturbed. This can be done by looking at the present degree of complexity in the vegetation. It is possible to say in very general terms that the more complex an area of vegetation the longer it will take to re-establish and, therefore, the more important it is not to disturb it during

---

* For more information on plants and erosion control read Gray and Leiser (1982).

site development operations. There are of course exceptions to this general rule, but it may help in making decisions about a site. Complexity is provided by high species diversity; several layers of vegetation such as a mixture of scrub in grassland; edges such as the edge of a wood or pond and the presence of extra habitats such as those caused by wet areas.

The most important site planning factors in relation to plants are to ensure that sufficient information is available to permit the survival of the most valuable areas of vegetation on the site and to work out how to upgrade the ecological value of the site.

Retaining or enhancing the ecological value of a site is important for recreation purposes as well as nature conservation. It adds another dimension to interest visitors to the site. A site planner who is sensitive to the local environment, even if starting with a bare site, can ensure that plant associations develop to reflect the local environmental variations. This can be done by managing the land in an appropriate way and controlling the range of plant species used in the different parts of the site. By doing this, conditions can develop within which habitats which act as niches for different species of wildlife can become established.

The development of an appropriate range of plant associations and habitats on a site will ensure a more interesting and stimulating setting within which the public can enjoy the experience of the outdoors, whilst at the same time ensuring that plants and wildlife can survive in these areas which are mainly given over to man's activities.

The next chapter deals with the information to be gathered about the social environment, followed by consideration of the people who will use the site in the future and their needs.

Carrying out the project work

Once you have completed reading through this section you should follow the programme of survey work described in Steps 6–8 of Part Five. Remember that every site is different, so it will be up to you to decide which information is relevant to collect for the particular project with which you are presently involved.

References

Bernatzky, A. (1966) Climatic influences of green and city planning, *Anthos*, 1, 23; (1969) The performance and value of trees, *Anthos*, 1969,1,125.

Courtney, F.M. and Trudgill, S.T. (1984) *The Soil, an Introduction to Soil Study*, 2nd edition, Edward Arnold, London.

Davidson, D.A. (1980) *Soils and Land Use Planning*, Longman, London.

Gilbert, O.L. (1989) *The Ecology of Urban Habitats*, Chapman and Hall, London.

Gray, D.H. and Leiser, A.T. (1982) *Biotechnical Slope Protection and Erosion Control*, Van Nostrand Reinhold, New York.

Harrison, Carolyn and Burgess, Jacquelin (1988) Qualitative research and open space policy, *The Planner*, Nov. 1988, 16–18.

Jarvis et al. (1984) *Soils and their use in Northern England*, Soils Survey of England and Wales, Harpenden.

Laurie I. (ed.) (1979) *Nature in Cities: the Natural Environment in the Design and Development of Urban Green Space*, Wiley, Chichester.

Mostyn, Barbara (1979) *Personal Benefits and Satisfactions Derived from Participation in Urban Wildlife Projects*, NCC publication, London.

Odum, E. (1975) *Ecology*, Holt, Reinhart and Winston, New York.

Olgyay, A. (1963) *Design with Climate*, Princeton, NJ.

Rackham, O. (1986) *History of the Countryside*, J.M.Dent, London.

Relf, E. (1976) *Place and Placelessness*, Pion, London.

Robinette, G.O. (1972) *Plants, People and Environmental Quality*, American Society of Landscape Architects, Washington, D.C.

Spirn, Anne W. (1984) *The Granite Garden*, Basic Books, New York.

Stiles, R. (1988) Engineering with vegetation, *Landscape Design*, **172**, April 1988.

6 Aspects of the social environment: land use, land management and landscape character

This chapter is only concerned with a very limited range of the aspects that relate to the social environment. It deals with the land use information that the site planner needs to obtain about the people who live on and around a project area. This introductory text does not attempt to cover the full range of issues the economic and social planners must consider when making their decisions (Hall, 1982; McLoughlin, 1969). The next part indicates how people tend to react to and behave in external spaces, but that too is only a limited part of the social environment.

The physical and natural environmental factors outlined in the previous two chapters interact to create a setting for man's activities. The way man has used the land in the past has a profound effect on present land capability.

Misuse of the land by general over-exploitation or by eradication of a particular resource may have rendered an area unusable, or have resulted in its being able to support fewer people or only support them at subsistence level. However, just as land may have been damaged by man's past activities, it can also have been improved. For instance, soil productivity may have been increased by drainage or irrigation schemes, or by a slow improvement in soil texture through careful husbandry. Potential for urban development may also have been improved by man's past activities; for instance, by schemes which have reclaimed land from the sea, brought drinking water to arid areas, or ensured an adequate supply of biomass by planting and carefully managed forestry.

In order to plan any area of land it is important to have an understanding of what man has been able to do on it in the past and of how the physical and natural environment have limited or controlled this. It is also crucial to site planning to understand the impact which man's activities have had on the environment, for often what is perceived as a natural environment is only held in that state by specific land use and land management activities.

The landscape, as it is seen and reacted to in the settled areas, is the result of an intricate series of interactions between man and nature. The landscapes that result are the settings, the backcloths, for human activities. Each landscape has a different character, as a result of the way that people have related to the physical and natural environment in the past. This landscape character can be very important to retain, as it reflects cultural heritage and the way people have used the land within the constraints of the local environment. Landscape is part of people's sense of belonging to a particular place.

Proposing a change in land-use or land maintenance and management activities is the normal end-product of a site planning exercise and such change invariably leads to landscape change. There is, therefore, a need for site planners to understand the factors that operate to keep any landscape looking as it does. Without that understanding no landscape conservation measures can be successful.

For all the above reasons the site planner needs to record how man has used the land around a project site in the past, as well as how it is used at present. This information helps to establish the parameters within which the site planning concepts and policies should be developed.

While in theory it might be best to go back as far as possible in time to understand how the present land-use pattern and landscapes have evolved, the site planner can rarely afford sufficient time and is forced to take short cuts. The site planner needs to establish how the present and past land-use pattern might affect the future development of the project site. As a first stage the site planner records the land uses that are on and around the project area at present.

Different information is required for sites in urban and rural situations. The information listed below gives some guidance about why land-use data is useful to the site planning process and the type of information that can be usefully gathered as a first step of the site survey and assessment. The site planner should be aware that as more is discovered about the site, it will often be necessary to return to a particular topic in more detail.

HOUSING

The built environment land uses

Shelter is a primary requirement of human life. People become attached to the place where their home is and the quality of that environment is particularly important to them.

The site planner needs to know in detail about any existing houses in the project area and in general terms about any residential areas around it. These are the residential environments which will be affected by the land-use change and for which the impact of the new development should be assessed by the site planner. The introduction of new land uses into any area with well-established settlement patterns can cause problems and be perceived by the people who live there as something that will detract from the quality of life. This concern is particularly strong if a non-residential land use is to be introduced. This is one of the reasons for the development of zoning legislation in many countries, to reduce the likelihood of conflict by having different land uses in different areas. Many land-uses are not compatible with housing but some are, provided that sites are planned and designed with care. The next chapter describes some of the factors which have been found to influence residents' satisfaction with the housing environment.

The site planner should record the details of any housing within the project area, unless the client has already made arrangements for the people concerned to live elsewhere, as might be the case when working for a large housing authority. Sometimes the site planner works on a housing renewal scheme which involves temporarily decanting a population while the area is rehabilitated. In such a case it is vital to have very detailed information about the people and their needs. This information is not gathered by site planners, as it requires detailed studies by social experts and housing managers. However, the site planner must ensure that a social survey is carried out and in such a way that it provides useful information for the replanning and design. To be of use to the site planner data is required on peoples' needs and attitudes to their external environment, not just the qualities they require inside the home and the need for social facilities. The next Part indicates the type of information that is useful to the site planner when planning and designing a site.

Record any housing immediately around the project area. It is useful to have information on the type of buildings, their approximate age, their condition and the way in which they are laid out and find out something about the people who live there. The level of information needed will depend on the particular development planned for the project area and the extent to which those living around the site might be expected to use the newly developed site. Sometimes this latter movement of people will be the desired end product of the site plan, in other cases an influx of local people could create tension between them and those for whom the site is being developed. The site planner has to be aware of these possibilities as the site plan is developed and aware that reducing the risk of social conflict might well involve extra expenditure for the client at the design detail stage. More detailed data can always be gathered at a later date if it is needed and the site planner should normally only gather general information about the adjacent areas at the stage of the first survey.

Should the surrounding housing be of historic or townscape interest, more detailed study will be needed to establish whether there are any characteristics which should be reflected in the new development. See the sections in this chapter on past land uses and visual qualities.

OPEN SPACE

Surveys into the use of open spaces and recreation areas have repeatedly shown that the majority of the population do not like to walk too far to a local open space; 400 m (a ten minute walk) can be taken as the normal limit for people to walk to one regularly (Part Three). For this reason the site planner can restrict the study of local open spaces to those within 400 m of a project site. The surveys of the use of open space have shown that it is only if such a space has very special features that people will make a regular effort to walk further to it. When an open space is beyond the 400 m distance people tend to use some form of transport for visits, except for the few who are keen walkers. Once people are in a car or bus, or on a cycle they are free to go further afield and are, therefore, less likely to use local open spaces. Instead they go to the particular space which has the facilities they require or to the space that has the type of setting they consider best fits the activity they want to pursue.

If a project area or any part of it is to be developed for public use, the above limitations on the distance people are willing to walk means that the people who use the site on a casual basis are likely to be those living within a ten to fifteen minute walk. Otherwise they will only come to it for a special interest or its special ambience, probably using some means of transport to get to the site, and they may create a parking problem that will have to be solved. The two groups will have different needs and expectations and the problem of how to find out what they want is dealt with in the next chapter.

SOCIAL FACILITIES

These include schools, community buildings, health facilities, clubs, shops, indoor sports and swimming facilities. The need for various social facilities relates directly to the characteristics of the local population. The local planners are the people to approach to find out what they and the social planners intend should be done to support the people living in and around the project site. Knowing what types of social facilities are or will be available can help in assessing the need for additional facilities which might occur as the project area is developed. This type of assessment can only be carried out by experts in social planning, but obtaining advice from them will be quicker if information has already been gathered on what already exists on the site and near it.

The type of project will determine the importance of gathering information on social facilities. When they are an important component, such as for housing schemes, then the site planner has to produce a site plan which allows people easy and direct access to all the facilities they require.

INDUSTRY, WAREHOUSING AND WORKSHOPS

A project site adjacent to or part of an industrial area can turn out to have many difficult site planning problems. For instance, the amount of noise emitted by the factories can make it expensive and difficult to develop a site for residential, commercial or recreational use. The noise from traffic servicing the factories can also be a problem. Air pollution problems, including unpleasant smells, are often associated with industrial processes and can make adjacent sites unpleasant places to visit. The flow of workers in and out of the sites can cause regular traffic jams and make access to a project site unnecessarily difficult. The spaces around the factories and warehouses may be in use for storage and be unsightly.

There are other less obvious problems associated with such sites. For instance, the owners of many factories and workshops provide little in the way of recreational facilities for their employees. This can lead employees to look for nearby spaces which can be used for informal relaxation on days when the weather is pleasant and they will occupy any unused land for their recreational activities. In addition some factories provide insufficient parking for employees and this can also lead to an unexpectedly high use of any new car parking facilities on the project site unless the problem is recognized from the beginning.

The site planner, therefore, needs to understand what any existing industrial land uses around the project site might mean in terms of pressures on the site. First the present problems of any industrial areas have to be identified with the aid of the local planners and then an estimate has to be made of how these might change in response to the development of the project area.

If the project area is to be turned over to an industrial use, then its impact on the surrounding land uses must be considered. The site planner has to work out what the worst impacts of the project might be in terms of noise, traffic, visual detractors, social behaviour patterns and then plan to minimize and if possible eradicate these through the site plan and design.

COMMUNICATIONS

These include roads, footpaths, bus routes, bus stops, railway lines, railway stations and car parks. Roads and the associated services are so expensive to build that the existing road pattern can be a major determinant of the future form of development on individual sites. Therefore, the site planner must know where the nearest access points are to the main roads. Early discussions with the local road engineers are important, as these can help determine how access to the project area can be arranged within the guidelines operated by the engineers. The site planner should not assume that just because there is a road adjacent to or near a site, access to it will be allowed. There are very strict rules and regulations about where lower category roads can join major roads and about access to the lower category roads from private access roads. The site planner needs to understand the local road hierarchy and the road safety rules applied by the local road engineers.

SERVICES

If services such as electricity, gas, communications cables, water and sewerage are known to be available in the vicinity of the project area, the site planner must establish that the facilities can be made available for use on site by contacting the relevant authorities. The question of the approximate cost of servicing the site will have to be raised at an early stage, as these costs can be high and the client will need to be informed. If the site is small, and in an urban area, it is possible to get a very rough idea of the services available to the site by looking out for man-holes.* In many of the more remote sites, linking to a sewerage network will not be possible and it will be necessary to investigate the use of cesspits for disposal of effluent. To do this the site planner will have to work with engineers and with the information already gathered on the local geology and soils.

Rural or urban fringe land uses

The site planner working on an unbuilt site in the countryside has to collect much of the information listed above, but also has to consider issues which are specifically relevant to countryside areas and which can determine the decisions made about how best to plan a site.

* In Britain if you look on the man-hole cover you can often identify what service is underneath.

AGRICULTURE, WOODLAND, FORESTRY AND EXTRACTIVE INDUSTRIES

Issues relating to agriculture and forestry were discussed in the previous chapter and basic data about agriculture should have already been collected by the site planner. The information about these factors and about the local vegetation pattern allows a preliminary assessment to be made of the relative value of keeping the land open for farming and retaining the natural vegetation pattern. As stated in the previous chapter, in ideal circumstances the site planner would be appointed at an early enough stage in the site planning for these factors to have influenced site selection. However, in most cases the site planner is employed well after the stage when it is possible to stop a development scheme happening on a particular area of land and so it is often too late to save the best land.

When the site planner is working on a project in a rural area or on the urban fringe, collecting information about the agricultural land immediately adjacent to the project area is important if the new scheme is not to detract from the agricultural landscape or make farming less efficient. In relation to the latter, agricultural productivity may be adversely affected if houses are built adjacent to fields. Children and adults may use the fields for informal recreation and sometimes to dump waste, dogs from the housing areas can disturb stock to such an extent that animals cannot be kept in fields nearby. The site planner has to consider in detail any conflicts of interest that might arise between land users and plan and design to minimize them.

Information on field boundaries and the pattern produced by them can have an impact on the way a project site is laid out in rural areas. This is because the distance that a project is visible in the open agricultural landscape is often greater than if the project is in an urban area. Therefore, if the appearance of the project area is not to detract totally from the rural landscape of which it will become a part, it normally has to blend with it. In most circumstances this is most easily achieved by reflecting the patterns, shapes, colours and textures of the landscape within which the project area is situated. For instance, by reflecting any local patterns in the distribution of woodlands and using similar woods to screen the new development.

The size of the farming units should be recorded and information gathered as to whether it is static or expanding. The site planner should find out from local agricultural experts whether there is any government policy to maintain, increase or decrease the size of holdings, as such changes can have a significant and rapid impact on a landscape. If possible find out how any subsidy schemes are affecting local agricultural production. This information will help in assessing the likelihood of change to the local landscape because of changing patterns of land management and land utilization.

Establish which area within which the project area lies is subject to national, regional or local government planning policies aimed at increasing the woodland or forest. If change is likely, attempt to establish, through talking to local agricultural and forestry experts, what types of change would be possible locally and then by talking to the local farmers find out how they think they might implement such policies. Find out too if any financial incentives for increasing the area of woodland/forest are available, as these might help to determine the final form of the site planning proposals. In parts of Europe such policies are being introduced and they might well have a profound impact on regional landscapes.

The economic viability of crops can change very quickly, particularly when the type of crop grown locally is determined by international economic forces. At the site planning level it can be useful to know what crops would naturally give the best yields on an area of land and how this natural capability can be altered by the use of artificial aids such as fertilizers and irrigation. Local agricultural experts could be asked about this as well as local farmers. Understanding the patterns which are visible in the agricultural landscape and associated with the use of the individual plots of land allows the site planner to decide whether to reflect or go against the locally prevailing pattern when proposing the site plan. To make this decision the site planner needs to work out what is appropriate in relation to the local landscape.

In many areas of countryside extractive industries are the main employers of labour and despite the environmental problems associated with them, they may be seen as vital to the survival of local communities. If a project site is near a quarry or open cast mining scheme, the site planner needs to discuss the problems associated with extraction and the processing of the material, with the local planners. The site planner should ensure that there are no adverse effects with regard to the project. When the project itself involves extraction, the site plan should show how the adverse environmental impacts are to be handled. In the latter case a proper environmental impact assessment will often be necessary before planning permission can be obtained.

THE LOCAL POPULATION

The people living in and around the project area

If the project site is likely to attract the local public, it is important to estimate how many people live within about half a kilometre of the site. It is useful also to obtain information about the age structure of the people living locally, as this will help in assessing how they might use the project site. Such information is normally available from local census statistics.

In most countries census information is recorded in great detail, but for most site planning generalized information about the people living around the project site is sufficient. Of course, if the project site is one that is already developed, very detailed information will need to be extracted from the records about the people living there and that information will need supplementing by social surveys. In some areas of the world the populations shift so fast that up to date information is not available even in a generalized form, in which case the site planner often has to rely on observation and best guesses, unless a proper survey can be undertaken. Local town planners are usually useful sources of information about population.

When extracting the population data from the census for site planning purposes it is useful to assemble it into a minimum of four age categories: children under eleven, young people aged twelve to sixteen, adults in the age range seventeen to sixty and older people over sixty. In different cultures other breakdowns might be more appropriate, but in Europe these general groupings can be used for guidance on the range of uses expected in the local external environment. It is also useful to obtain information from the census data on the proportion of women in each age group. Their life style and recreation patterns are different in almost every culture and proper provision is rarely made for their special requirements in the external environment.

The next chapter deals with how the site planner can use information about people to establish the requirements of the different site users and indicates the differing patterns of use of various age groups.

GATHERING INFORMATION

In gathering information about social and economic factors for the site planning process the site planner must be aware that the decisions taken about social and economic issues have a direct effect on what happens on individual sites. It is important, therefore, for the site planner to hold discussions with those responsible for local social and economic planning, to identify whether there are any particular problems or issues which should influence the detailed development of a given area of land. The size of the site and the complexity of the development proposal will influence the extent to which the site planner should become involved in such problems. In the first instance the site planner should check with the local town or rural planners.

It is often useful to gather information on local unemployment trends, as different patterns of using land and facilities often emerge in areas of high unemployment. It is also useful to gather information on the local social and cultural mixes, as these too can influence the way people use the external environment, as has been well illustrated by Cooper Marcus (1986).

HOW PEOPLE USE THE PROJECT AREA AT PRESENT

Many development sites are used for some other activity than that generally planned. If nothing else they may be derelict sites which people use as short cuts or for casual recreation. Disrupting well established, if unofficial, patterns of use can lead to unnecessary conflicts between the existing and future users and in extreme cases to vandalism by people who feel that they have lost a resource which was valuable to them. Therefore, even when the site has not been developed previously, it is important to gather information about who is doing what on the site at present.

In many cases it will be possible to cater for existing uses such as through routes during the site layout stage, but in others, such as the loss of the only area of open land accessible to the public, the issues involved will need to be resolved by the local planning authority.

The next chapter gives details of how to obtain detailed information about the needs of a local population in relation to their external environment. However, it is always worth being as observant as possible about how people use a site at present and during any site visits keep a photographic record and make notes. Some parts of a site may be more attractive to people in their present state than others. The site planner should attempt to establish why and whether this is of any importance to the future design.

Past land use and historic features

Any landscape is a palimpsest, i.e. what we see as the landscape today reflects what has happened on that area of land in the past. Each layer is piled on the previous landscape, but that is only partly obliterated as the new layer is established. Evidence of natural as well as man made changes which have happened on any area of land, is there to be interpreted. It is only the wilderness areas which show no or little signs of man's activities. Traces of man's historic activities remain in almost every landscape, particularly in those areas where substantial populations have settled, although they are often difficult for the untrained eye to detect. While such traces are important because they add to the local sense of place and are part of the local landscape character, they can also turn out to be of economic value because of their historical associations. Historical features have helped stimulate tourism throughout the world.

Understanding landscapes in terms of their historic development is, therefore, important if such landscapes are to be interpreted in a manner which will make them of recreational as well as educational and academic interest. Landscapes as evidence of history are likely to become more, not less important in the future, particularly when tourism is increasingly playing such an important part in many national economies. Traces of the past should be seen by the site planner as a valuable cultural resource, not something to be bulldozed away in the interests of short-term profit.

Site planners rarely have time to become involved in an in depth study of the history of their area. However, it is important that they do not overlook any potential of the project area for special development related to its historic context and that they do not inadvertently destroy important cultural links. The site planner has to take short cuts to establish whether there is anything in the area of historic interest and, when any objects or sites which might have such interest are found, should discuss the findings with the local history experts.

Examining maps of the wider study area for any features of prehistoric or historic importance can be a useful first step in identifying the occurrence of historic remains. Most developed countries have detailed topographic maps which also indicate these features, but in many countries no systematic nationwide survey is available. If there is a lack of mapped information, the best people to approach to discuss the likelihood of local sites of interest will be those working in the nearest university or museum on archeology or history.*

Indicate on the plans any objects or sites of interest on or near the project site. The existence of such sites can help the site planner to develop ideas on the direction which footpaths might take from the project area; designing footways which take the user past interesting features adds to the likelihood of the routeway being used for strolling. The latter is an important aspect of leisure time activities which are often overlooked by planners and designers.

One of the problems with maps showing historic sites is that they overlook the more widespread but less spectacular features – the walls, the old roadways, the stone stiles, the footbridges which are part of the grain of a local landscape and often of some antiquity. The site planner has a very useful role in identifying these older objects and places, where possible identifying them as features for retention and incorporation in the site planning proposals.

If information on historic development has not already been assembled for the area or if it only concentrates on the important buildings, one of the ways to get an idea about the historic development of an

---

* In Britain you will find good local history sections in most public libraries and also local history societies in many areas.

area is to plot all the old artifacts (man-made objects). It is normally fairly easy to recognize when something has not been built or made in the recent past, since the weathering processes give them a look of age. In most countries buildings and other structures connected with the time before local industrialization stand out as different from those built since. It is, therefore, at least worthwhile mapping the pre-industrial, early industrial and present day buildings and structures. In those parts of the developed world where industrialization flourished in the previous century, many of the features of that early industrial period are seen now of as much interest as those of the earlier historic periods.

Do not just concentrate on structures but also look out for any obviously man-designed landscapes – parks, estates and gardens can all contain evidence of past styles of design worth retaining for their historic interest.

In areas where everything was built at the same time and it is difficult to find anything of special interest, this part of the site planning exercise will be superfluous. In that case just do a quick check of the area to make sure nothing of interest has been overlooked, which could be reflected in the form or style of development.

The discovery of any historic place or feature on the site can be a great advantage, as it adds to the potential recreational and educational interest of a site and will often help make the place a more attractive setting for many uses. However, if the site is being developed for other uses, such as high-density housing or industry, the finding of a special historic feature could lead to problems. In many countries the feature would have to be investigated thoroughly by archaeologists prior to development. The site may turn out to be so valuable that, as with sites of particular ecological importance, parts of it have to be protected.

Professional advice is essential if, for instance, any obviously old bits of pottery, coins or other man-made objects are found on the site.

Land ownership and planning controls

In many countries there are legal controls over the use of land. It is important to understand how these affect the site as well as the land immediately adjacent to it. In Britain, in particular, there are very strong controls over the detailed form of the buildings and their design as well as on the use of the land, but in other countries provided the zoning laws are adhered to, there is often greater freedom for the site planner and designer.

Thorough discussions with the local planners are needed to establish how the strategic, district and local plans influence what can happen on and near the site. What sort of buildings the local planning authority will allow, at what densities can development take place, how much open land must be retained, how must car parking be dealt with; these are some of the questions that need to be answered by the planners prior to any detailed site plans being drawn up.

In addition information is needed on any special controls, such as tree preservation orders or conservation area status, or special requirements on materials, heights of structures etc., which might apply to the project area. It is important to know all these things before making decisions about how the site should be planned and developed, otherwise the client's time and money can be wasted.

In many countries once the ideas for the site plan have been developed, it is necessary to approach the planning department of the local authority to obtain their agreement to the scheme and to check if special building or planning permission is required. It is important to establish this at an early stage, as it can influence the programming of the development project.

In Britain, it is usual for all except very minor changes of land use to need permission from the local authority. The local planners and development control officers are usually very helpful with advice on the procedure to be followed and the information which the client must provide. Even if the site is owned by the local authority, it is still necessary to go through this process. If planning consent is required by law, then the local authority must process this consent for itself as well as others before work begins on site. If the project does not involve building operations, then there is a whole range of work that can be carried out without the need for planning permission, but it is always better to discuss the proposal with the local planning department and explain what is intended.

Landmarks   To feel secure, people normally need to have the feeling 'I know where I am'; without it they can experience a sense of alienation (Part Three). In part at least people develop this feeling through using landmarks to orientate themselves. A landmark in this sense is any feature, natural or man made, which stands out from the general scene and is remembered by the individual. It is not just the prestigious local focal point: it can be a rock of a particular shape, an outcrop of rock forming a cliff, a group of rocks, a clump of trees, an individual tree of a different sort or shape from the others in the area, it can be a church tower or any building different from the others around it. The list is endless and psychologists have shown that in a local neighbourhood even small-scale objects, which to an outsider seem insignificant, such as a shop on a corner, are the landmarks that make up our mental map of the area in which we live.*

* For further information on the importance of landmarks see K. Lynch (1960).

CONSIDERING THE APPEARANCE OF A LANDSCAPE   **Landscape**

Making aesthetic judgements is always a difficult task, because each of us has very different ideas about what we like to look at (Part Three). Self-awareness about attitudes to aesthetic issues is an important first step for any site planner. Becoming aware of particular reactions to different scenes will help in making decisions about site planning issues. If a person knows what they think and why, then the attitudes can be explained to others. Being able to express reactions clearly allows the site planner, through discussion and then through user surveys, to understand better the reactions of others.

There can be no generally accepted rule as to what constitutes beauty. Landscape architects have searched in vain through recent decades for some common measure of aesthetic quality and in doing so have realized what complicated issues are involved.*

All our senses are involved in the human reaction to a scene. How we experience a scene is not just a matter of objects perceived through the eyes. It is also, among other things, influenced by the relationship between the objects in view, the sequence in which they are experienced, the culture in which we have been brought up, our level of education, our past experience and even our state of well being. The best we can hope for as site planners is a general consensus amongst those who use and those who occasionally visit a site on the merits of its visual attributes. The site planner needs to know which objects and areas are considered relatively attractive, and perhaps, therefore, worth considering for preservation, and which areas can be changed.

It is important not to neglect the built-up areas in any consideration of landscape. To the landscape architect and planner, the built environment is as much a landscape as the rural and wilderness landscapes. This can often be difficult for those not involved in the profession to accept, as the way in which the word landscape is used in the English language has meant that it is bound up with the way we express our feelings about the countryside and natural beauty. However, the wider definition of the word landscape is an important basic concept to the site planning process, as it allows us to consider the whole of the outdoor environment. Landscape within the built up area is sometimes referred to as townscape.

VISUAL ATTRIBUTES

An understanding of why a site looks as it does is vital to planning any site, since every change the site planner proposes in relation to land use

---

* For further information see the issue of Landscape Research devoted to the topic Landscape Evaluation in Planning Rural Areas, Vol. 6, 2, Summer 1981.

or method of land management will also change the landscape in some way, sometimes subtly, sometimes obviously.

Consideration of the visual aspects of landscape is a complex issue. Where the site planner is not a landscape architect then a specialist needs to be co-opted into the site planning team to give advice on the particular qualities of the local landscape.

The landscape that we see is partly the result of features over which we have no control and partly the result of things we can control. For instance, we have no control over the form of the land, as it has evolved through the actions of erosion and deposition on the basic geological structure. These actions have resulted in the valleys, hills and drainage systems which make the skeletal framework of all our landscapes. We also have no control over the regional climate and that severely limits what can be produced from the land, as well as what will naturally grow on it and, therefore, controls the overall texture and colour of the surface.

How people use and manage the land is particularly important in influencing the detail of the landscape – the scale of the local enclosure, and the local colour and texture of the landscape (Beer, 1987a). It is these latter elements of the landscape that site planners can control through the planning and design process. It is the way a site and its buildings are set out and the way the site is clothed with vegetation which determines the appearance of the local landscape; the site planner controls all these to varying degrees on different sites and, therefore, influences the local landscape.

Landscape types and their maintenance and management

Many of the techniques evolved to classify or consider landscape have been worked out in relation to relatively large areas of land (Smardon *et al.*, 1986). To adapt such methods to the small scale of site planning would be a long involved task and require the expertise of an experienced landscape architect. The site planner can, however, take a short cut and instead of attempting to adapt landscape evaluation techniques, can concentrate exclusively on the factors over which man has control, on the way the land is used, the elements (components) of each landscape and the method adopted locally to manage the land and the landscape elements. This short cut gives the site planner some understanding of the detail of the local landscape and it only requires a little more field work to supplement the information that will already have been gathered by a site planner working through the process described here.

In some instances the whole of the project site and the adjacent land will have a similar landscape which can all be defined as of one type, in others there will be distinct differences. In the former case the study will not take too long.

IDENTIFYING LANDSCAPE TYPES FOR SITE PLANNING PROJECTS

Site planning, unlike landscape planning, needs a very detailed breakdown of information about the local landscape. At the site planning level landscape types can be identified by using the information already gathered on land uses and then subdividing the particular land use to indicate the areas with different visual attributes. This normally works at site planning level only, because at that level individual land uses generally have similar visual characteristics. The site planner then lists the components of each landscape subdivision and assesses which of those detract from the visual qualities of the area and which enhance them. Information is also recorded on how each of the landscape components of the subdivisions are managed. This may seem laborious but given that it is only done for the land within the project area, unless it is a complex site, it often takes very little time.* Two examples are given below for sites in an urban landscape.

The land use is a playing field

It is all one landscape type mainly composed of short close mown grass which is maintained by gang mowing ten times a year. The elements (components) of the landscape are the playing surface, a club house and a small area for car parking, and an area of rougher grass surrounding the whole site with board fencing around the perimeter. The whole area appears bleak. However, the appearance of the area is slightly enhanced by being kept litter free and the playing surface regularly mown. The factors which detract from the visual quality are: the fence which is in a poor state of repair, the strip of grass between the fence and the playing field which is mown too often for wild flowers to thrive and too infrequently to appear neat and tidy, the building which needs painting, the wooden balcony which needs repairing and the car parking area which needs resurfacing. Whilst adequate as a playing surface the full potential of the area as a recreation facility is not realized, as it does not attract people who are not involved in sports, despite the fact that there is ample space for them to move around.

---

* It is important to beware of confusing the word landscaping with planting. This is very often done in planning and architectural circles where the planting added to a site development is referred to as the landscaping. Try not to use the word landscaping at all. The landscape that we see is not just composed of plants but is a result of the individual appearance of all the different elements that make up the landscape and the way they interact with each other, and the basic landform.

The land use is low-density, low-rise public housing
It consists of three landscape types:

The housing and associated gardens and culs de sac
The houses are fronted by short gardens totally enclosed by tall privet hedges, many of which are not looked after by the tenants. The gardens open on to 4 m wide roadways which are surrounded by 2 m footpaths. The asphalt footpaths and road surfaces are in a poor state of repair with crumbling kerbs and weeds growing in the cracks. The lamp posts are large and made of concrete: some are leaning at an angle, patches of grass and weeds grow at their base. Telephone posts and wires produce an untidy wire-scape; many of the posts are not upright. The whole area appears very 'down at heel', dilapidated and poverty stricken and there is no sign of maintenance activities. The quality of the environment could be improved instantly by increased maintenance, but the problem of the tenants' attitudes to their own environment and their willingness to take responsibility for it would need study.

The through roads and their associated grass verges
The roads appear wide, although the carriageway is only 8 m wide. The road is lined by grass verges which are 2.5 m wide and there is a 2 m footpath between the verge and the front gardens. The verge is broken up by driveways and the grass is mown three times a year. A few gardens still have hedges, but most have been removed and replaced by randomly planted shrubs set in grass. There are no large trees and a few medium and small trees. The concrete lamp posts and telephone posts dominate the scene and many of them lean at curious angles. The road and pavement surfaces are well maintained and the grass verge is regularly mown. Litter is a particularly severe problem in the area of the corner shop. The roadway is used for night-time parking, despite the fact that every house has a driveway and garage. The appearance is very bleak and open. The visual image of the housing area acquired by outsiders passing through the area is in the main gained by use of these roads. The image could be improved substantially by changing the view from the road.

Small areas of open space
The open spaces are the spaces left over after building; they are not designed for public use. They mainly consist of grass, which is regularly mown. A few random shrubs have been planted in an attempt to decorate the areas, but no attempt has been made to turn them into attractive spaces which the inhabitants might want to use for various activities. Litter accumulates and adds to the impression of these being wastelands. Skilled landscape design could make these spaces a useful part of local landscape and again improve the visual image of the area.

With the information gathered using the process suggested here, the likely impact on the local landscape of the site planning and associated land and landscape management proposals can be assessed and useful discussions entered into with landscape architects about what might happen to the landscape of the project area. It is also a process which will allow communication with the local community and the site users about the elements that comprise their landscape and the ways in which they could be better maintained. This allows for a very real level of public consultation on the appearance of landscapes, as it can sidestep the issues related to perception and aesthetics.

The influence of visual image on the inhabitants' perception of their home environment and why it is important for the site planner to be concerned about it is discussed briefly in the next section.

LANDSCAPE CHARACTER

Site planning schemes should usually aim to reflect the local landscape character in some way if they are to be regarded as successful, otherwise they will be seen as schemes which detract from the local scene (Beer, 1987b).

All landscapes are composed of patterns, textures and colours; they are a result of the way in which the surface of the earth is clothed by vegetation or changed by man's agricultural and non-agricultural activities, except in wilderness areas. It is very important to identify these factors, for they influence how we see landscape. If a pattern is broken, or different texture or colours are introduced, we produce a different and perhaps alien landscape. Sometimes as site planners and designers we want to draw attention to a site and in that case might deliberately introduce alien elements so that the new landscape stands out. More often, however, we try to blend in with the surrounding landscape, to enhance its particular landscape character.

Views

The views of a project area from without and the views into it will often play an important part in developing ideas for the future planning of the site. It is useful, therefore, to know the types of views available and to get an impression from consultations with local people and visitors of the views they would like to have retained or screened. The site planner needs to remember that viewing is a two-way operation; people looking in from outside might not like what they see, whereas those looking out might be happy. The site planner's problem is to strike a balance. Objects which detract from the scene should be located where they are least visible, or arranged so that they are screened by the introduction of new visually acceptable elements in the landscape.

INTER-VISIBILITY

It is useful to work out where the different parts of a project area are visible in the surrounding landscape. There are elaborate and time consuming methods of doing this, such as by plotting cross sections from the contour data on the topographic maps* or by feeding topographic data into specially devised computer programs. One of the most simple, and appropriate for small site planning projects, is to walk through all parts of the study area and record on a 1:25 000 map what can be seen of the land beyond the boundary of the site and then go to those areas and look back towards the site to check what is visible. However, any site planning projects which involve substantial development of large-scale structures require that more accurate techniques are used, such as those available using specially developed computer software.

VISUAL QUALITY OF THE VIEWS

It is necessary at an early stage in the site planning process to identify which views from the site should be preserved as they are, which could be enhanced and which should be screened.

Inevitably judgements about this are subjective. It is important, therefore, to involve the local people and/or regular visitors to the area in making assessments. If no contact with local people is possible, the judgement of an individual site planner, perhaps supplemented by that of other members of the team, can be used. However, make sure that in any statements about visual quality it is explained how these judgements were arrived at so that others understand their limitations.

A relatively simple but systematic way to record subjective judgements of visual quality is to give each view a score. Give the first view looked at a score of 10, whatever the view is like, then score up or down for each of the following views. For instance: the next one might be much less good and given a score of 5, the one after that appears slightly better than the first so the score is 11 and the next is much better so the score is 15. The actual numbers used do not matter. What is being done with this process is to consider the relative merits of all the views from the site – it does no more than allow a ranking of the views from and to the specific site.

It is normally best not to take the ranking too literally as it gives an undue sense of scientific exactness. It is best to sort the views at the most into five quality categories, such as the following:

* A useful summary of the techniques which can be used for this is available in Chapter 16 of R. Smardon *et al.* (1986) section by S.G. Alonso, *et al.*

- Very good views, which must be kept open.
- Good views, which ought to be kept open.
- Moderately good views, which could be used with advantage.
- Poor views, which ought to be screened.
- Very poor views, which must be screened.

This information is useful as it allows the site planner to decide where visitors might like to sit or walk to enjoy views. It also helps to decide the views that detract from the scene, so identifying where screens should be placed.

There will inevitably be conflicts between what is best for the future users of the project area and those living around it. It is the resolution of such conflicts of interest that makes site planning and design so interesting and challenging.

Site planning in essence

Site planning is essentially about trying to get a good fit between the needs of people and the environment. Site planning is about the right thing in the right place; to establish what is 'right in a particular area', it is necessary to understand the local landscape and then to use this understanding to develop appropriate types and forms of development. When the uses fit the landscape, then an area can develop its own beauty which relates to appropriateness rather than aesthetics. Site planning does not neglect aesthetics, but aesthetic issues only form part of site planning. Through site planning we can determine to keep a particular feature for aesthetic reasons (say a long-distance view framed by a certain group of trees) and we can also aim to introduce a certain sequence of visual experience to add to the aesthetic pleasure of visiting a site and to design the detail of parts of the site to achieve particular aesthetic effects.

There are occasions, such as when faced with a totally flat and featureless site, that the site planner considers developing a plan based solely on people's needs in terms of facilities and spaces, rather than on a concern for the local landscape character. In those circumstances aesthetic rather than other physical environmental considerations can be a major factor in determining the form of the plan as well as the landscape which the planner aims to develop.

Whatever the circumstances, attempting to make a match between the physical environment and peoples' needs is how the site planner ensures that a site develops its own special character. It is this development of a special and yet appropriate character which is so often neglected by those involved in making plans for sites, and when it is neglected we can end up with the same dull uniformity everywhere.

The next part outlines how to gather information about the needs of the people who will use the site in the future and how to determine the settings which it might be appropriate to develop on the site to meet these needs. Part Four shows how the information gathered about the local physical, natural and social environment helps to identify how best to locate uses on the site and produce the settings required by the users.

Carrying out the project work

Once you have completed reading through this section you should follow the programme of survey work described in Steps 9–11.

References

Beer, A.R. (1987a) *Conserving the rural landscape: some notes on design issues, Department of Landscape*, University of Sheffield.

Beer, A.R. (1987b) *Landscape conservation*, Department of Landscape, University of Sheffield.

Cooper Marcus, Clare and Sarkissian, Wendy (1986) *Housing as if People Mattered*, University of California Press, Berkeley.

Hall, P. (1982) *Urban and Regional Planning*, Penguin Books, London.

Lynch, K. (1960) *The Image of the City*, MIT Press, Cambridge.

McLoughlin J.B. (1969) *Urban and Regional Planning: a Systems Approach*, Faber and Faber, London.

Smardon, R. *et al.*, (1986) *Foundations for Visual Project Analysis*, Wiley Interscience, New York.

Part Three
Spaces For People

Once the site planner has gathered as much information as is readily available about the natural and physical environmental aspects of a site and its surroundings, the next stage before any plans for the site can be drawn up is to consider in detail who will use the site, how and for what. Here, the main concern is with the 'outside' areas: with the spaces between buildings and with open areas of land. However, when working in the built environment the site planner should always bear in mind that the internal and external uses of a site are inextricably linked and must be planned and designed together (Canter, 1977).

Chapter 7 highlights some of the issues that face the site planner trying to identify present as well as future user needs. Chapter 8 presents some basic information about people's activities and their associated environmental requirements to help the site planner decide on the best approach to site layout and design.

Too often, sites are planned and designed in relation to the designer's own life experience and opinions, without adequate understanding of how those most likely to use a site, who may have different outlooks and needs, might wish to behave within it.

With all the evidence since the 1960s about people's reaction to high density housing, why did it take almost twenty years before authorities ceased to build that sort of estate? By ignoring people's needs in relation to their housing environment many local authorities may still be paying off the loans raised to finance the building of the large housing estates of multi storey buildings forty years after the buildings have been pulled down (Beer, 1982).

One of the concerns is that some of the developing countries are copying the type of planned development which in Europe and the US has been linked to social problems (Cooper Marcus and Sarkissian, 1986). There is some evidence that attitudes towards the urban housing environment are cross cultural and, therefore, that many of the same social reactions to 'hostile' housing environments are being exhibited among the occupants of such housing estates in developing countries

(Al-Noori, 1987). Mass housing is a form of development which requires very careful design in conjunction with sound management, in particular when it involves the less affluent.

The slow reaction to the problems highlighted by sociological studies appears to indicate a barrier to communication between different professions and between the professions and the politicians. Greenbie (1976) pointed to the difference of interests between those involved in pure research, such as the scientists and social scientists, and those involved in having to make design decisions.

The aims here are to give guidance on the main ways in which the available information on people's behaviour in different environmental settings might influence the site planner's decisions, and to show how that information might be used to develop effective arguments to influence the client's thoughts.

References   Al-Noori, W. (1987) *The environment outside the dwelling, a case study of new housing in Baghdad*, PhD thesis (unpublished), University of Sheffield.

Beer, Anne R. (1982) The external environment of housing areas. *Built Environment*, **8**, No. 1.

Canter, D. (1974) *Psychology for Architects*, Applied Science Publishers, London.

Canter, D. (1977) *The psychology of place*, Architectural Press, London.

Canter, D. and Stringer, P. *et al.* (1975) *Environmental Interactions*, Surrey University Press.

Greenbie, B. (1976) *Design for Diversity*, Elsevier, Amsterdam.

Environmental settings and the quality of life 7

This chapter introduces a few of the ways in which such experts as environmental psychologists and social scientists have approached the problems associated with defining human environmental needs.

Over recent decades a fairly general recognition has developed that land use and land management planning is required at local, regional and national as well as international level to ensure human well-being and even survival. With such strategic planning issues to be dealt with, alongside the basic social and economic needs of a local population, it is perhaps not surprising that the less quantifiable aspects such as those that influence the quality of human life have been rather neglected. The intention here is to attempt to redress this somewhat, by concentrating on the factors influencing the quality of life at the local level, looking at the question of what makes some sites more satisfactory settings for human life and activity than others. The reader who needs to understand more of planning issues in the wider sense is referred to basic texts on planning (Cullingworth, 1972; Fabos, 1985).

Environmental settings

The concept of the 'environmental setting', or as it is sometimes termed the 'behavioural setting', has been gradually gaining ground as a tool to aid site planning and design. The concept implied by the word 'setting' is perhaps best understood by thinking of the spaces that form the city. These spaces are the basic support system for human activities, the settings for all outdoor activity. It is possible to think of the whole of the outside as a sequence of spaces, some small and intimate, others vast and seemingly limitless. The concept can apply to much of the countryside too, particularly in Britain with its relatively small-scale landscapes.

PLACE AND SPACE

Humans tend to understand their immediate environment in terms of the sequence and qualities of spaces that make up the areas they most use. Knowing exactly where one is and how that space relates to the others around it is of vital importance to all humans; the feeling of being lost and the fear associated with that feeling is an overwhelming one. The studies which the psychologists have carried out of mental maps (sometimes termed cognitive maps) have shown that people carry images of places in their minds and knowledge of how these places relate to each other.

It also appears that people take this knowledge further and most important have a clear image of what they define as home territory. People can also clearly describe the territory through which they move regularly on their way to work, school, recreation or the shops. Each of our mental maps of our home territory and regularly used territory is unique in some way, as can be simply tested by asking your friends to draw a plan of your common home territory. According to the psychologists this is because all humans construct their personal mental image of places in relation to the way each individual experiences their environment.

VISUAL CHARACTERISTICS OF SPACES

Each space has different visual characteristics to do with shape, scale, relative height of the edge, the appearance and degree of transparency of the edge, the appearance of the floor as well as of the sub-spaces within the major space. It is these differences which allow us to distinguish easily between spaces. The differences are further emphasized by the way each space relates to other spaces, the occurrence or not of natural elements within the space and its sub-spaces, as well as the amount and type of human usage of the space.

As Lynch (1960) suggested in *Image of the City*, the concept of 'edge' is crucial to understanding spaces in the city. The 'edges', whether formed by landform, vegetation or structures, or a mixture of elements, play a major part in creating in our minds the image of a place. Lynch identified five elements related to our understanding of space in the city: 'edges', 'paths', 'nodes', 'districts' and 'landmarks'. He saw these as the building blocks out of which we structure the city, both in terms of how it is perceived and how it must be designed.

The landmarks of an area have a particularly strong influence on memory of place, although it is noticeable that different people have different recollections of what constitutes a local landmark, even if they agree about the major landmarks. Landmarks tend to be objects – they can include the local shop, a tree, cross-roads as well as the more obvious objects like church towers, water towers, town halls, other large buildings or major landscape features. Out of his studies Lynch developed the concept of 'imagibility', or as it is sometimes termed 'legibility', the idea that each particular place has an image that can be interpreted easily and clearly remembered.

FACTORS INFLUENCING PERCEPTION OF SPACES

It is not just the image of a particular space which determines how it is perceived and understood. Perception of the special characteristics of an individual space also relates, amongst other factors, to the sequence and types of spaces passed through on the way to the space, to the other spaces seen from the particular space, to past knowledge of the space and of similar spaces, to the state of mind, to past experiences of the natural environment, to the individual's cultural, educational, social and economic background, to aesthetic sensibilities and to such factors as state of physical well being. It also relates to the evidence of human activities (noise, dirt, smell), who is in the space when it is visited or observed and what the visitor feels able to do or prevented from doing when there. This combination of factors influencing people's perception of space makes it very difficult for the site planner and designer to think clearly about how to plan and design an individual space.

SITE PLANNING, ENVIRONMENTAL SETTINGS AND THE SENSE OF PLACE

As site planners our first function is to plan and design to allow a specific range of activities to take place. To do this it is necessary to work out the range of facilities that will be required to allow these activities to be performed. It is also necessary to ensure that the site will be managed in such a way that the planned activities can take place. Finally, and for site planning most important, it is necessary to ensure that people will experience the place as being a satisfactory setting for their activity or activities. In part this involves using the characteristics of the existing place and understanding their role in how people experience place; in part it involves developing new places with new characteristics.

People react to and experience environmental settings as the place in which their daily or occasional activities take place. The site planner, therefore, has to assess the effectiveness of any proposals. Firstly, by attempting to work out whether the proposals for its future layout and design make life easier for those who will use the site, that is by supporting the activities that will need to occur. Then, by working out what will make the site a sufficiently satisfying and interesting place to encourage people to stay and enjoy being there. If a site layout and design does not aspire to do these things, it probably will not work well for the user or the client. In such circumstances the client will be faced with the additional costs involved in putting the site right at a later date.

Linked to the issue of environmental settings is that of the sense of place. The work done by Kevin Lynch (1960) was one of the earliest studies in this field and for the site planners it remains one of the most useful. Despite his and others' work an understanding of the importance of the sense of place seems to have been missing from too many designed schemes in the past decades. The design professions have continued to be criticized by the psychologists such as Sommer (1969) and Canter (1977) for making erroneous assumptions about human behaviour and concentrating on form rather than how spaces are likely to be used. These authors both stress the importance of creating places that mean something to people. Relf (1976) in his short book *Place and Place-lessness* presents some interesting insights into the issues involved in place.

MAKING SITES LIVABLE

As the site plan is developed a good site planner asks the question: 'what will it be like to: take the children for a walk, go to the bus stop, take a cycle ride, go to the shops, go to school, park the car, go to the park, stroll in the sports ground, watch the football game, fish?' and so on.

As Lynch and Hack (1984) said, the site planner's role is to make the spaces people inhabit fit for habitation, but another equally important role is to make them livable. As Lynch pointed out, the factors which affect habitability are often governed by what happens outside a site. Dirt, road noise, polluted water, polluted air, such factors are only really curable by planning actions dealing with areas much larger than individual sites and, therefore, the subject of strategic plans. However, the alert site planner can do much to limit the impact on the site users of these externally created problems. For instance, by using some of the methods of ameliorating poor environmental conditions described in previous chapters and by proposing ways of laying out the site which make the best of any assets existing in the local environment. When, however, we deal with the question of livability, then we begin to enter the difficult realms of human psychology.

Knowledge of how humans behave in relation to their environmental settings and why they react as they do is still limited. Therefore, it is difficult to work out what people will consider is a livable environment. Knowledge of how people are likely to react to given situations, what will please them so that they continue to use a space, what will alienate them so that they do not use a space, or even what makes people feel free to vandalize a space is lacking. We know surprisingly little about human perception and what does and does not engender a sense of satisfaction in humans.

Yet without this information how can the site planner plan and design. In attempting to consider this problem here it is not being suggested that environmental determinism, with all its inflexibility, is the answer. Rather an approach is being proposed which accepts that the quality of the environment does have a major influence on the way in which people perceive the quality of their lives and, therefore, cannot be ignored by the site planner.

It is often fairly straightforward for the site planner to establish what the major outdoor activities of a site are likely to be. They derive from the function of the site. For instance, on a city site the buildings which are erected for a specific planned function determine to a large extent how people will need to use the areas immediately outside. If there are no buildings, the activities which the site is supposed to cater for will derive from the functions allocated to and permitted on the site. More difficult is the identification of the factors which can be used to understand the attributes which an environmental setting should have if the setting is to support people's needs adequately. The remainder of this chapter deals with the various means by which these factors might be identified and approached.

How people experience environments

The ways in which people experience environments are summarized in Box 7.1.

Some of the evidence to support this summary is set out below. However, it should be noted that all responses to environment are mediated by language, that is the way people communicate with others from their local culture and from other 'cultures'. Symbolic meanings and values have been shown by Burgess, Harrison and Limb (1988) to be important in understanding how people relate to, and use, settings.

Kaplan (1973) developed a model of how people experience and make sense of the built environment. He showed the importance of being able to gather information about the environment and suggested a person's cognitive map included four domains as indicated in Box 7.2.

For an environment to be satisfactory for the user it has to allow the user to gain the information required to understand it. It has to be an environment that people can make sense of, to offer novelty, challenge and also an element of uncertainty to stimulate the intellect, and it has to permit choice.

There is no straightforward way of describing the relationship between people and the spaces in which they live, work and play. A host of factors impinge on reactions to spaces and places. Site planners and designers, therefore, have a complex task in identifying the factors that

BOX 7.1

**The factors that
influence how
people understand
and experience
environments**

1. The senses: people's first contact with the environment is through the senses:

    sight
    hearing
    smell
    touch
    taste

2. Needs: people have basic needs which lead to an instinctive reaction to the information received through the senses:

    survival (physiological needs – food + water + shelter)
    security (physical and psychological needs)
    belonging (to a group and a place)
    expression of individual identity (the need for the self to be worth while)
    experience a sense of self-fulfilment (the achievement of aspirations)

3. Desires: to fulfil these basic needs people have a built-in desire to acquire knowledge about their environment; they are driven to do this by the need to experience satisfaction:

    knowledge (to understand present and to be able to predict future occurrences)

4. Aesthetics: people's knowledge as well as social and cultural conditioning, and their past experiences result in their developing sensibilities:

    what is seen, heard, smelt, touched and tasted is filtered by past learning and experiences and judged qualitatively by the individual

need to be considered if they are to design places which support the human activities that take place in them.

When considering the part that the environment plays in our perceptions of the quality of our lives, it is often easier for us to identify what people do not like about their immediate surroundings than to discover what they like. For instance, we know that people do not want us to plan and design areas in which the inhabitants are afraid to venture out after dark, areas where even in broad daylight people live behind locked doors, areas which look so like wastelands that they seem to accentuate local poverty, shopping areas which are so empty at night that people fear visiting them, city parks which local people perceive as places too dangerous to visit. The list of the mistakes that have been made in recent

1. recognition:
      knowing where you are
2. prediction:
      knowing what happens next
3. evaluation:
      knowing whether what happens next is good or bad
4. action:
      knowing what to do

Box 7.2

The domains of an individual's cognitive map

years is extensive, but how are we to use this information positively in an attempt to produce environments less likely to be perceived as alienating?

Maslow (1967) suggested that it is possible to identify the basic needs of human life; these are set out in Box 7.3.

As site planners we need to ensure that all these basic requirements will not be hindered by the environmental setting. By looking at the research carried out by psychologists and others, we can begin to identify the characteristics of a setting which cause people to feel satisfied or otherwise with their environment. In addition we can supplement that information in relation to individual sites by our own observations of people's behaviour and reactions.

A place has to support the human functions for which it is being planned and designed. It should be designed so that it relates to the human scale and allows people to use it without risk. If as a minimum this is not done, a site will not work as a satisfactory setting for people's lives. But a site also has to provide stimulation for the human mind to

- The first essential is that the physiological needs are met – that we are able to assuage hunger and thirst.
- The second is that we feel secure and have a place to shelter and are able to keep ourselves warm.
- The third is that we feel we belong to a group or society.
- The fourth is that we are free to express our individual identity in some way.
- The fifth is that we live in an environment which allows us to experience a sense of self-fulfilment.

BOX 7.3

Basic needs of human life

allow us to feel satisfied. People need to feel that a place belongs to them; for them to feel good in it, a site has to have a stability about it.

THE HUMAN HABITAT

One of the ways to start working out what would make a successful human habitat might be to see what can be learned from the scientist's approach to creating habitats for animals. It is known that each animal thrives best if certain physical and natural characteristics are present. For instance, in zoos it has been found that the nearer it is possible to get to a replication of these natural conditions the more content, long-lived and healthy the animal. Surely then the answer is to see if we can identify the supports that humans require. However, this is not as easy as it might seem, for humans are one of the most adaptable creatures on earth.

Humans survive in an immense variety of conditions. They do not always thrive in them, but they survive. Unlike other animals people can construct elaborate habitats to support their needs, even in the most hostile physical conditions. Perhaps it has been that very adaptability which has allowed those involved in the planning process (the politicians, the planners, the developers, the financiers and others) to be involved in the construction of so very many unworkable human habitats in cities, habitats which so obviously have not supported the users' daily needs and instead alienated people. Newman (1976) and Coleman (1985) have both studied in depth the alienation that can result if individuals feel they have no control over their environment; their work has indicated the importance of a concern for the human habitat as a social support system at the local level and emphasized the need for site planning to take place on the basis of a full understanding.

Given all the cultural diversity amongst the human race, can we even begin to think how we might produce more acceptable habitats? Habitats which support people's daily needs rather than create difficulties and barriers for human activity. Is it just naive idealism to even begin to think that it would be possible to take the planning of human habitats further than the basic provision of an infrastructure? That is what the site planner has to decide in relation to each site.

The key to why we need to be concerned about each part of the city as a supporting habitat for human life is that it is to everybody's advantage if populations do not feel alienated from their immediate environments and instead each area becomes a 'settled' area of a city. Settled areas of cities normally have less turnover of population and have a reputation for being safer and more secure. There is normally less vandalism, the people who live there have more pride in their immediate environment.

In addition, the cost to the city of looking after such areas is likely to be lower because of the lower maintenance requirements.

INFORMATION AS A BASIC REQUIREMENT OF SURVIVAL

In *Humanscape: Environments for People*, edited by Stephen and Rachel Kaplan (1982), you will find one of the most useful collections of articles about people and environments available to site planners. Anybody intending to become deeply involved in site planning should refer to it. Here it is only possible to deal with the topics in a very superficial manner.

A common characteristic identified by psychologists is that humans need a continual supply of information about their environment to survive and thrive. As Kaplan (1982) pointed out, information alone is not enough. People also have to care if they are going to make the effort to gather the information that is presented to them through the environment. It has been shown that in fact people are strongly motivated, not only to use information, but actively to seek it and to seek reasons to use it. This drive to know more is balanced by a need to control the quantity of information absorbed. As Kaplan said, 'people crave new information and are at the same time repelled from information too far from what they can comprehend and deal with'.

People need to understand, to make sense of their environment. They like the excitement of learning; they get bored if there is nothing new in a situation. Perhaps going back to the needs of our ancestors to survive in hostile environments, humans are driven to make sense of the information they receive about the environment. To enable them to do this it has been suggested that people have an in-built desire for involvement with their environment. It has been suggested that much human motivation and emotion is information based and that this is one of the reasons people are so aware of their environment, so fascinated by it.

THE ROLE OF FASCINATION

Kaplan (1982) states that people like to feel fascinated. Fascination can take the form of becoming interested in and involved with what is potentially educational, dangerous or important to the individual in some social way. Kaplan considered this to be one of the reasons why humans have, in psychological terms, such a strong reaction to wild life. Although some of the reaction relates to survival instinct, perhaps some is also related to inherent pleasure in being part of the natural world. The latter has been indicated by recent research into the attitudes of urban dwellers to natural life in the cities (Burgess, Limb and Harrison, 1987).

Kaplan also considers people's fascination with things green – whether gardens, wilderness, parks or even house plants to be part of this link with the natural world.

Hebb (1982) considers that it is a fundamental part of living things that they must be active – both the brain as well as muscle. The environment stimulates both and without that stimulation mental function and physical health have been shown to deteriorate. Fascination with the environment is seen as a basic requirement of survival and not just a manner of behaviour adopted to fill people's leisure time.

MAKING SENSE OF ENVIRONMENTAL INFORMATION

People are curious about things and they like to have something to explore. They are fascinated about things that relate to themselves, but they are also fascinated about things that relate to their group. People also like to feel challenged and they like to win. In site planning terms these factors too can be important. If there is nothing to explore, if there is nothing to fascinate people, if there is nothing for people to do, then a site will be less liked by the users.

In an essay on the quality of living, Farber (1966) makes the following relevant statements: 'Most of us need to aspire, to create, to give, and to belong'. It is not that people need to do all these things all the time, but only that they need to be able to 'find some mode of expression'. He states 'Social planning is indispensable in a crowded world' but it also has to include a recognition of our 'non-material needs'.

Farber also identifies altruism as a characteristic of humans. It has been described as 'intrinsically motivated'. Many trivial gestures of daily life are driven by altruism, but they are often the gestures which make life in crowded communities bearable. Without some level of altruism few community projects could ever begin, let alone thrive. Altruism relates to the human need for informal contact with others and site planners have to bear this in mind.

Farber considers that some form of struggle is necessary for humans to feel satisfied with their world: 'Security cannot make up for the loss of adventure; comfort for the lack of hard creative work; nor togetherness for the lack of true companionship'. When this is applied to site planning it suggests that there is a need to have a challenge in an environment, a need for people to be able to do something, a need for people to have the opportunity through contact with others to make friends. His statement implies that the perfect environment which did not involve people in doing something or struggling against something, even if it were obtainable, could never make people happy with their lot. His insight goes far to explain why wilderness landscapes make such good recreation environments, allowing people to struggle in groups or alone against relatively hostile natural environments.

THE HUMAN NEED FOR A HOMEBASE

In an article discussing the contrasts between man and the other primates Washburn (1972) stresses that the environmental conditions within which *Homo sapiens* (modern man) developed have changed considerably over the last 50,000 years. He further suggests that the ability of man to cope with these changes indicates a high level of adaptability. Washburn suggests that the present rate of social and environmental change is much greater than anything in the past and whether the rate of adaptability is sufficient to cope with the changes is, he thinks, open to question.

Humans are remarkable among the primates in that they require a location to which they can return and where they can expect to be helped by fellow humans, a place that will be there every night – a homebase. Other primates, for instance, normally do not help sick members of their group. Humans have developed a level of co-operation linked to the home base which is far ahead of that exhibited by most other primates.

Another way humans differ from them is in the amount of land they use. For instance, primitive human beings – hunters and gatherers – used hundreds of square miles of land, whereas no other primate ever uses much more than 15 square miles. Humans have the built-in ability to know hundreds of square miles and have a brain which can allow them to place themselves exactly within that known area.

THE NEED TO BELONG TO A PLACE AND GROUP

As well as having developed the ability to locate themselves accurately within large geographical areas, humans have also developed a strong sense of territory. In particular, this is still very important among primitive tribes. As Greenbie (1981) has described when discussing proxemic and distemic spaces in the context of site planning, people can clearly define their land and what belongs to others. Even westernized modern man, used to the concepts involved in travelling the world, still tends to vest an emotional importance in an area of land identifiable as home or nation.

IMPLICATIONS FOR SITE PLANNING

These factors are important to site planners as they imply that for people to feel satisfied with their environment, they need to understand where they are and they need to identify with the place they call home.

SEEING LANDSCAPE

This is not the place to attempt, even superficially, to investigate the vast literature that exists on how people see and how they interpret what they see. A useful introductory text for those working in site planning or design is the book *Foundations for Visual Project Analysis* (Smardon *et al.*, 1986). Part Two of that book deals in some detail with the basic visual process and how we interpret what we see. However, it is useful for all involved in site planning to be aware of quite how complicated a field of study this is and the factors which make it so. Without a grasp of this it is difficult to understand the complexities involved in the apparently simple task of identifying the beautiful landscape.

Psychologists have pointed out that when we look at the world we see what we have learnt to believe is there, we see in terms of our education, we see what we have been conditioned to expect. The apparently simple act of seeing is, in fact, very complicated. From the time we are born we try to learn to understand the world and to make sense of it, as we move round in a world of objects we quickly have to learn to understand spatial relationships, the positioning and arrangement of each object, its shape, its colour and its use. Without this information we would be perpetually confused. It does, however, take time to learn to read all the visual messages the environment gives us. We do this most readily when we see a benefit to the self or to the group of learning quickly.

Each individual to some extent learns independently and, therefore, it is perhaps inevitable that there are differences of opinion about the detailed composition of a scene. However, it can be shown that despite the differences, there is a great level of agreement between people with similar backgrounds, a common level of education, common life experiences and common cultural background. This factor has a bearing on the finding that those within the design professions tend to see things in a different way from the general public of which they are a part (Greenbie, 1989). It is one of the worrying factors of which site planners and designers have to be aware, that they are in danger of having different values from the people for whom they are designing.

The different ways that individuals see have been studied in detail and perception psychology has shown us that although each individual lives in a personally understood environment, the individual's perception and attitudes are influenced by the society of which the individual is a part and the place to which the person belongs.

Group images undoubtedly exist and are related to the sharing of similar needs, ideals and loyalties. This 'public image' has been identified as a basic bond of any society or sub-group of society. From this it has been argued that any society will have certain norms of perception which prevail at particular times, with minor differences identifiable for different classes, different experience of human habitats and for unique individual experience. For this reason there is considerable agreement on the extremes of ugliness and of beauty within any society. It can be said that the eye of the beholder has been trained to fit into a prevailing cultural pattern.

An issue which adds to the problems of arriving at any consensus of opinion about the qualities of a scene is the way the brain operates. The brain is programmed to simplify the information it receives through the senses; if it did not do that it would be overloaded with information. Studies have shown that it is only when people first see a scene that the brain absorbs the maximum amount of the available information. The more the scene is experienced the lower the level of awareness. It could be likened to the brain categorizing the scene and then not needing to look again at the detail to know all that is necessary about a scene. This is a necessary limitation, as the brain has to have a mechanism for disregarding what it has already decided is known and safe and concentrating on the new. It has been suggested that this is a basic psychological mechanism to allow us to identify quickly the alien and perhaps the hostile in a scene. Perhaps the level of alertness created by experiencing a new scene is one of the reasons tourists have been found to put greater value on a scene than those who live locally. The fact that the brain suppresses from consciousness that with which it is most familiar is another reason that site planners and designers have to be systematic when they record a scene, so that what is there is recorded, not just what is thought to be there.

The way people see things can be observed to have changed through history. Mental images of what constitutes beauty in a landscape change with time, just as fashions in clothes, furniture and architecture change. This is the factor that made much of the research carried out in the 1970s into a quantifiable means of identifying beautiful landscapes so dubious.

There is no fixed unchanging norm of beauty. In the eighteenth century the poets and travellers described the upland landscapes of Britain as ugly fearful wastelands. Those same landscapes came to be seen as of great and special beauty by the middle of the twentieth century. The fact that opinions can change over so short a period in human history must make all planners think very hard about what beauty really is and critically assess any systems claiming to be non-subjective methods for identifying the beautiful landscapes. Landscape beauty is very much of the particular place. It is concerned with the total environmental qualities of a place, not just the components of the scene. The concept of landscape beauty is, therefore, part of a continuous discourse about nature, landscape and society. The visual symbols we use to interpret what we see both shape and are part of the cultural context. 'Reality' is continuously re-presented and re-interpreted over time.

Landscape aesthetics has been a subject of detailed study by landscape architects, artists, writers and other academics. The reader will, however, find the book *The Experience of Landscape* by Jay Appleton (1975) a very useful guide to the issues that have been addressed and the factors that impinge on aesthetic awareness. The major differences of opinion only are referred to here.

At one extreme are those who insist that landscape aesthetics can only be understood by looking at landscape in the way it is viewed by the artist – the painter, the novelist, the poet. This is in itself an impossible task, as we do not really know how they see a scene. On the other side are those who can loosely be called the ecological school of landscape. These people have based their opinion of what constitutes landscape beauty on Frazer Darling's contention that 'a landscape in ecological repose is also one which has the power to create content in the minds of human beings'. Quite what is meant by ecological repose is as vague as what is meant by beauty as interpreted by the artist. Does it rule out farmed landscapes as beautiful scenes, does it mean that only the wilderness landscape can be held in high esteem?

It is worth noting that what is ecologically beneficial may not be aesthetically pleasing in 'picture' terms and that conflicts of interest will inevitably arise in site planning. The site planner's role is in part to resolve such conflicts. That can only be done by deciding what must have priority on a local site and in many cases that decision will relate to strategic planning decisions beyond the control of site planners.

There are circumstances when we have to give relative values to landscapes so that we can determine where we can most happily contemplate change. In these circumstances, how a landscape is judged must be a local affair. Deciding the value of a local landscape is as much to do with the local history and cultural development and the social condition of the local people, as it is to do with the land and the objects on it. In some cases the need to preserve undisturbed a relatively natural landscape will be the dominant factor, in others the need to preserve a highly designed landscape which obeys well defined artistic rules of a particular historic period. In one situation it will be appropriate for the site planner to be working on a site plan and design obeying the formal aesthetic principles of a particular period (Jellico, 1975), in another such principles will be virtually irrelevant.

It is the appropriateness of the solution to the problem and place that matters to the site planner and designer. In Britain the Countryside Commission has drawn up a straightforward method of landscape assessment which has been designed to by-pass the problems outlined above. Their document *Landscape Assessment: a Countryside Commission Approach* (Countryside Commission, 1987) stresses the importance of the site planner asking the question 'why is the exercise being conducted' and shows that it is only when that has been done that any attempt should be made to choose criteria to judge or evaluate landscape. The suggested approach also shows that it is necessary to take account of the 'objective' and 'subjective' qualities of a landscape, in terms of the human response as well as the objects in and form of the landscape (Meredith,1987). It suggests various methods for field survey and how the information can be analysed by breaking landscape down into areas of similar character.

It is a method which allows non-experts as well as experts to understand what makes each part of a landscape special and different from the others. This allows an evaluation to be made by judging each area of the landscape against the criteria which were defined at the outset. It is an uncomplicated approach to a complicated problem, which relies on the expert site planner producing information in a manner that will be understandable to the public and decision-makers.

Site planning and human environmental preference

What sort of environments would support human life? As the Kaplans (1982) questioned, 'What kind of environment would be suited to a knowledge-hungry organism, one concerned to comprehend and to explore, and yet quite limited in how much (information) it can handle at any one time? What kinds of environments do humans prefer? What properties must environments possess to enhance people's well-being and effectiveness?' One of the issues which has held us back from dealing with these questions in the past is the implication that pre-ference involves something frivolous, suggesting something decorative or an unnecessary extra rather than something essential for human life to thrive. The Kaplans point to the scientific evidence that in evolu-tionary terms makes this is a false interpretation.

The evidence is that for survival, organisms prefer an environment within which they are likely to thrive. They dislike and shun environ-ments which harm or hinder them: 'preferred (human) environments will in general be ones in which human abilities are more likely to be effective and needs are more likely to be met' (Kaplan, 1973). Kaplan points out that people are not necessarily aware of their needs and further that their needs will on occasion include idiosyncratic elements as well as distortions related to the prevailing social and cultural climate and individual's experience of life. Preferences must be seen as import-ant indicators of the environments in which people can be constructive and effective.

PLACES IN WHICH PEOPLE CHOOSE TO LIVE

Once people are living beyond the basics of economic survival and have some freedom of choice open to them, they seek to live in places which please them. The identification of the characteristics of these places would be a good starting point for the site planner intent on investigating the content of preferred environments. If, as has been suggested above, it is important for places to hold a level of fascination for the user, then what characteristics are needed for that?

Complexity and diversity, mystery, legibility and coherence have been identified as important characteristics, not just as characteristics of the scene, but also in the way in which the place impinges on the other senses.

COMPLEXITY AND DIVERSITY

For people to find an environment fascinating, it must have complexity and/or diversity so that they become involved with it.

MYSTERY

It has been shown by Appleton (1975) and others writing about the aesthetics of landscape that mystery is an important element in involving us in environments. For instance, if a path winds out of sight ahead of people they tend to want to find out what is there, they become intrigued.

LEGIBILITY

While people need complexity to involve them and keep them interested and mystery to pull them onwards, they need also to be able to make sense of their environment. It has, therefore, to have coherence and structure so that the parts make a whole. This is where Lynch's concept of legibility as an attribute of any environment becomes a useful aid to the site planner. In site planning terms it means a place has to be sufficiently legible for our brains to comprehend, that it has to be coherent. Coherence helps make sense of the experience of a place. As the Kaplans stated, such an attribute is a comforting feature in any landscape or townscape, reassuring us that we can predict that the places we have yet to experience will also be understandable and therefore not threatening to us. Coherence without diversity can, however, result in deadly dullness.

THE INFLUENCE OF PAST EXPERIENCE

Environmental preference is not just related to the place itself, it also involves the previous experiences of the individual. The individual's knowledge and expectations have a bearing on preference. An environment, therefore, need not be familiar to people for them to like it. What matters is that, because of past experiences, it can be comprehended and linked in the mind to previous places. This is where the aspects of environment that are often described as being appropriate, 'having a sense of rightness', come in to site planning. If, as site planners and designers, we can work out what is 'right' as a supportive environment, we can incorporate those ideas into the planning process.

PREFERENCES VARY BETWEEN INDIVIDUALS AND GROUPS

Human beings, through their very adaptability and the variety of experiences they have in their lives, are bound to have varying preferences. The site planner cannot, therefore, aim to please everybody all of the time. Site planners have to attempt to identify the common ground as a starting point and then look at the particular needs of the individuals who will use a site.

Lynch (1960) writing on the city stated '...there is always more than the eye can see, more than the ear can hear, a setting or a view waiting to be explored. Nothing is experienced by itself, but always in relation to its surroundings, the sequences of events leading up to it, the memory of past experiences'. 'Moving elements in a city (people and their activities) ...are as important as stationary parts.' The site planner has to be aware of the experiences available to people on the way to and from the site as well as within the site. Decisions about a site should not be taken in isolation; except when it is an island, it is always part of something bigger.

People too are part of what is observed in the city and other landscapes, so their presence influences preference for particular places. As writers on urban design have illustrated (Lynch, 1960), the individual's perceptions of the city are fragmented and partial and mixed with the other concerns of daily life. A city is ever changing in its detail and this too is a continual source of fascination to the inhabitant and visitor. It is important to the users of its spaces that throughout these changes the city remains understandable. This is normally achieved through the basic structure remaining relatively constant.

Lynch (1960) suggests that a good environmental image creates an impression of harmony. This sense gives its possessor an important sense of emotional security. In contrast fear comes with disorientation. Lynch suggests that people need their home territory to be distinctive. Much of the evidence gathered by the social scientists since his studies, showing how people like to adapt and change their plot or frontage, would seem to support this contention (Cooper Marcus and Sarkissian, 1986). Lynch sees a 'vivid and integrated physical setting, capable of producing a sharp image, play(ing) a social role. . .'. He sees such images as forming part of the collective memories of the group to which the individual belongs. As he pointed out, common memories of the home town are often the first point of contact between individuals away from their home territory.

On occasion humans do appear to like some sense of disorientation, but only when it occurs within a framework which is familiar; the disorientation of the maze for instance. Complete chaos is never a pleasure.

Carr (1967) developed Lynch's and others ideas about how people react to city environments into a list of criteria to help the city planner. Among these are criteria which suggest the city planner should:

1. make available in the immediate neighbourhood a wide variety of environmental settings which each individual could choose to experience, the use of these areas to be encouraged by the way in which they are connected;
2. enhance the visual qualities of the setting to emphasize the uniqueness of the place so that people develop individual attachments and group perceptions.

The implementation of Carr's proposals would go far to compensate for the loss of diversity in the city and other landscapes which has concerned many authors. For instance, Watt (1972) saw the large number of diverse elements which have in the past formed the city being replaced by a small number of similar entities. He points out that all the arguments for keeping old buildings and areas really hinge on the desire to keep a diverse city or landscape – to satisfy our preference for such relatively fascinating scenes. The modern drive for efficiency and productivity is seen as part of the basic problem, as such an economics-driven concept is inimical to diversity. Leaving out the question of damage to the natural environmental aspects of the human habitat, there is a danger of the world becoming more bleak for humans, if economic factors alone guide land use policy. In extreme cases a lack of diversity could be associated with all the disastrous social consequences for society which are associated with harbouring dissatisfied populations.

Human adaptability and stress

As has been indicated humans can and do survive in habitats which are neither optimal nor preferred. Their in-built adaptability allows them to do so – but the cost to the individual and to society of the adaptations that people make may well be great. The environmental factors that cause stress have been discussed by the Kaplans (1982).

BOX 7.4

Some of the factors causing stress

- crowded environments, particularly when people are too poor to pay for the social support structures which can make such places bearable for the better off;
- the level of aggressiveness in the local community;
- feelings of not being in control of one's own daily life, including lack of control over who enters one's home territory;
- feeling a lack of privacy (aural as well as visual);
- feeling that one's worth as an individual or as part of a community is not recognized by society at large, including feeling that 'they' (the local housing authority, the government, the private landlord) are determining what sort of environment one lives in, from its appearance to how it is maintained.

ENVIRONMENTS MUST MAKE SENSE TO THE USER

The Kaplans have suggested that environments of which it is difficult to make sense create such an overload of information for the individual that this causes the individual to be alienated and to fail to become involved with that environment. Environments which are too difficult to understand do not allow people to become involved. Environments where there is nothing to stimulate people do not attract them to become involved. The environment that does both has been seen by the Kaplans as particularly stressful.

Factors which cause people to experience stress and, therefore, to have difficulty in adapting to an environment are identified in Box 7.4 .

CROWDING AND STRESS

Crowded situations can also increase the likelihood of irritability and aggression and have been seen as a cause of stress in many societies. Greenbie (1974) has suggested that the important factor is how space is structured to accommodate crowding. Crowding has been linked with health as well as other social problems. One of the key factors in causing stress in high-density housing has been the number of children in relation to the number of dwelling units. A study by Westminster City Council (1980) showed that when there were more than five or six children per ten dwellings, the level of vandalism and crime rose.

HOSTILE ENVIRONMENTS BREED A SENSE OF AGGRESSION

People living in environments which they experience as hostile have been shown to have fewer friends. They have also been found to feel little or no involvement with a local community (Appleyard and Lintell, 1972). This, it has also been suggested, can lead to aggressiveness in individuals. Aggressiveness normally means that a local community is unsettled and the people dissatisfied with their immediate environment; it can be associated with high levels of vandalism and crime.

Crowding is a particular problem for human beings. It forces them to react to protect themselves. It has been shown that the greater the crowding the fewer the friends people have, whereas the reverse might have been expected (Greenbie, 1976).

The impact of crowding on people's attitudes to their environment appears to be modified by local cultural and social attitudes, but further work needs to be done to establish the mechanisms. For instance, what attitudes enable the people of Hong Kong to exist and thrive at far higher densities than could be contemplated in most Western European cities. Is it family networks, or are other factors involved?

NOT BEING IN CONTROL OF ONE'S OWN DAILY LIFE

Strangers both fascinate us and threaten us. This is such an important factor that, when there are too many strangers, we feel alienated from the environment containing them. This is probably one of the mechanisms at work alienating many from crowded environments. It is also one of the reasons that it is important for site planners to indicate clearly who owns which piece of territory within a site. No territory should be ambiguous – it should be clear which is public and which private. In that situation people know when they have a right to challenge the stranger within their territory.

Provided that the people of an area are not strangers, it appears that people can cope with the stress of density. However, in new developments people are almost inevitably strangers. The site planner has to attempt to compensate by doing everything possible to increase the sense of control individuals can have over their own territory.

All over the world the problems associated with poorer people in high-rise, high-density housing cause concern. Except where there is a tradition of community support, as in Hong Kong, resulting in successful high density housing, it is only the relatively rich who can pay for the infrastructure of security and control that allows people to cope with the stressful social conditions inevitably associated with high densities. It has been shown that adopting strategies which aim to redesign such estates to make them feel less hostile for the inhabitants does work. The re-designs work best when the site layout is changed so that it consists of a smaller number of dwellings accessed from each entrance point; when there is an area of land that belongs specifically to the group or its members around the entrance; when the residents have a clear view of who is entering; when there is a caretaker; and when the residents are clear about which is their territory and which is the responsibility of others. The level of crime and vandalism appear to drop when people experience their home environment as less hostile and develop a sense of pride in being able to identify their community.

Many of Oscar Newman's (1972) suggestions, which were seen as so contentious when first proposed, have with time been shown valid and many of his prescriptions to work. Alice Coleman (1986) developed his thesis in relation to similar British housing estates and came up with similar suggestions for redesign. It must, however, always be stressed that design alone is never the answer. Many social and economic factors also have a part to play in the way people behave towards their local environment. The site plan can, therefore, only influence people's lives to some extent.

The most basic issue seems to be that if people feel they have some control over what is happening in their area, they can cope with a certain level of environmental stress. If not, then there will be problems.

PRIVACY AND PERSONAL TERRITORY

The anthropologist E.T. Hall (1966) suggested that each person is surrounded by an invisible bubble of personal space. He showed that people prefer to maintain themselves without overlapping with the bubbles of others. People will space themselves out often at fairly regular intervals.

The relationships between people alter the bubble, it differs with close friends, acquaintances and strangers. There are strong differences between cultures. Sommer (1969) carried out intensive research into the way people behave when sitting in spaces which Rutledge (1985) discusses in his book *The Visual Approach to Park Design* with reference to site planning and design. Greenbie (1982) in his book Spaces took the ideas about personal territory further and developed them in a manner which directly relates to the needs of the site planner.

Privacy is about the right of each individual to control what the world knows about him or her. Westin (1967) suggested that four basic states of privacy can be identified; these are shown in Box 7.5.

It is important for the site planner to get this right. There are acceptable distances apart that people prefer in different social settings. These differ with culture, but the distances that are acceptable in the local

BOX 7.5

States of privacy

1. solitude:
   complete visual privacy;
2. intimacy:
   privacy as when people are part of a small social unit, for instance the family when it is alone;
3. anonymity:
   privacy as when the individual is in a public place but is able to observe without feeling observed – people merge with the local landscape – without this they cannot relax in public spaces; they feel threatened;
4. reserve:
   the psychological barrier against intrusion allowing us to remain ourselves within the group situations which are part of all human life.

culture are important for the site planner to understand. A design must allow people to perceive that they have sufficient space to choose between social interaction or privacy.

Another aspect of privacy is noise. It is the noise of others invading our privacy that we so resent. For instance, noise generated by the children of friends and family is more readily tolerated than that of strangers' children – because of the expectation that there is some possibility of controlling it.

THE PSYCHOLOGICAL, CULTURAL AND SOCIAL ASPECTS OF EXPERIENCING ENVIRONMENTS

The remainder of this chapter looks specifically at what is known about people and their attitudes to the natural environment and open spaces, specifically in cities, as this is of crucial importance to site planners.

Nature and 'green' in life and in cities

The word 'green' has become an accepted shorthand for the natural as opposed to man-made elements of our landscape. For site planning 'green' is particularly important as it constitutes a major part of the diversity that is required to make places satisfactory settings for human life. Much can be done to improve the livability of cities through a concern for 'greenness' – through the preservation of and introduction of plants and wildlife. In Part Two the importance of plants for human survival and for maintaining the quality of the physical environment has been discussed. Here it is people's attitudes towards 'greenness' as an environmental experience which is dealt with.

In recent years the word 'green' has even developed political connotations. The more people become aware of the damage that has been done to man's habitat and the natural world which supports the existence of that habitat, the more they appear to become 'green' in their thoughts and actions. Whether this new interest is too late or not to save the human habitat we cannot know. However, as site planners we can now take it as axiomatic that we must do all we can to preserve and to introduce nature and 'greenness' on every site where it might be possible and appropriate.

NATURE MATTERS TO EVERYBODY

Whether we are aware of it or not, nature matters to everybody. For instance, as soon as people's incomes rise above the basic level of survival, many buy plants for their yards or balconies. When they are richer they move to 'green' suburbs and when they are richer still they acquire houses surrounded by 'green', even if they still work in the town. It is often argued that is done by people to indicate their status, but it is also done to please themselves.

Several recent research projects in the UK have investigated people's attitudes to green space in cities. Barbara Mostyn (1979) and Alison Millward and Barbara Mostyn (1989) have looked at reactions to natural areas in cities and Carolyn Harrison, Jacquelin Burgess and Melanie Lamb (1988) at the role of urban green in people's lives. The studies undertaken by these researchers have illustrated how much more valuable at the site planning level qualitative information is about the environment, than that produced by quantitative studies. This section highlights some of the findings of the qualitative studies.

Many of the conventional social research methodologies appear to make it difficult for people to describe why they like particular places and environments. For this reason the direct questionnaire asking people what they want open areas to be like has been of little value. This is probably because much of the reaction people have to environment is at a subconscious level; people are unable to articulate these feelings when asked directly. This adds to the site planner's difficulties, particularly when attempting to develop ideas about the special qualities and characteristics of each environmental setting.

As we have already seen, it is probable that some human needs are inherent in all human beings – the need to feel safe and secure in our home territory for instance. However, it must also be recognized that many needs are culturally derived, so that, depending on the characteristics of the culture in which we grow up, we will feel more comfortable in some environments than others. As site planners our role is to develop settings which support modern life in all its diversity. Even within a 'culture' there are many different groups, each applying their own set of meanings and values to interpreting their environment. Those meanings and values can change rapidly as people create their own culture; it is not something static.

Mostyn's research into people's attitudes to natural areas within cities which was undertaken for the Nature Conservancy Council was carried out mainly through group discussions – this method was chosen as it overcame the problems inherent in asking people about concepts which they had never even realized existed, let alone influenced their lives. People normally say they act spontaneously if asked why they do something in an open space or they cannot give any reasons. Through group discussions it was possible for the researchers to gain some insight into their inner motivations and feelings. Groups of five to six people were asked non-directive questions to establish their fears and desires in relation to spaces in the city and in this case natural spaces. Examples of the questions which were used include : 'what comes to mind when you think of (a particular) open space', 'how would you describe that place to someone who lives in another city'. The individuals in each group were also asked to do a drawing depicting their feelings when they were at a specific open space. These special qualitative research techniques uncovered the real motivations and feelings experienced by people visiting the sites.

The spaces people were talking about during the research were often very small (from 3 to 12 hectares), some of them only the width of an old railway line. They had all been developed as natural or wildlife areas. The major findings of this research are listed below.

THE FINDINGS FROM THE GROUP DISCUSSIONS

The lessons that Mostyn was able to draw from her studies included the benefits and disadvantages indicated in Boxes 7.6 and 7.7.

THE FINDINGS OF THE OBSERVATION STUDIES
OF BEHAVIOUR

The observation and tracking studies carried out as part of their research project by Millward and Mostyn were also very interesting. Research into human behaviour has always had to contend with the fact that there is a discrepancy between what people say they did in a space and what they actually did; this applies as much to leisure activities as to any other behaviour. There is no deliberate intention to mislead the interviewer in

A sense of belonging is important if a space is to thrive
Almost everybody who had been involved in community schemes talked about their local natural area as my valley, my trees, our place. The people saw the fact that they had been involved in planting trees on the site as being symbolic of putting down roots. Years after the event individuals were still able to identify my tree, my nest box. There was a strong contrast between such attitudes to spaces which had been developed with the aid of the local community and those that had been imposed by outsiders where everything was described as theirs, the local government's. Mostyn recorded less vandalism where people used the words my or ours.

All types of people, not just nature lovers, are interested in nature in cities
Mostyn's studies showed that the full range of people in any community are likely to become involved and that there were no common personality characteristics to account for an interest in nature. All ages, all occupations proved to be interested.

People comprehend the recreational value of wildlife and natural areas in a city
People alter spaces to increase the recreational potential of the natural areas, for instance by creating a jogging track. Adults see them as important places for children to learn about themselves. The research showed that people were even aware of the work they had undertaken on conservation (planting, pruning, wall building, hedging) as having had recreational value; for example letting off steam whilst learning a skill.

BOX 7.6

Community benefits from local open spaces

this, it is just that people are often unaware of the detail of what they are doing as they move through an environment.

The observation studies in the natural areas showed that 50% of the users were adults. This conflicted with what people had said about their use of the spaces. They had implied they only went with children. In the interviews people had said they liked being near the water, but in fact people were rarely seen to approach the water's edge. Tracking of individuals for up to half an hour showed that two-thirds of the users of the space stopped frequently to look at nature – flowers, shrubs, birds and yet when interviewed about their use of a site, this was rarely mentioned. This type of survey produces very different information for the site planner than the traditional questionnaire which typically can only establish that people walk through a space. Such a survey finds out

BOX 7.7

Benefits to the individual

Emotional benefits
People talked about the relief of escaping from their home environment by going to the area of natural land, of experiencing it as a paradise, of the sense of being alone and away from it all, of the peacefulness (remember several were just small patches of land in the city so it is interesting to note that the perceptions and reality differ greatly). Some people even said they were able to feel that they were in the countryside. In many cases a sense of pride, that this special natural site was in their neighbourhood and that they had been involved in its development, was expressed.

Intellectual benefits
Through the group discussions it became clear that people were aware that they had gained something from seeing nature at work, from finding out about local history and from the learning of new skills.

Social benefits
People said that they felt they could be more friendly and could get to know people more easily in the natural area, there was more community spirit and that people were more responsible for things. Teenagers had enjoyed being seen as useful members of society.

Physical benefits
People spoke of being out in the fresh air, feeling more alive, feeling fitter. Parents spoke of the fact that they felt the area was safer because their children were away from the traffic.

The disadvantages to the individual of being involved with natural areas

Almost all the disadvantages related to a feeling of a lack of control over events.
People spoke of the personal upset it caused if vandalism happened on their land.
People disliked the areas looking untidy, they wanted them to look well managed; otherwise they considered it meant the place was uncared for.
People spoke of feeling let down if things happened too slowly after they had been suggested.
People wanted others outside their local community to know what a

good place their natural area was. Publicity and visibility of the site were seen as important. Without this they felt undervalued.

Fear of loss
The fear that their natural area would be taken away from them by the authorities or developers was overwhelming. Some even spoke of stopping themselves liking the place for fear of being upset when it was destroyed.

Dislikes
People disliked it when there were not enough colours in the site. (In Britain, if native vegetation alone is used there is a limit to the variety of colour that can be introduced into a natural scene, but this disadvantage can be overcome by careful choice of species and the judicious addition of exotic species).

nothing about the qualitative aspects of the experience of using the space for a walk.

The tracking also revealed other behaviour patterns. About two-thirds of the users made some form of social contact during their walk – nodding, talking, smiling. The majority of users stuck to the paths, despite there being no restrictions on moving off them, so disturbance to wildlife was minimal.

PARALLEL DISCUSSIONS WITH THE LOCAL PLANNERS

As a supplement to their research with the users Millward and Mostyn carried out a series of investigations with the officials who had been responsible for initiating the schemes. These showed that the planners and designers had felt that the public would really prefer a formal traditional park to a natural site. But none of the users had suggested this; in fact they had wanted natural parks to have more nature.

The planners had also thought the sites ought to be bigger, but the users liked what they saw as small natural parks, they had spoken of their familiarity with the sites and how they felt they could grasp that size of space and, therefore, feel safe in it. The planners had expected that the natural areas would encourage more trouble amongst teenagers, but in fact there was less. Teenagers expressed their feeling of freedom there.

Both the planners and the users talked about the importance of wardens on the natural sites, although in fact it was the site without one which was the most used. Although the planners considered the sites were for everyone, women were still being partially deterred from using them by a sense of unease since the observation studies did show that women were more likely to use areas when a warden was there. The sense of unease experienced by women was researched in more detail by Burgess, Harrison and Limb (1988) in their study of open spaces in Greenwich. The findings of their research suggest it would be foolhardy to reduce the number of park staff as it would have a direct impact on the number of women feeling able to use parks.

There has been a tendency for parks and natural places to be seen as dangerous places in cities, but there is much more crime on the streets than in parks. For the site planner it is important to ensure that any space in the city is understood by the user to be someone's responsibility. It must either be seen to belong to me and my group or to a specific other person or their group. It is the ambiguous spaces, where no one feels responsible, that people become afraid to enter. As soon as a space, and particularly a group of troublemakers associated with it, inspires fear, then it will not work as a space to support human activities – whatever those activities might be.

The public involved in the discussions saw the role of open space in cities was to make them more livable. When people do not use open spaces it is because they do not know what to do there, as well as the more obvious problem of safety. Once the people involved in this research had been educated into the experiences available in natural areas, they often preferred them to conventional parks. In planning terms what matters is that the full variety of experiences of both the formal and informal environments is available.

WHAT ARE THE OPEN SPACES OF A CITY?

Harrison, Burgess and Limb (1988) carried out research for the Economic and Social Research Council and the Countryside Commission into people's attitudes and values of green space in cities. They held in-depth group discussions with selected inhabitants living near parks in the London Borough of Greenwich and interviewed over 200 people living in the same areas. The research project aimed to explore social and cultural dimensions of popular values for open space – how people 'read' the urban green – how they interpret it.

Their study is particularly interesting as it became clear that the public perception of open space in a city was different from that of most trained planners. In the discussions people defined open space not just as parks and gardens, that is spaces specifically set aside for public enjoyment, but as urban green areas in general. 'Walks along the river-side, round the houses and on the way to school; waste places seen from the top of a bus or used by children, streams and scrubby bits; farmland, woodland, golf courses, cemeteries and squares in shopping centres were all encompassed...' in the phrase open space (Harrison and Burgess, 1988).

The users experienced green as part of the totality of the city, not something separate. Urban green was shown to be part of the lives of all the participants in the group discussions which formed the basis of this research, regardless of social class, income, racial origin or place of residence.

The research showed that people were aware of being in contact with urban green on a daily basis. They were aware of the enormous sensual pleasure they experienced from contact with nature – seeing sunsets, experiencing seasonal changes, the smell of leaves and flowers, walking on springy turf, watching insects, birds and animals involves us all with nature. Such experiences provide everybody with contrasts with the sterile built environment which comprises too much of our cities.

The group discussions which formed the basis of this research were held as in-depth discussions over a series of six meetings. They took place with two white working class groups, one white middle class group and one Asian women's group. The aim was to identify the similarities and differences between the perceptions of the different groups in relation to their attitudes to open space in cities.

COMMON ATTITUDES TOWARDS OPEN SPACE

Some of the most common attitudes arising from these discussions as recorded by Harrison, Limb and Burgess (1987) are listed in Box 7.8.

DIFFERENCES BETWEEN THE SOCIAL GROUPS

The research by Burgess, Harrison and Limb indicated significant differences between the social groups in their perceptions and attitudes, (Box 7.9). This contrasts with earlier psychological research which suggests the major differences are based on individual psychological processes.

THE IMPORTANCE OF OPEN SPACE FOR COMMUNITIES

It turned out to be those who lived in the environments most deficient in open space who attached the greatest importance to open space. They wanted it as both social space and living space. As far as the site planner is concerned the most important finding of this research has been that

BOX 7.8

Attitudes towards open space

Nature is fun
All classes and cultural groups reflected this attitude. They liked being outside, being aware of the seasons, being aware of the natural world, sliding on ice, kicking leaves around in Autumn and they liked fresh morning air.

People talked particularly about animals, birds and insects that they remembered having seen. Although they were aware of the plants, these were a secondary satisfaction. It was the bird, animal and insect life that stood out in people's minds. A feeling of wonder and awe was often expressed in relation to wildlife. People expressed a desire for contact and were curious about how nature worked.

Throughout the discussions it became clear that the group members were aware of being in daily contact with nature and, in particular, animals. When asked, as part of the group discussions to describe what certain landscapes, as portrayed by photographs, would be like it was the animals and wildlife that were frequently mentioned.

Open space in a city has a symbolic value
Even people who did not go into open spaces considered them important; they had a symbolic value.

Childhood territory
Discussions relating to childhood showed that everybody remembered being able to define their own territory. They also had vivid memories of the qualities of their childhood landscape, whether it had been natural or built up. Almost everybody seemed to talk about their childhood as a golden age and all believed that experiencing nature was important for children. There was common agreement that through the experience of nature children learnt social values, that if children learnt to respect nature they could learn to cope with society. Most parents, therefore, wanted contact with nature for their children.

The loss of variety in urban areas
It became clear in the group discussions that people recognize a loss of variety in urban areas and think of institutional landscapes, including parks and playing fields as part of this, thinking of them as cold and featureless. They wanted intricate designs and fascinating designs. They wanted more opportunity for unplanned and informal social interaction. They wanted a rich variety of natural and social experiences to be available to them and their families and friends.

BOX 7.9

Social differences in attitudes towards open space

Social groups
The middle class group were more self-conscious in their awareness of enjoying landscape, experiencing it as something to be looked at and thought about. In contrast, those in the working class groups experienced landscapes as something to be inside and primarily as a setting for their social life.

Men and women
Men regarded open space as a setting for their own activities, whereas women persisted in most valuing open space as a place for their children. Women and men who were parents were the most hostile to the bare, bleak playing fields and park areas managed as if they were savannah. It was only those involved directly or indirectly in sports who did not see that these areas were lacking as social settings.

Women want to feel free to use open spaces without fear
It was noticeable in the discussions that not many women saw the use of open space as part of their rights. Women are afraid to go into many open spaces, especially woods. Yet as they talked about these feelings, it also became clear that they wanted those experiences for themselves and re-sented the fears which stopped so many of them going into open spaces and woodlands on their own. The research showed that to a major extent women's fears related to the cultural/social context of their lives. Media coverage of attacks on women and children, as well as the reality of their actual experiences, further inhibited their use of open space.

Ethnic groups want parks as social spaces
The ethnic groups, in this case from the Indian sub-continent, showed some differences of attitude. For instance, those born outside Britain tended to transfer their own childhood experiences to their reading and understanding of the significance of various landscapes. All the Asian women in the sample perceived open spaces in Greenwich as dangerous and explained this as fear of gender as well as racially inspired attacks. At the same time they wanted the parks to be social places – places for extended family outings and social interaction.

Natural landscapes and danger
There was recognition of the problem that interesting natural landscapes were the most dangerous to go into. This was blamed on vandalism and criminal behaviour, linked with various forms of attack on the person. But this situation was also linked by the groups to the breakdown of the community spirit rather than the type of landscape. The presence of sympathetic parks staff was seen as a major means of overcoming this. There was no demand for such landscapes to be removed from the city.

people look for diversity of experience of open and greenspace right on their doorsteps. They do not want open space far from their homes in distant oases called parks or public open space. What they want is open space on their doorstep, freely available for all sections of the community. In this context, the fact that women are inhibited from using many existing open spaces is a crucial design and management issue which has to be addressed by the site planner. These issues are discussed further in the next chapter.

It is important that the reader working on planning greenspace in cities goes to the original research as the findings can only be briefly summarized here.

References   Appleton, J. (1975) *The Experience of Landscape*, John Wiley, New York.

Appleyard, D. and Lintell, M. (1982) Environmental quality of city streets: the residents' viewpoint. In Kaplan, S. and R. *Humanscape: Environments for People*, Ulrich's Books, Ann Arbor, Michigan.

Burgess, Jacquelin, Limb, Melanie and Harrison, Carolyn (1988) Exploring environmental values through the medium of small groups. Part One and Part Two. *Environment and Planning* A, 20.

Canter, D. (1977) *The Psychology of Place*, Architectural Press, London.

Carr, S. (1982) Some criteria for environmental form. In Kaplan, S. and R. *Humanscape: Environments for People*, Ulrich's Books, Ann Arbor, Michigan.

Coleman, A. (1986) *Utopia on Trial*, Hilary Shipman, London.

Countryside Commission (1987) *Landscape Assessment: a Countryside Commission Approach* (CCD 18), Cheltenham.

Cullingworth, J.B. (1972) *Town and Country Planning in Britain*, Allen and Unwin, London, four editions.

Fabos, J.G. (1985) *Land Use Planning, from Global to Local Challenge*, Dowden and Culver, New York.

Farber, S.M. (1982) Quality of living, stress and creativity. In Kaplan, S. and R. *Humanscape: Environments for People*, Ulrich's Books, Ann Arbor, Michigan.

Greenbie, B.B. (1974) Social territory, community health and urban planning. *Journal of the American Institute of Planners*, 40, 74–82.

Greenbie, B.B. (1976) *Design for Diversity*, Elsevier, Amsterdam.

Greenbie, B.B. (1981) *Spaces: Dimensions of the Human Landscape*, Yale University Press, New Haven.

Greenbie, B.B. (1989) *Space and Spirit in Modern Japan*, Yale University Press, New Haven.

Hall, E.T. (1966) *The Hidden Dimension*, Doubleday, New York.

Harrison, Carolyn and Burgess, Jacquelin (1988) Qualitative research and open space policy, *The Planner*, Nov. 1988, 16–18.

Hebb, D.O. (1982) The causes of fear. In Kaplan, S. and R. *Humanscape: Environments for People*, Ulrich's Books, Ann Arbor, Michigan.

Kaplan, S. (1973) Cognitive maps, human needs and the designed environment. In *Environmental Design Research* (ed. W.F.E. Preiser), Hutchinson and Ross, Stroudsberg, Pa.

Jellico, G. and S. (1975) *The Landscape of Man*, Thames and Hudson, London.

Kaplan, S. (1982) Attention and fascination: the search for cognitive clarity. In Kaplan, S. and R. *Humanscape: Environments for People*, Ulrich's Books, Ann Arbor, Michigan.

Lynch, K. (1960) *Image of the City*, MIT Press, Cambridge, Mass.

Lynch, K. and Hack, G. (1985) *Site Planning*, MIT, Cambridge.

Maslow, A.H. (1967) A theory of metamotivation: the biological rooting of the value-life. *Journal of Humanistic Psychology*, 7, 93–127.

Meredith, Josephine (1987) Beauty and the eye of the beholder, *Countryside Commission News*, 29.

Millward, Alison and Mostyn, Barbara (1989) People and nature in cities, *Urban Wildlife Journal*: No. 2, NCC publication, London.

Mostyn, Barbara (1979) *Personal Benefits and Satisfactions Derived from Participation in Urban Wildlife Projects*, NCC publication, London.

Newman, O. (1972) *Defensible Space*, Macmillan, New York.

Relf, E. (1976) *Place and Placelessness*, Pion, London.

Rutledge, A.J. (1985) *The Visual Approach to Park Design*, John Wiley, New York.

Smardon, R.C. and Palmer, J.F. and Felleman, J.P. (eds) (1986) *Foundations for Visual Project Analysis*, John Wiley, New York.

Sommer, R. (1969) *Personal Space: the Behavioural Basis of Design*, Prentice Hall, Englewood Cliffs, NJ.

Washburn, S. (1972) Aggressive behaviour and human evolution. In *Social Change and Human Behaviour* (ed. G.V. Coelho and E.A. Rubenstein) NIMH, Washington DC.

Watt, E.F. (1982) Man's efficient rush towards deadly dullness. In *Kaplan, S. and R. Humanscape: Environments for People*, Ulrich's Books, Ann Arbor, Michigan.

Westin, A. (1967) *Privacy and Freedom*, Atheneum, New York.

Westminster City Council (1980) *Living at High Densities*, London.

8 User requirements

'Making places that fit human purposes is the task of site planning. Two things have to be understood: the nature of the site, on the one hand, and how its users will act in it and value it, on the other' (Lynch and Hack, 1984).

The identification of environmental needs is central to site planning. If site planners or any other type of planner ignore human needs, they risk producing environments which alienate people. Although we are as far as ever from truly being able to identify experiential needs, the site planner has to plan and design while recognizing that an issue does exist and cannot be ignored. In the past when towns developed slowly within a local cultural context, people were able to adjust to the new with apparently little problem. Nowadays new site developments can be big and fast moving, and their form and detail organized by people with no contact with the locals; the results can be very costly mistakes. If for no other reason than economics we have to bring a consideration of human experiential needs into site planning. As the Kaplans (1982) said, 'the role of the physical environment in human experience requires a fresh look'.

The previous chapter introduced some of the increasing quantity of information that is available to site planning from those researching in environmental psychology. It will already be apparent that this material differs from much of that which forms the basis for Part Two, where to a large extent the data presented is based on a body of established information. This chapter presents further material about people and environmental setting.

Because of the lack of hard information about user needs, the site planner has to use a variety of approaches to the problem of finding out about the experiential qualities of settings. Some of these are indicated in Box 8.1.

In a book of this length it would be impossible to deal with all these subjects in detail. Instead the issues are introduced and the reader is referred to a range of books on specific topics.

BOX 8.1

Four ways of obtaining useful data on user needs

1. be familiar with the type of research mentioned in the previous chapter, knowing where to look for information which will allow general guidelines to be drawn up;
2. be familiar with the literature available on the special needs of specific groups in society, for instance children, disabled people, as well as adults at various stages of their life cycle; obtain information on the facilities that will be needed to allow each activity to function;
3. be familiar with the studies of particular environmental settings, that is where to find information on people's behaviour in housing areas, schools, open spaces and parks, etc.; obtain information on the type of settings which allow a particular activity to be considered a satisfactory experience;
4. use public participation as a means of finding out and providing the public with what it wants.

Public participation

Public participation is crucial to successful site planning. The public participation movement of the 1970s and early 1980s was largely directed at attempting to find a means of finding out what the public wanted. The advantages and disadvantages of the systems which were developed to liaise with the public in relation to site planning matters have been discussed elsewhere (Hester, 1983; Appleby, 1978; Heder and Francis,1977). From this work it would appear that it is at the site planning level that the public participation process is at its most effective. It is at this level that an identifiable group of people can be expected to react with considered opinions about precisely defined spaces, spaces which they or people like them will use.

The questionnaire is the most common means used by planners to try and find out what people want. There are, however, problems with all forms of questionnaire designed to involve the public in helping to plan or design a site. Questionnaires can only deal with people's reactions to that with which they are already familiar. All people can only respond to questions about facilities and environments within the limits of their own experiences, whether these experiences are direct (that is the person involved has physically experienced the activity, facility or setting and so is able to report a reaction) or indirect (that is experienced only at second hand through the media or hearsay). Questionnaires are much less useful as a predictive planning tool. People can describe their reaction to what already exists, but are less good at describing what they would like in the future.

Another problem with questionnaires as far as the site planner is concerned is the sheer quantity of information derived from them, which can lead to paralysis of the planning and design process. The site planner has to be very careful to consider the purpose of any survey and the limitations on its usefulness in advance of drawing up the questionnaire.

The site planner initially has to decide the minimum range of information about the users which will be needed to begin planning a specific site. The easiest way into this is for the site planner, with the aid of the client and users, to draw up a user requirement brief.

The aim is firstly to construct a scenario of the activities that might take place in the future within the area to be covered by the site plan – the activity list and secondly to develop this to describe the range of experiences that the site users will be most likely to appreciate and which will allow them to make maximum use of the new site – the environmental settings.

To gather the required information the site planner must decide when it is appropriate to rely on the client's own description of the way a site will be used, when to ask people direct questions about behaviour and requirements, when to try and find out their opinions, for instance through non-directive discussions, when to observe how people use a site (whether it is the site in question or a similar site) and when it is appropriate just to draw on the previous experience of the members of the site planning team. Lynch and Hack (1984) in *Site Planning* indicate a range of methods which site planners can use to identify user requirements.

Drawing up a user brief

This includes developing a scenario of site activities and appropriate environmental settings. Dealing with people is a subject which is well dealt with in the architectural press and so only those issues mainly related to outdoor areas are examined here. It is, however, essential that the site planning team recognizes this as an entirely artificial division and one where the limitations of looking at a problem from one side only must be overcome by the way in which the team works. Overcoming any artificial division is best done by the site planning team developing clear lines of communication between those concerned mainly with the construction of a building and those concerned with the manner in which the total site must work. It is the totality that will matter to the user, so the site layout and design has to support not just the activities in the building, but also those in the spaces around and beyond the building.

A list of the main activities that will happen on and immediately around a site can be drawn up by working with the client and the future users. It is common to begin this investigation by identifying all the different user groups. Depending on the problem, these can be age groups, interest groups, cultural groups or a mixture of them all. Age differences are always important as people tend to be interested in doing different things at different stages of their life cycle. It is the changes which occur in user requirements as the local population structure changes that are the major reason that site plans always have to be flexible and adaptable and can rarely be considered fixed answers to a problem.

IDENTIFYING THE MAJOR ACTIVITIES

The major activities are those which are essential to the proper functioning of the site. This list has to include all the activities that will happen on a site, not just the outdoor activities.

To plan and design the external environment, it is essential to realize that the activities which happen outside are directly linked to the activities inside any buildings on or near a site and to their function. At the user requirements stage, therefore, the site planner has to ensure that all decisions are taken on the basis of a clear understanding of the relationship between the way a building or group of buildings is used and what needs to happen immediately around it to support that use, and the needs of the people who use the building.

In relation to site planning major activities will normally be identified in relation to the land-use category to which the site is allocated: the site is mainly intended for houses, shops, industry, education, recreation, food production, extractive industry, etc. or for any combination of these land uses.

IDENTIFYING THE SPIN-OFF ACTIVITIES

Once the list of the major activities has been drawn up, it is necessary to expand this to examine what could be termed the spin-off activities. These are activities in which the site users are likely to become involved as a result of the development of the major activities within the site, as well as those on the adjacent land or nearby sites.

For instance, if a site is to be developed for offices the major activity in the external environment is likely to be the daily movement to and from the work place, with all the associated car parking, delivery and servicing requirements to be met by the site plan. The spin-off activities will be the need for outdoor sitting areas for lunch breaks, routeways for lunch time strolling, spaces for more active outdoor recreation, and in good climates outdoor meeting areas. In addition, the owners are also likely to be interested in the image which their building presents and to require a setting that they consider reflects their status, so that the visitor as well as the regular site user is exposed to a sequence of experiences which create the required image.

IDENTIFYING THE ENVIRONMENTAL SETTINGS

The second stage of developing a user requirement's brief is to deal with the problem of identifying and describing the range of experiences that should be available to the site user if the user is to gain maximum usage of the site.

To do this the site planner either has to identify the experiential needs of a known group for whom the site is being planned or, as is more often the case with site planning, to use studies of similar sites and user groups elsewhere as the basis for extrapolating the likely requirements of future site users. The site planner must aim to describe the settings that would be most appropriate to develop within the site. This involves providing a brief which goes well beyond a list of the activities people first think of when asked what they want to do on a site.

Harrison and Burgess (1988), as part of their studies into methods for exploring the value of amenity land, have tested a variety of research techniques to identify the concepts, beliefs and values of most importance to people in relation to open areas of land. They include methods such as depth interviews, participant observations, once-only group discussions and in-depth group discussions. Such qualitative research methods are invaluable for studying environmental values and gaining insight on user requirements.

IDENTIFYING HOW PEOPLE MIGHT USE A SITE

As well as working out the main activities and the spin-off activities for which facilities must be provided on a site, the site planner has to try to anticipate where people will naturally congregate and how they will move into and out of a site and move through it.

Predisposed behaviour can be viewed as a user need. For instance, woe betide the designer who tries to close off an established routeway through a site with anything less than an insurmountable barrier. The old routeway will just reappear even if there is no allowance for a path. Denying people the right to do something that they have been used to should only happen after careful consideration of the consequences — it will normally only work if the user can understand the gain in terms of its advantageous impact on their immediate daily life.

Those who have observed people in spaces (Rutledge, 1985; Whyte, 1980) have drawn attention to the way people attract people. These observations are useful in that they demonstrate the snowball effect on where people want to follow certain activities. Such factors have to be allowed for in the site plan. It means that the site planner cannot operate by just imposing a predetermined idea of the best location for a particular activity.

Activities are rarely independent; they nearly always attract other activities to them and can repel others. Some activities can happen almost anywhere (strolling). Some need certain physical characteristics (rock faces for climbing) or natural environmental characteristics (particular species of plants or particular habitats to attract birds for the ornithologists). Some are totally dependent on the availability of specific man-made facilities (to a large extent organized sports and athletics come into this category).

User satisfaction

In the search to find a means of understanding the user's needs, the social scientists found that one of the simplest measures was to assess the relative degree of user satisfaction with various aspects of the physical environment. In the main they did this by asking people to evaluate their reactions to particular aspects of an existing environment. A simple method for the non expert is to ask questions which allow the respondent to reply using a five-point scale of satisfaction. Such a scale allows the respondent the opportunity to describe their reaction from highly satisfied to highly unsatisfied. This simple technique can be made more useful by asking the respondent to name the things or features which cause them to feel satisfied or dissatisfied. Properly carried out and with the right level of statistical checks on validity this method can provide a great deal of information about any existing situation and allows the site planner to assess what is working for the users and what is not, what needs to be added or removed from the site.

User satisfaction studies have been used extensively in an attempt to evaluate the success of various housing schemes, for instance, the Department of the Environment in Britain (1981) in a *Survey of Tenants' Attitudes to Recently Completed Estates*. Such post-occupancy studies were undertaken from the late 1960s onwards.

Chapter 7 summarizes some of the factors involved in the way people experience space. Box 7.1 deals with psychological needs and it is in relation to these that user satisfaction studies are particularly relevant. Consideration of psychological needs omits the vital question of whether the space works for the people who use it; this is also a crucial part of the experience of using and being in a place and being satisfied with it. To answer this question it is necessary to identify the activities which will occur on a site and then build the physical structures or settings to allow them to happen.

Every site is different and every group of people is different, so any information gathered about likely activities, for instance, by looking at the present use of the site and its hinterland or by looking at other similar sites, can only be seen as a starting point for developing activity lists for a project. The site planner needs to work with the client and user on the drawing up of such lists as well as to refer to the literature available about human activity in a variety of settings.

ACTIVITY LISTS

In the first instance the major activities derive directly from the land-use. Plans may be required for one or a combination of uses and people will do something slightly different on each site because of their particular needs. Some of the possible uses are listed in Box 8.2.

The list in Box 8.2 does not attempt to be all-encompassing; it is intended to give an indication of the many different types of land-use

---

BOX 8.2

A range of the land uses for which site plans can be required

1. Residential
    family home or cluster of houses or block of apartments
    care unit for a specific social group
    holiday homes or hotel
2. Educational
    nursery school
    primary level educational establishment
    secondary level educational establishment
    tertiary level educational establishment
3. Commercial and retail
    shop or shopping centre
    town centre or out of town centre
    retail warehouse
4. Industrial
    workshop or factory
    group of manufacturing units or business park
    water supply
    power production and supply
    waste disposal
    extraction industries

5. Health and social welfare
       surgery or health centre
       specialist health facility or hospital
       specialist care centre
       cemeteries
6. Leisure
       individual recreational facility
       family recreational facility
       group/organization recreational facility
       public garden or park
       outdoor sports centre or indoor sports centre
       water sports or camping
       nature/wildlife area
       allotments
7. Farming or forestry
       crop or animal production
       fish production
       timber production
       biomass production
       water storage
8. Conservation
       nature reserves
       recreational experiences
9. Wilderness
       habitat preservation
       recreational experiences
       unusable land

with which a site planner might be asked to deal and for which activity lists will need to be developed.

How the site planner proceeds from the stage of having identified the land-use category depends on what the project is. If it is a land-use such as housing, the client can often be fairly precise about requirements and in such cases the site planner will find a wealth of research information about peoples' activities and behaviour patterns in such environments on which to base decisions (Cooper Marcus and Sarkissian, 1986). If it is for recreation the site planner will often find that the client can be definite about requirements for a given number of sports pitches or a given area of open space, but is unlikely to have thought further about the multitude of activities that take place in open areas. There is, however, a growing literature relating to people's behaviour in open spaces (Rutledge, 1985; Whyte, 1980).

If, however, the project is a land-use such as industry, the client is unlikely to be precise about anything except the manufacturing process, the office space and parking space requirements. There is little literature on people's needs in such environments, since until recently the environment has been seen as unimportant by many business organizations. It is only recently with the growth of prestigious science parks and business parks that in Britain substantial numbers of business men and industrialists have come to realize that working in an environment with a good image can have economic as well as social advantages for them.

Useful literature

The books recommended here are just to get you started. In drawing up activity lists for different land-use categories you should use their extensive bibliographies to follow your line of enquiry. You should, however, always remember to supplement this research by talking to the users ·or similar social groups whenever this is possible.

All land-uses:
Alexander, *et al.* (1977) *A Pattern Language.*
Housing Areas:
Cooper Marcus and Sarkissian (1986) *Housing as if people mattered.*
Recreation in cities:
Wurman, *et al.* (1972) *The nature of Recreation*, a handbook in honour of Fredrick Law Olmstead.
Parks:
Rutledge (1985) *A visual approach to park design.*
City streets and shopping areas:
Whyte (1980) *The Social Life of Small Urban Spaces.*
Schools:
Adams (1990) *Learning through Landscapes Project.*
Countryside recreation:
Patmore (1983) *Recreation and Resources: Leisure Patterns and Leisure Places.*

An example of making an activity list – a housing area

If the proposed land use is housing, for instance a client wants 100 units built on 4 hectares of land, it might at first seem that this bald statement of intent is itself sufficient to allow a site plan to be prepared. Indeed a developer could fairly easily fulfil such a brief by placing 100 houses and the required roadways and services on the site. But the difference between that approach, which is the one which explains many of the housing layouts built in the recent past in Britain (Beer and Booth, 1981), and the development of a housing scheme based on a proper assessment of the site's potential and the user needs, is substantial. Housing is the most common form of development. It is the largest user of land after agriculture and forestry in most countries, yet it is often built with little real assessment of user needs or of the long-term cost to society and to the site owners of failing to meet their environmental requirements.

The site planner, particularly when working on higher density lower income group housing, needs to be able to go beyond the bare essentials of knowing that the facility (in this case the houses) has to be put on a site. It is normally the site planner who has to work out what sort of environment would be most likely to meet with the users approval. If this is not done, vandalism and crime can escalate unnecessarily as the inhabitants react to an unsatisfactory environmental setting.

Factual information required prior to the production of a site plan

The basic component of any housing site is the dwelling unit. In the past, and in some countries still, such a unit was closely linked with the family unit. Houses still tend to be thought of as containing families. However, in many societies this is no longer so and houses can be inhabited by single adults alone or in unrelated groups, by single people raising children, by couples without children at home, as well as by the conventional family. In many western countries the number of households that can be defined as families having children at home are now a minority of households. Young people in particular are increasingly demanding the right to their own home as soon as they leave their parent's home. This, together with the increasing number of elderly people wanting to remain independent, has led to an escalating demand for dwelling units.

The site planner needs to find out who it is intended should inhabit the houses once they are built and whether limitations on occupancy are to be dictated by the income of the inhabitants (their ability to afford to buy or rent), or by a housing distribution policy within the control of a local government or other agency. Such factors will determine the social, economic and age/sex structure of the inhabitants and have a strong impact on how an area should be designed.

In addition to the number of units to be provided on a given area of land the site planner, therefore, tries to find out about the special characteristics of the future population of the site, the preferred type of unit, the preferred form of the development, as well as the client's intentions with regard to community facilities and access to the transportation network.

Box 8.3 indicates the type of information that should be assembled; it relates to the context of northern Europe and should not be seen as a check-list which would be applicable everywhere. The activities associated with a particular land use will vary from place to place and between cultures as well as between the social groups in any society. A locally applicable list will always need to be generated and this should take account of everything discovered by talking to and interviewing the local

BOX 8.3

Examples of the basic information required for a housing area plan

1. number of dwelling units
    number
    range of sizes
2. the present and future population
    age and sex structure
    employment structure
    income groups
    lifestyle and social groups
    level of disability
    car ownership levels
    home ownership levels
3. type of dwelling units
    individual houses, row houses, apartments, bungalows
    communal homes
4. form of dwelling units
    preferred layout (streets, clusters)
    scale of private outdoor areas
    scale of communal outdoor areas
    distance allowable from service vehicles to front doors
    distance allowable from parked cars to front doors
5. community facilities on and off site
    shops, schools, libraries, health and other social services
    recreation facilities within and beyond the site
    distance to facilities
6. transport networks
    access from the site to the major road system
    access from the site to local footpaths and cycleways
    access from the site to the public transport system.

people, as well as research into the people who are likely to use the site.

Box 8.4 illustrates the type of list a site planner draws up for each site. It indicates some of the major and spin-off activities for which appropriate sites will have to be found on the site plan and enables the site planner to identify the range of experiences that might be developed on the site.

In parallel with consideration of the appropriate environmental qualities, the site planner also has to work out the locational restrictions on each activity. In this way it becomes possible to identify the activities which are fixed in certain positions on a site, those associated with other activities, those which should not be located next to particular activities and others which are totally flexible and can be sited as the plan develops.

Boxes 8.3 and 8.4 have been drawn up in relation to a housing area. A similar set of charts can be drawn up for any of the other project types listed in Box 8.2. The site planner must do this for every project so that there is a full understanding of the activities that have to be allowed for and the facilities that will be needed to support them. Such a list needs to be prepared prior to considering experiential needs.

BOX 8.4

The major and spin-off activities that happen in and around the home

1. activities inside the home
    sleeping
    cooking and eating
    relaxing: watching TV, listening to the radio
    playing games and working on hobbies
    storing belongings: food and household goods
    washing: the person and clothes
    cleaning
    entertaining: friends and relatives
    homework
    household maintenance
    sitting or standing looking out of the window
2. activities related directly to what happens inside the home but often occurring immediately outside the house
    drying clothes
    getting goods into the home
    cooking and eating
    entertaining
    looking after pets
    children's play
    growing plants: flowers, shrubs, vegetables, fruit
    keeping pets
    keeping animals and birds for food
    sitting on the doorstep or in the garden
    sleeping in the sun
    participating in hobbies involving large-scale objects
3. activities that happen outside in the vicinity of the home as an essential part of living there
    children's play
    parking the car and leaving or arriving in it
    sitting or standing to watch and talk to:
    the family, friends, neighbours and passers-by

going to the shops
going to the schools
going to the bus stop
going to the post box
going for a stroll
walking the dog
walking the pram and/or toddlers
jogging for fitness
joining an informal street ball game
knocking a ball around a pitch/against a wall
playing a formal sport
sitting outside
waiting on the corner for friends
contact with the delivery services:
milk, foodstuffs, home delivery of meals, newspapers, post
contact with people carrying out repairs and maintenance

THE INFRASTRUCTURE REQUIREMENTS

As well as gathering information about the activities, the site planner also has to consider at this early stage the infrastructure of water, sewerage, power, telecommunications, roads and footways, which will be required to support the major and the spin off activities. The availability of such an infrastructure will have a strong impact on the quality of life. Without such facilities a site cannot function. If they are not available it can mean that it is inappropriate or impossible to develop a site for a particular use.

The costs involved in providing the infrastructure have often become a major component in site planning decisions. They dictate that a certain layout is adopted in preference to others as it reduces building costs to a minimum. This will be discussed in greater detail in the next section, but here it should be noted that information needs to be collected on the costs involved in providing the various facilities. In addition information is needed on the yardsticks that are most appropriate to use in estimating the relative efficiency of different layouts in relation to infrastructure costs. As with any other factors in site planning it is not necessarily the cheapest option in capital terms which is the most cost effective in the long term. Maintenance costs and factors such as the gain that can accrue from having a site which attracts higher rents or sales prices also have to be taken into account, as does the need to protect the environmental qualities of an area, whether physical, natural environmental or experiential.

To work out the range of settings which need to be provided within the site, once the site planner has developed a list of the activities that should be catered for on a site, the next stage is to consider the environmental qualities that might be needed to support use of the site. The following paragraphs summarize some of the factors of which the site planner ought to be aware when making decisions. The list is by no means exclusive and has been derived in the main from planning and landscape design literature.

Box 8.5 summarizes the reasons why the site planner should be aware of people's experiential needs at the site planning and design stages. Awareness of such issues can help the planner to generate ideas on how best to lay out a site so that it can develop the environmental qualities that will encourage people to go to the site and like using it.

This predisposition to environmental awareness encourages the site planner to work towards providing people with a site that as far as possible satisfies their environmental needs.

In Box 7.1 some of the major factors which influence people's experience of environment were set out. It is important for that to be taken further now, to identify what actions the site planner might take towards providing more satisfactory environments which people can enjoy and feel pleased to live in, work in, or play in.

Ideally the site planner needs to meet all the requirements set out in Box 7.1. In particular the site planner can do something to influence the diversity of sensory experience available from a site and can influence

1. instinct: the need for environmental information:
   people become aware of objects and the spaces created by those objects through their senses;
   people have an in-built need to understand and to classify what they perceive;
   people need to know whether what is sensed is new and perhaps dangerous to survival;
   people are at their most alert when involved with something new or threatening to the senses;
2. result: environmental awareness:
   people are aware of their environment at all times;
   people assess the environment in terms of levels of satisfaction with the experiences it offers;
3. action: the site planner builds on this involvement as:
   people are predisposed to be fascinated by their environment and involved with it.

BOX 8.5

People are predisposed to be involved with their immediate environment

the sense of security and belonging that people feel in relation to a site. In housing areas the site planner can also allow the user the possibility of individual expression and self-fulfilment through achieving their aspirations. Through the manner in which the design is tackled, a site can be made comprehensible to the users, whilst at the same time presenting them with sufficient interest to fascinate them and involve them with the site. The site planner can also aim to produce environments which are judged aesthetically pleasing within the terms of the locally prevailing culture and so add to people's satisfaction with their local environment.

It was stressed in the previous chapter that the site planner should never be misled into thinking it is possible to attempt total control of environmental factors and people's perception of them. It is important that this is kept in mind as ideas for future settings are developed. The site planner should also be aware of the constraints imposed by our limited state of knowledge of people's reaction to environment. People will often not react to environments as we expect them to. All that can be attempted by site planners is a better fit between proposals and what the users eventually do on the site.

THE FIVE SENSES AND THE ENVIRONMENT

Some of the ways in which people experience their environment through the senses are given in Box 8.6.

ENSURING DIVERSITY OF SENSORY EXPERIENCE

A key issue for the site planner, and the one over which the site planning team has the most control, is the possibility of diversity of sensory experiences. Box 8.6 indicates some of the ways in which people use the five senses to gather information about their environment. This table can be used as a starting point to develop ideas for particular sites. It allows the site planner to determine that there are sufficient interesting experiences available on a site and that any problems with unpleasant effects on the senses can be mitigated.

CATERING FOR PEOPLE'S PSYCHOLOGICAL NEEDS

In the previous chapter it was suggested that certain human needs in relation to the environment may be instinctive and others learnt. It is important to identify how to create environments which can support those needs. The fact that people can learn the need to be involved with certain types of environmental experience, and that this adds to their

Sight

Sighted people learn most about their environment through seeing it. People most often experience their immediate environment first through seeing objects and groups of objects placed on a surface of land. They see how the objects and land relate to each other, they observe the spatial sequences which result from these arrangements. They use sight to recognize places and so learn to know and keep track of their location in space. They identify sights as containing natural and man made objects. They observe wildlife and people and learn to identify the dangerous from the safe. They identify danger from others and the environment through applying acquired knowledge to the information they are receiving through sight. They identify home territory through sight and can quickly identify those who do not belong in it. People hold mental maps of their home territory and other well used territories, if what they see is memorable, this helps to develop a clear image – landmarks are important.

Things see can be classified by the site planner as unique, rare, common, ubiquitous.

Sights can be judged by a site user as a beautiful, pleasant, unpleasant, ugly or offensive experience.

Hearing

After sight, hearing is the most important sense for understanding the environment. People find out about the needs of others and give them messages, mainly through hearing and speech. People identify certain types of danger through hearing. They experience the presence of people, birds and animals through hearing as well as sight. Through hearing the rustle of wind in vegetation and the noise of running water, they have a heightened awareness of involvement with the natural environment. Through hearing they can be aware of the bustle of life and the roar of transport systems and industry.

Things heard can be classified as unique, rare, common, ubiquitous.

Sounds can be judged by a site user as a very pleasant, pleasant, unpleasant, offensive or unbearable (certain noise levels can make people physically ill) experience.

Smell

This is the next most important sense to site planning. People do not have a very strongly developed sense of smell compared with many animals. In certain circumstances they can smell other animals and identify the presence of people. People instinctively dislike the smell of decay and they tend to like the smell of fruits, leaves and flowers, probably all part

BOX 8.6

The five senses and environmental awareness

of the mechanism for knowing what is safe to eat. Smells can signify danger to life from fire or chemicals. The foul smells associated with many industrial processes and their waste and the smell of sewage and rotting household waste can deter people from living in certain areas, even when the concentration of smells is very diluted and only occasionally intrudes on a site.

Smells can be classified as unique, rare, common.

Smells can be considered by the site user as very pleasant, pleasant, unpleasant, offensive or intolerable experience.

Touch

This is of importance to site planning because it is the way in which the blind find their way around. People have a highly developed sense of touch which enables them to identify and manipulate objects. People can feel texture as well as shape and size. People will often consciously touch strange objects such as sculpture to develop a better understanding of them. People often unconsciously touch familiar objects as they move through an environment. Children use the sense of touch more than adults.

The feel of things can be classified as unique, rare, common, uncommon. Feel can be considered by a site user as a very pleasant, pleasant, unpleasant or offensive experience.

Taste

Of relatively little importance to site planning. The taste of things enables people to identify what is safe to eat as well as what it is pleasant to eat. The presence of available edible fruits can add to the pleasure of being in a place where they can be picked. The pleasures associated with eating and drinking can be accentuated in outdoor settings particularly if associated with special events.

The taste of things can be classified as unique, rare, common, uncommon or poisonous.

Taste can be considered as a very pleasant, pleasant, unpleasant or offensive experience.

satisfaction with the quality of their life, is important to site planners. It is one of the factors which suggests that the site planner should attempt to do more than just reproduce the environmental settings which are within the present range of knowledge of the user. Over the period of the past 20 years considerable changes in people's lifestyles have been noticed; the site planner needs to be aware of these and what the trends might mean in terms of what should be provided on a site.

Kelman (1958) suggested that people can learn certain lifestyle needs. He stated that they do this by learning through their daily life what makes them feel satisfied. He has identified a certain pattern to this:

1. The first stage is imitation: people do or experience something just to copy others, to please others, to be with others or to be accepted by others.
2. The second stage: people recognize that they have gained a sense of satisfaction from doing or experiencing something.
3. The final stage: people recognize that they would miss the activity or the experience if they could not be involved in it; it has become an important component of their satisfaction with the quality of their lives.

This is a model that seems to apply to all environments and is particularly important for site planners. It provides the expectation that, provided people can experience some form of satisfaction, the new environments and activities will be accepted and absorbed into local lifestyle. An instance of this factor at work is that, as recently as the early 1970s, wild areas in cities tended to be regarded as only a sign of dereliction. However, with the development of the urban wildlife movement and the deliberate construction of wildlife areas in cities, there has been a change of attitude. Local inhabitants can nowadays become very upset if anybody suggests reducing the size of or removing their wildlife area (Mostyn, 1979).

FACTORS INVOLVED IN PERCEPTION OF PLACE

It is important for the site planner to be aware of the way people react to places if they are to plan satisfactory settings. Box 8.7 summarizes some of the factors involved.

Awareness of the factors listed in Box 8.7 can be expressed through the individual experiencing: happiness, satisfaction, dissatisfaction or unhappiness.

Security: a crucial requirement on any site

The level of security that people experience is of the utmost importance concerning their willingness to become involved with a place or space. The importance of security for the way in which people perceive the quality of their lives is born out by a recent national survey in Britain which investigates the factors influencing the public's perception of quality of life in cities (Rogerson *et al.*, 1989). The findings, which were the result of a national opinion survey amongst all major social and

BOX 8.7

Some of the factors involved in perception of place

1. The foremost instinctive reaction of the individual to a place is one which identifies it as:
   My place
   Your place
   Their place
   No-one's place
   The enemy's place

2. Spaces can allow people to feel a relative sense of:
   security or insecurity
   belonging or alienation
   fear or ease
   awe or friendliness
   delight or horror
   fascination or indifference

3. Associations are inspired by spaces and places. These can develop through:
   the space being involved in direct links with past events in a person's life
   indirect links in that the place reminds the user of another place or type of place, or an event in the user's life or known of through the media or historical association
   memories of home/ work/ education/ play/ people

4. People like knowing a space well and being familiar with it but they also like new experiences, they like being fascinated so they:
   search for the new
   search for the different
   yet they want these experiences all within the limits of something known or understood if they are not to be overwhelmed by uncertainty

economic groups, indicated that the levels of violent crime and non-violent crime were taken to be the two most important measures of quality of life in a city by the public. Table 8.1 which is based on work by the Glasgow University Quality of Life Group using data derived from the Mintel *Regional Lifestyles* Survey (1988), indicates the ranking of the factors that people use to judge the quality of their life in cities.

The information in Table 8.1 emphasizes the need for the site planner to be concerned above all else for the security of those who use a site. The traditional site planning reaction to this issue is to eliminate any objects where intruders might lurk. The unfortunate by-product of such an apparently logical approach is to create townscapes and landscapes

Table 8.1 A summary of the relative importance of the factors the public use to assess the quality of life in cities

Factor	Significance
Violent crime	The most
Non-violent crime	
Health provision	
Pollution	
Cost of living	
Shopping facilities	
Scenic quality	
Cost of owner occupation	
Education facilities	
Employment prospects	
Wage levels	
Unemployment	
Climate	
Sports facilities	
Travel to work time	
Leisure facilities	
Quality of council housing*	
Access to council housing	
Cost of privately-rented accommodation	The least

* In Britain council housing means housing provided by local government.

Table derived from Findlay *et al.*, 1989.

which so lack visual interest that their sterility appears to evoke alienation and that in turn seems to encourage vandalism. It is ironic that many of the schemes designed to deter vandalism are now among the most highly vandalized. A useful study of vandalism presented in a way which relates to site planning was undertaken by Wilson (1978).

A better approach is for the site planner to encourage the development of settings which are cared for by local people and within which they take responsibility to control intruders; settings which have all the richness that humans need to hold their attention and so allow them to become involved with the site; for the site to become theirs.

To develop the feeling that a place is relatively secure to be in, a place needs to exhibit certain features. These are summarized in Box 8.8.

It is now realized that many of the large housing estates built in the 1960s and 1970s, with the intention of improving the quality of housing available to the poorer people in society, have become ghettos. Many do not exhibit the features identified in Box 8.8, instead they have features such as long corridors linking several buildings and a multitude of

BOX 8.8

Features which encourage an impression of security

1. The setting needs to be legible and comprehensible, so that the users, even occasional visitors, know exactly where they are within the space or spaces that it comprises.

2. The setting needs to provide sufficient information so that the users can predict the nature of the adjacent spaces in whichever direction they decide to move.

3. The users must be able to see who else is in the immediate neighbourhood and identify how those people relate to themselves, that is whether others are friendly or unfriendly.

4. The users must be able to determine from the setting who is responsible for the place, to whom each area of land belongs. They must receive clear messages from the setting which enable them to distinguish who has the right to be in a particular place. The setting also has to indicate through its characteristics the range of activities that is appropriate in that place, within the constraints of the locally prevailing culture.

possible exits which make them very vulnerable to troublemakers and criminals. As Clare Cooper Marcus and Wendy Sarkissian (1986) point out in their consideration of security and vandalism, many of the failures of public housing schemes in the USA have been attributed to vandalism, crime and the fear of crime. Once crime takes hold as a problem on an estate, it becomes very difficult to stop it escalating beyond control. The fear of crime seems to breed more crime and the 'outside' becomes considered unsafe. Alice Coleman's (1986) studies of some London housing estates indicated similar processes at work in Britain in similar environments.

A variety of solutions have been suggested to make housing estates safer places. Oscar Newman's pioneering work on housing estates in New York (1972) identified the areas with the highest crime rates as enclosed spaces within the buildings and grounds of high rise estates; the spaces which residents could not control or survey. The stair-wells, elevators, screened-off parts of lobbies, hall-ways, roof-tops and any unclaimed ground were experienced as unsafe. These are the spaces which no individual or group feels they own.

It has been suggested by Newman (1972) and others that a clear hierarchy in terms of ownership of space, from private (belonging to the individual or family unit), to semi-private (belonging to a group of people who all know each other at least by sight), to public (belonging to the local authority or other public body) helps to deter the development of a high level of crime. There must be no ambiguity about the type of space. To ensure this happens, each of these types of space needs to be designed in a different way. Only then will the required level of security have a chance to develop. Clare Cooper Marcus and Wendy Sarkissian (1986) go into some detail about the various design approaches that can help to develop the required level of security in different types of territory. In addition they deal with the security topics listed below. The reader is referred to their book *Housing as if People Mattered* for full details and possible design solutions to security issues. The information below summarizes some of their suggestions.

1. Access should be controlled by creating site entry barriers. It is not always necessary for these to be physical barriers. Greenbie among others has shown that certain design solutions which in effect do no more than symbolize a barrier are sufficient to suggest the transition from one type of space to another.
2. The routes which strangers can take through a private or semi-private area need to be controlled. This can again be done by careful design and does not always necessitate the introduction of solid barriers.
3. Lobby areas must be fully open to surveillance by inhabitants, or only accessed through locked doors which allow entry to a small group of dwellings. Hidden corners should be eliminated. Corridor access should be eliminated unless a means of surveillance and full control of access can be introduced.
4. The view from the home of the entrance to the unit should be unobstructed.
5. The arrangement of buildings should be such that informal surveillance of the external spaces and access points is ensured. Informal surveillance is probably even more important than proper policing or caretakers, although in difficult situations those are important additional factors in developing a secure setting. It is the people casually looking out of windows, sitting outside watching their children, talking to their friends, who make an area feel safe to be in. In some circumstances people need visual privacy to feel comfortable, in others the feeling of being watched can help an area to feel safe. The site planner has to strike a difficult balance and work out where privacy can be given without compromising security. The adopted design solution will be different in relation to the particular problems of each site.
6. The level of lighting is very important and no site plan is complete until this has been sorted out. Lighting which does not have excessive shadows is best. All heavily used areas should be well lit, with particular attention paid to those areas where informal surveillance is at a relatively low level.

The sense of belonging and feelings of individual identity

These are important factors in determining whether people accept a place as their responsibility. That a place is understood to belong to a person or group has been seen to be important to the development of a sense of safety in that place. Site planners need to aim for situations in which people will feel involved enough about what happens in a place to attempt to control who enters it and what happens there. To do this an individual or group have to identify with a place, describing it as my or our place.

A wide variety of factors are involved in developing the impression that a place belongs to particular people, factors such as actual owner-ship of the land, or a sense of attachment to something held dear, but few of these are in the realm of site planning. One of the few ways that the site planner can influence the development of the required associa-tion between people and place is to ensure that a place has charac-teristics with which people are proud to be associated.

In relation to housing, for instance, the feeling of pride in one's neighbourhood has been shown to link strongly with the general level of satisfaction with the housing environment. Poorer people in particular have shown dislike for feeling that they have been put into houses too different from what they perceive as the middle-class norm (Cooper Marcus, 1982). It is only the more affluent who willingly accept 'way out' designs. They do that partly at least because they are expressing their status and wealth through the form of dwelling they choose to inhabit and therefore feel pride in that.

The desire to feel proud of where one lives is reflected in the import-ance people give to the impression of the approach to the dwelling for the visitor. If it is classified as a satisfactory experience, it has been shown to play an important part in people's assessment of the quality of their home environment (Cooper Marcus, 1982). In relation to this it is interesting to note that the bias towards the home as a favoured place tends to make inhabitants rank the appearance of the block containing their dwelling unit above other similar blocks, even if they are almost identical. The fact that people are predisposed to want to like where they live and to want that place to have a satisfactory appearance is useful for site planning. It implies that, if the site plan can go someway towards creating the sort of setting which people like and feel proud of, there is a chance that the people who live there will take over and adopt the place as theirs. Once that happens the level of security experienced by the inhabitants and visitors tends to improve and the maintenance require-ments associated with high levels of vandalism to drop (Cooper Marcus and Sarkissian, 1986).

Surveys (as described by Cooper Marcus and Sarkissian, 1986) have identified various features on housing estates which people dislike and like (Box 8.9). Eliminating those disliked from site plans and designs,

1. Dislike
   looking at blank walls
   poor views from their windows
   a closed-in sensation
   looking at very large unused spaces
   a lack of vitality
   poor provision for children's play
   poor levels of up-keep
   high noise levels
   lack of privacy
2. Like
   experiencing the spaces they see as intimate
   looking at greenery
   experiencing the estate as open
   seeing long distant views
   seeing lots of people moving around
   the estate being well looked after

BOX 8.9

Some of the features that people tend to dislike or like in their housing environment

or modifying them so that they are found to be acceptable, is a useful way for the site planner to ensure acceptance of a scheme by the users. Incorporating those features the public tend to like also helps ensure acceptance of the design solution.

There is no significance in the ordering of the above lists and it will be noted that there is also some contradiction in them. For instance, it appears that people both want long distant views and an open feel to their housing area, but at the same time want it to have an intimate scale. The site planner has to juggle these different requirements at the site planning stage. The relative importance of the factors has been found to change from site to site and culture to culture. What is important, however, is that these are factors which can be influenced by the way the site planner reacts. There are many other factors which influence the development of the inhabitants' attachment to their home environment and the reader is referred to the book *Housing as if People Mattered* (Cooper Marcus and Sarkissian, 1986) for further identification of these.

Aesthetics and people's perception of their immediate environment
As noted in the previous chapter, aesthetics is an important but illusive subject for site planners, as it is for anybody else involved with people's qualitative judgements. There are unfortunately no fixed rules about aesthetics which can be applied universally, but rules have been identi-

fied by various authors which apply at least within given cultures and
sections of society.

Aesthetics is not just about what is seen, it is about everything that we
experience. Our aesthetic judgements are based on our acquired knowledge, our social and cultural conditioning, plus the multitude of past
experiences which differ for each individual. People react to what they
see, hear, smell, touch and taste through the filter of their past learning
and experiences. All people, not just those who consider themselves
highly educated in such matters, are able to give their judgement about
the aesthetic value to them of a given experience. That judgement may
differ significantly from person to person.

The differences of opinion in relation to aesthetic issues mean that the
site planner almost inevitably has to consult expert opinion on the
aesthetics of a culture. This is not unreasonable since the expert too is
part of a culture; for site planning purposes someone has to define the
aesthetic objectives of a culture if ideas about how to plan and design are
to be developed which fit the local needs.

It has already been pointed out that people can only react to questions
about the sorts of environments in which they would like to live through
the filter of their own experience. Therefore, to risk basing designs for
the future on people's present level of sensitivity to aesthetics without
reference to expert opinion, would be to risk producing environments
which will soon be rejected as appropriate to the changing needs of that
group of people. It is in trying to assess how people's sensibilities are
likely to develop over time that the expert in aesthetics has an important
role to play and this is why landscape architects, architects and civic
designers must be fully trained in the aesthetic requirements of their
culture.

Pleasing people's sensibilities is a sure way to add to their satisfaction
with their immediate environment; an understanding of aesthetic principles is, therefore, central to site planning but almost never the dominant
consideration. The site planner has to use all the knowledge available
from the field of aesthetics, particularly on how people make value
judgements, before taking decisions which will allow the development of
settings which satisfy people.

There are, however, some occasions when the aesthetic principles
developed by the experts dominate the site planning process and the
design solution, deciding the form and detail of the development.
Aesthetic considerations can dominate when the site planner is dealing
with a client who is commissioning a design solely for individual use, for
a limited range of people with highly developed aesthetic sensibilities, or
for image-making purposes. For instance, an individual house and associated private gardens, a club house and associated grounds, or an
organization requiring a particular image to be associated with their
company. In such circumstances the whole approach to the layout and

design is more akin to that associated with a work of art. The key to knowing when this approach is appropriate is the importance which the client puts on image rather than other user requirement factors. This ties in with the research findings set out in the previous chapter, which indicate that the better-off people are (in our society that normally equates also with a higher general level of education), the more likely they are to experience landscape as something to be appreciated through looking at it rather than just as something to be in.

Another instance when the understanding of aesthetic principles can dominate the decision-making process, is when a site has historic links. To retain or return to the landscape or townscape of a given historic period requires that the site planner has a full understanding of the design principles within which the design was originally evolved.

The site planner should be aware how people can react to spaces
In the concern to identify the experiential needs of the user, the site planner also has to be aware of a further factor, that spaces as total physical entities can engender reactions which influence people's perception of spaces. The exact impact of the space on an individual cannot be fully anticipated, but as site planners we need at least to be aware that people will react positively or negatively to any place that we are involved in forming through the site planning and design process.

The main characteristics of a place

Box 8.10 identifies some of the characteristics of spaces which can be controlled by the site planner and designer.

THE ROLE OF 'GREEN' IN DEVELOPING SPECIAL LOCAL CHARACTER

One of the most important aspects of site planning has become the preservation and addition of plants and natural habitats.

The previous chapter presented evidence that nature and 'greenery' is something that most people want in their daily lives. They want it on their doorsteps, not tucked away in parks, not inaccessible in distant countryside. In Part Two the conservation reasons for the preservation and introduction of plants were mentioned and the way plants can be used to ameliorate the urban environment was introduced.

There is other evidence of the psychological importance of 'green'. This includes medical observations which show that: people in hospital looking towards trees and plants can make a speedier recovery than those looking at walls; people who have been stressed and ill have

BOX 8.10

A summary of the main characteristics of a place which can be controlled through a site plan

1. Spaces in the city and countryside should be planned to allow both the performance of a function and at the same time give people the intellectual stimulation they require to feel satisfied with their immediate environment – the environment they live in, work in, travel through, play in and even profit from.

2. Spaces should have sufficient richness and diversity to stimulate our senses if they are to hold our interest. They should be sufficiently diverse to allow intellectual stimulation. For instance, the human need for intellectual stimulation could be one of the reasons why gardens are so popular for city dwellers, for they provide perpetual interest and fascination through the flowering sequence of plants and other changes that occur in the vegetation through the seasons.

3. Spaces should provide a situation in which people can meet informally. People's need for interesting experiences could be one of the reasons why people have been observed to cluster together even when there is plenty of space. This snowball effect probably works because people like to observe others and to have the chance of interacting with others.

4. Spaces should be complex enough to challenge our senses and yet cohesive enough for us to understand the space and be able to feel secure within the space. They need to be organized so that people can understand them and their relationship with other spaces. A space must be legible enough to be distinct from others if people are to avoid feeling lost. People need to know where they are. They need to recognize a place as known or unknown. They need to describe places to others.

5. Spaces need distinctive characteristics which enable a sense of place to develop. This is important, as it links to the development of a sense of being on home territory, or the territory of the neighbour-hood or of a social group – any group to which the individual feels a sense of belonging. Children have been shown to have an acute awareness of their territory as being a local place, even if the territories that many adults think of as theirs are modified by the local social, cultural and economic factors. It is important that people can feel secure in any space, but most particularly if that space is their home territory. It should be clear who 'owns' each part of the land.

6. There should be privacy where privacy is needed and openness and contact where it is not required.

7. A space ought to be of a human scale if it is to feel comfortable to the users. Spaces in which people feel insignificant tend to inspire awe and fear and except where this is a deliberate intention, ought to be avoided when developing spaces for daily use. One of the major

problems for the site planner working where large modern buildings are to be erected, is to produce external spaces which have a scale to which the people entering and leaving the building can relate, so that they are encouraged to make good use of the outside area and yet to develop spaces which have some relationship to the often immense scale of the buildings.

recovered faster and stayed healthier for longer when they are in contact with pet animals.

City dwellers tend to have a negative image of many parts of the city which can cause dissatisfaction with the quality of life. Therefore, any characteristics such as 'greenery' which are viewed positively need to be multiplied if city livability is to be perceived to improve.

Parks and gardens have been valued for centuries for giving people living away from the countryside contact with nature. This argument, backed up by the planning philosophy that it was good for the health of the urban population to have access to open spaces, was used to justify the spread of urban parks in the nineteenth century.

The possibility of going into green spaces is considered to ease the burden of urban life by city dwellers and to give added opportunities for social interaction. To make cities more livable people want easy access to spaces where they can have contact with nature and which also delight their senses. Taken together the research by Burgess, Limb and Harrison and by Mostyn and Millward, which was discussed in the last chapter, produced a basic list of the characteristics which people want from outdoor areas in cities. These are set out in Box 8.11 and Box 8.12.

---

1. Places where contact with animals and birds and the more attractive insects like butterflies is possible
2. Places with visual variety
3. Places which are full of plants and give an experience of greenness
4. Places where children can learn about nature and social life through contact with animals
5. Places to loiter in and watch the world go by
6. Places which are conducive to harmonious social interaction, where it is possible to meet people casually, people one would not otherwise come across
7. Places to chat while children play
8. Places for family outings

BOX 8.11

The characteristics which people want from outdoor areas in cities

BOX 8.12

City dwellers would like greenspaces on their doorstep

1. Small spaces available to all, not open spaces which consist of a series of no-go areas
2. Spaces to give a variety of visual experience locally with colour on the doorstep. Its availability in parks is no substitute. People do not want city greenspaces as substitute countryside, they want them to be different.
3. It is important to people that the local open spaces do not appear neglected

The need for comprehensive greenspace planning

It is important to stress that it would be wrong to imagine that when an area of a city has social problems, minor tinkering with the open spaces would alone make any real difference to the social climate. Only major social and economic change can do this. However, environmental improvements which can be associated with community involvement in any changes can make a very real difference to the attitudes of people to their local environment.

Planning and describing the special qualities of each space within the city is ultimately the main concern of site planning. Connecting the different spaces that comprise a local environment allows site planners to plan and design a total system. This linking is important in that it allows more diversity of experience to develop than otherwise would be available within one area of the city. Greenspace plans which propose the environmental attributes and qualities achievable in each part of the city are needed for every city if site planners are to know how their area fits into the total city environment. Where such plans exist, the site planner has an added level of guidance on the best method of dealing with a specific site.

Preparing briefs for environmental settings

What does all this information about peoples' needs and attitudes mean to the site planner? How does this help us create 'behaviour settings'? Lynch and Hack (1985) described behaviour settings as 'small localities, bounded in time and space, within which there is some stable pattern of purposeful behaviour, interacting with some particular physical setting.' Lynch saw behaviour settings as 'in part self-regulating, changing their surroundings to maintain themselves, while also adapting to their surroundings'.

Watching how places work as behaviour settings is often more use to a person learning to be a site planner than any official survey of behaviour. Rutledge (1985) produced an excellent book on how human behaviour patterns should affect the way parks are designed. One of the methods for learning more about behaviour patterns is the type of observation study where you sit down and make a sketch of the setting that you are viewing and then annotate that to indicate how the users behave within the space. Such an elementary survey tool is of enormous use to site planners; it makes us watch and attempt to understand what we are seeing in a way which allows us to communicate effectively with designers. Rutledge considers that this type of study enables us to predict behaviour in other similar settings and so allows us to explore how we might integrate predictions of behaviour into our design process. Understanding the factors which lead us to design in a certain way then provides the basis for post-occupancy evaluations. Without the latter process designers will never learn from their mistakes and will continue to produce one-off designs based, as often as not, on nothing more than the the designer's own instinctive reaction.

Types of behaviour are actions – what people do. Site planning and design can make these actions easy and straightforward or hinder them. Design does not totally dictate behaviour, but neither is it without influence on behaviour – a design may encourage a certain reaction. By applying the site planning process we attempt to generate settings which will support a diversity of behaviour, whilst at the same time allowing what has been identified as the major function of a place to proceed.

The settings required for each activity need to be described so that the site planner and designer understand their characteristics, and whether fixed characteristics are required or whether there is flexibility. This has been termed drawing up performance standards. Both Wurman *et al.* (1972) and Hester (1983) have described the process in detail, showing that performance standards can be described for each activity by considering the 'who, what, where and when'. For instance, if a 'children's play setting' is required in a housing area, looking in detail at children's behaviour can help the site planner to recognize the different activities that must be catered for. A detailed consideration will show that it is not possible to cater for children's play just by providing a play area. In fact children are always on the move as they play and will want to play everywhere within a site; they will also benefit from playing in a multitude of different settings because of the greater levels of diversity of experience.

If a satisfactory play setting is to develop, the site plan needs to indicate the appropriate range of experiences and related activities that should be available to children of different ages within and near the housing site. The appropriate maximum distance from the home for each activity and the facility (structure, surfacing and/or equipment) needed to support all the the activities. The site plan also needs to indicate how children might be expected to use any facilities provided and whether that facility should be separate from others, or is related to an activity which can be integrated with a range of others. This information can be translated by the site planner working with the designer into a description of the spaces, the settings that will be needed within the site for the proper development of children's play. If children are likely to be attracted to nearby but off-site facilities, decisions will also be needed at the stage of drawing up the site plan on the provision of good safe access routes.

All site planning decisions are constrained by costs. The site planner, therefore, has to calculate the probable cost of providing the ideal setting for children and then consider what can be afforded. In discussions with the client it is as well to remember that there are high costs in terms of vandalism associated with making no or too little provision for children. The cost of providing for children's play is not just related to capital costs, since there are related maintenance and management costs which can rapidly escalate if the children abuse the provision.

The site design translates the description of facilities and settings into places for play. How this is done is discussed in Part Four. Here the subject of performance standards will be considered at greater length, as it is a crucial concept in relation to site planning and the link between that and the design process.

PERFORMANCE STANDARDS

These are necessary as a means to ensure user requirements can be met. It has already been stated that the detailed analysis of user requirements is basic to site planning. The solutions developed by the site planning team from this analysis can then be evaluated by the user: the user can judge the extent to which the solutions satisfy their environmental needs. Drawing up performance standards for each activity and for the spaces in which they occur is the bridge between these two situations. Wurman *et al.* (1972) have introduced a very straightforward means of describing environmental performance based on a method designed for use with local communities. It was specifically designed to help the community reach conclusions about the environments they wanted locally to support their activities.

Wurman *et al.* (1972) describe how it is possible to think of each activity independently and decide what is required for it to happen. Box 8.13 illustrates this process.

This is a long list but if you think through two or three of your favourite outdoor activities, you will see that it enables you to describe the best location and best spatial characteristics for those activities as

1. whether it is a relatively active or inactive pastime
2. whether it is an activity which interests certain age groups only or is done by everybody
3. whether it is an activity which requires a specific space or item of equipment
4. whether it requires great deal or a small area of land
5. whether it happens in one fixed location or involves the use of linear space
6. whether it requires flat land or slopes of varying degrees
7. whether it is a very common activity requiring daily doorstep access, an occasional but locally required activity, or
8. whether it is relatively rare and can be travelled to
9. whether it requires a track of its own or can use the tracks provided in the city for walking and driving
10. whether it requires specially constructed facilities such as buildings, shelter, safety equipment on site, or any special amenities
11. whether it is strongly affected by time, temperature, weather, or unaffected by any of them
12. whether it benefits from a natural-looking setting or a formal setting, or is unaffected by the type of setting
13. whether it has special maintenance requirements in relation to surfaces or equipment

BOX 8.13

To decide the characteristics of an outdoor recreational activity ask the following questions

well as the people who would be involved and the equipment that would be needed.

DECIDING WHERE THE ACTIVITY SHOULD BE LOCATED

This is determined by several factors, the main being the demand for availability of the activity and the presence of the correct physical setting (this can be one that is already in the vicinity and has all the appropriate characteristics, or it can be one which is created by the site planning team to meet a demand).

For instance, if it is a leisure activity which people take part in daily, then it will need to be within 400 m of each home. This has been shown by a variety of studies in various countries to be the maximum distance the majority of people will regularly walk to do something. Beyond that distance only the really keen and energetic tend to go regularly.

In relation to a new housing estate the site planner needs to try and locate all the activities identified as required on a daily basis by the inhabitants within 400 m of the home. If every activity needed a separate setting this would be an impossible task, but many activities can and do happen on the same piece of land. Look back at Box 8.4 and then obtain a plan of any housing area and work out where it would be best for those activities to occur. Which are the garden (or private outdoor space) activities? Which are the front doorstep activities? Which can happen at up to 400 m from the home? Which would the more energetic groups in society be likely to travel further afield for? What other activities can you think of from your personal experience that might happen in or near a housing area and where would they be best located?

It is worth noting in relation to this that once people get into a car or bus to travel to a specific activity they become relatively independent of the homebase. They can travel to any place in the town and adjacent towns, or the countryside where their requirements will be met. However, it is really only the more affluent who can travel in this way and for the poorer sections of any community it is important that the activities which they want to participate in are available locally.

If you look at your assessment of the best location for each activity in the housing area, you will see just how many ought to occur on the same area of land. This poses another problem for the site planner. It means that it is necessary to see which activities are compatible and which will need their own special area. People can sit and watch, sit and talk, play tag, watch the birds and insects, smell the leaves and flowers, watch the water splash from a fountain, play marbles, skip, push the pram and stroll round, all in the same area – quite happily coexisting and in fact benefiting from a greater level of diversity of experience, just because the place is busy. However, if the inhabitants want to play more vigorous games these have to be held elsewhere to avoid unnecessary accidents. If the games are formal they may well require properly defined pitches, which also means that they have to be separate from other activities. Even the use of children's play equipment with moving parts like swings and roundabouts has to be separated from other uses for safety reasons.

Making decisions about the location of activities and the type of experiences that should be available to the users involves the site planners and designers in having to work constantly backwards and forwards. Each decision has an impact on the decisions yet to be made. To get the right fit between activities and spaces is a challenging and fascinating process involving working with the information gathered about the physical and natural characteristics of the site and its surroundings, as well as with the information about the user needs.

One of the most neglected activities in the literature produced by recreation experts and yet the most common of all is going for a stroll. Strolling along city streets and through open spaces and the countryside is a daily activity. Most people walk to the shops, around the city centre, to the bus stop, to school or somewhere else each day. It is on these walks that we have the most contact with our local environment and through this activity we become aware of living somewhere which interests us and fascinates us or is alien and hostile to us.

In Britain the many recreation grounds and public open spaces planned and provided in the last forty years have been justified in the main as the places where a given sport will take place. The result has been bare bleak grasslands without any of the diversity that might stimulate use by non-sportsmen. Too often it is not the open spaces which attract people during their leisure time for there is nothing to do there, nothing of interest to watch except for people walking their dogs. It is no wonder that the streets are perceived as more interesting. There at least there is some life, some chance of catching a glimpse of other people and their activities, a feeling of not being totally isolated.

It is the presence of lots of people of diverse age groups strolling around and sitting watching and talking which makes us feel that spaces are safe. If a space just attracts one age group or people involved in one activity, it can alienate others. If open areas within the city are to be safe, they need to be designed to bring in a wide spectrum of society involved in a diversity of activities and until they become busy places they need to be supervised by wardens. There would be no difficulty about turning our bleak wastelands of playing fields into more widely used areas. All that is needed is for a consideration of the other activities that could be encouraged there and the construction of the settings which would support those activities, and, of course, the money to finance the works. But if the return for this different approach to open spaces was a lowering of the vandalism rate, as has been suggested by the research of Mostyn (1989) and others, this could be money well spent by any community.

CONCLUSION

Site planning, if properly carried out, will lead to richer more stimulating environments. Improving the quality of life in cities does not imply an inherent increase in the quantity of publicly looked after land, nor of associated costs to the community of supporting such land. It implies the reverse in many ways. If the whole townscape becomes richer in terms of the variety of environmental experiences it supports, then the present level of open space will in many cases suffice.

In Britain almost all the parks and major open spaces could benefit from a rethink in relation to the way they function for the local community, as well as for their more occasional visitors. The smaller recreation grounds or public open spaces, which dot the large estates built from the 1930s to the 1970s, provide the required number of square metres of open space per thousand of population, but would also benefit from replanning and redesigning to meet the needs of modern urban populations. To do this the funding of the larger open spaces within cities needs to be reconsidered and the cost to society of not providing adequate recreational opportunities at the local level for the mass of the population has to be part of that equation.

Above all, a change of approach is needed at the level of the site plan, so that small scale spaces, rich in visual interest, wildlife and the opportunity for informal activities and social contact, are incorporated into the design. This richness can be provided as much in people's gardens and in the streets and parking areas as in any officially designated open space, but in order to meet people's need the whole range of spaces is needed. Whatever public land is made available within any site must be managed and maintained at the level appropriate to the setting that is created and when necessary wardening must be allowed for. If this cannot be managed then it may well be better that all land, except that needed for circulation, is in private care, although such a drastic solution could lead to all the problems associated with lowering the level of diversity of experience available to the local inhabitants.

The next part deals in detail with the mechanism for drawing up a site plan. It indicates how the information about people, gathered through the examination of human activities and environmental needs suggested here, must be co-ordinated with the information about the land and its physical and natural environmental characteristics before a site plan can be made.

Carrying out the project work

Once you have completed reading through this section you should follow the programme of survey work described in Step 12 of Part Five.

References

Adams, E. (1987) Teachers, architects and planners: collaboration in education. *Bulletin of Environmental Education*, nos 191/192.

Adams, E. (1990) *Learning through Landscapes Project* (in press), Hampshire County Council, Winchester.

Alexander, C., Ishikawa, S. and Silverstein, M. (1977) *A Pattern Language*, Oxford University Press, New York.

Appleby, M. (1978) Organizing participatory public decisions, paper presented to 9th World Congress of Sociology, Uppsala, Sweden, Division of Environmental and Urban Systems, Virginia Polytechnic Institute and State University, Blacksburgh, Virginia.

Beer, A. and Booth, P.A. (1981) *Development Control and Design Quality*, Sheffield Centre for Environmental Research, Sheffield.

Coleman, A. (1986) *Utopia on Trial*, Hilary Shipman, London.

Cooper M., Clare and Sarkissian, W. (1986) *Housing as if People Mattered,*

University of California Press, Berkeley.

Department of the Environment (1981) *Survey of tenants attitudes to recently completed estates*, HMSO, London.

Findlay, A. *et al.* (1989) Whose quality of life, *The Planner*, 75, no.15.

Harrison, C., Limb, M. and Burgess, J. (1987) Nature in the city, *Journal of Environmental Management*, 25, 347–362.

Harrison, C. and Burgess, J. (1988) Qualitative research and open space policy, *The Planner*, Nov 1988.

Heder, L. and Francis, M. (1977) Quality of life assessment: the Harvard Square planning workshops. In *The Methodology of Social Impact Assessment* (eds Finsterbush and Wolf), Dowden, Hutchinson & Ross, Stroudsberg, Pa.

Hester, R.T. (1983) Process can be style, participation and conservation in Landscape Architecture, Landscape Architecture, May/June 1983.

Kelman, H.C. (1958) Compliance, internalization and identification: three processes of attitude change, *Journal of Conflict Resolution*.

Millward, A. and Mostyn, B. (1989) People and nature in cities, *Urban Wildlife Journal*: No. 2, NCC publication, London.

Mostyn, B. (1979) *Personal Benefits and Satisfactions Derived from Participation in Urban Wildlife Projects*, NCC publication, London.

Patmore, J.A. (1983) *Recreation and Resources: Leisure Patterns and Leisure Places*, Basil Blackwell, Oxford.

Rogerson, R.J., Morris, A.S., Finlay A.M. and Paddison, R. (1989) *Britain's Intermediate Cities: a comparative study of the quality of life*, Glasgow Quality of Life Group, Department of Geography, University of Glasgow.

Rutledge, A.J. (1971) *Anatomy of a Park*, McGraw-Hill, New York.

Rutledge, A.J. (1985) *A Visual Approach to Park Design*, John Wiley, New York.

Whyte, W.H. (1980a) A guide to people watching. In Cooper-Hewitt Museum, The Smithsonian Institution's National Museum of Design, *Urban Open Space*, Rizzoli Publications, New York.

Whyte, W.H. (1980b) *The Social Life of Small Urban Spaces*, The Conservation Foundation, Washington, DC.

Wilson, S. (1978) Vandalism and 'defensible space' on London housing estates. In *Tackling vandalism*, (ed R.V.G. Clarke) Home Office Research Study no. 40, HMSO, London.

Wurman, R.S., Levy, A. and Katz, J. (1972) *The Nature of Recreation*, London MIT Press for the American Federation of Arts and Group for Environmental Education, Cambridge, Mass.

Part Four

The Site Plan

This part summarizes the range of work a site planning team has to undertake to produce a site plan.

Chapter 9 indicates how to assess site potential using information previously gathered about the site and user needs. Chapter 10 deals with the content of a site plan and the preparation of design briefs.

Exploring site potential 9

It is at this stage, after a thorough analysis of all the issues related to the future development of a site, that the site planning team begins to make decisions about the site's future development. If the sequence of work described in Parts One, Two and Three has been completed, all the information required for the assessment of the site potential and drawing up the site plan should be available to the site planning team.

Collecting the information is not enough by itself, it is making sense of it that is important. It is often a difficult task as almost all sites, even small ones, can be complex. Out of the mass of information that becomes available the site planner has to decide what is crucial to the problem in hand; what should happen where on a site and how it should happen.

The site planner can begin by looking for patterns in the information gathered, patterns which will give a clue as to the best approach. An approach has to evolve to allow both for the conservation of the natural environment and the development of new human habitats to support the need for a satisfactory quality of life; the problem is to find a way to link the two to produce guidelines for development. Such a pattern rarely 'jumps out' at the site planner, it only emerges after spending a great deal of time studying the information. To develop an idea of what might be a suitable approach to solving the problem, the site planner often uses a thought process involving a series of loops. It entails repeatedly trying out different ideas and attempting to understand their implications both in relation to people and the natural environment. It involves gradually developing an understanding of the essence of the place and then a strategy for dealing with the problem. This understanding of the 'place' comes from a combination of the impressions received during repeated visits to a site (the subconscious understanding) and from a systematic interpretation of the data gathered during the site inventory phase (the conscious understanding).

It is very often the subconscious understanding which triggers the spark of an idea which eventually can lead to something special developing on a site. Even when a site is to be almost totally redeveloped and the new place will bear little relationship to the old, this thought and ideas process is still relevant. If the site planner does not develop ideas about what the experience of being in that place is to be like in the future for users and visitors, then it is highly unlikely that a satisfactory environment for human activities can be planned or implemented. Any site planner who fails to spend a considerable amount of time on and in the vicinity of a site and where possible in the company of the users, is highly unlikely to be able to produce a site plan which will satisfy the users or relate to the 'place'.

Parts Two and Three detailed the type of information that a site planner should expect to gather. However, a major part of the fully trained site planner's skill is in deciding which of the mass of possible information it is essential to collect. This decision should only relate to the particular problem posed by a specific site and its future uses. Every site plan has different problems, so the information needs will always be different. There is no magic recipe or formula always applicable; only the skill of the experienced site planner will enable short cuts to be taken. The key for cost effective site planning is the identification of the minimum level of information needed for decision-making. In drawing up that list of the minimum information requirement, the site planner should always remember there is normally the opportunity of obtaining more information if that proves necessary.

Some survey information will always be required, however straightforward the problem. For instance, a topographic plan will be needed as a base plan for the survey stages and to act as the base for the site plan. Information will also always be required about the users and their needs. Beyond that the information which comes into the decision-making process depends entirely on the site and the problem.

Assessing the site's potential

Drawing up an assessment of the site's potential in relation to the proposed development is the stage where the expertise of the trained site planner is at its most useful to the multi-disciplinary planning team. On a big project most of the background information can be gathered by the various specialists in the team using the expertise of their particular field of knowledge, backed up by information gained from outside experts. The problem is to bring all the disparate information together, to make sense of it.

Drawing up a site potential plan is the method landscape architects have evolved to deal with this problem. Through it they attempt to make sense of what has been discovered about the site and its users. It is a plan which attempts to distil the essence of the site. To produce it the site planner normally uses a large base plan of the site and its surroundings, recording graphically either on the base plan or on a series of overlays the factors which make the site special. The factors causing the site to change even without any new development being implemented also need to be identified, as they highlight any land and landscape management problems inherent in the site.

The site potential plan should indicate all the assets and liabilities within the site and in the area immediately surrounding it; the decision as to what is an asset and what a liability relates to the proposed development. It is useful if the drawing that results from this exercise summarizes the factors which will constrain development and the factors which present opportunities for a variety of different approaches for coping with the new development. The site planner has to produce this summary in a way which the whole site planning team and the client can understand. A consensus needs to be reached about the implications of it for each particular part of the planning and design process. When it is possible to arrange discussions with the future users, they too should discuss the implications of the site potential in relation to the environmental qualities they would like to develop within the site.

Assessing site potential cannot be defined as a fixed process. Even for a specific problem, ideas about the relative importance of different aspects of the site and its users will change as concepts are developed to deal with the projected development, and different ways of doing things are tested.

In most circumstances the site planner and other designers involved in a project are working towards an understanding of the site so that the site's existing characteristics are respected and reflected in the proposals. This is, however, not always the case. There are instances where site planning decisions may go against the natural feel of a site so as to deliberately introduce something new and different, something which stands out as alien in the local landscape. But to do this it is essential that the site planner and designers understand the implications not just for the site, but for the landscape of which it is a part. The full site planning process still has to be adhered to even when it is intended to obliterate most of the existing site.

In most circumstances the site planner is working in a situation where a site has already been chosen for a particular use; the site planner's role is working out a best fit. Sometimes, and if site planning were to be a really effective part of the planning process it would be more common, the site planner is asked to locate a suitable site for a specific activity or to work out the best use for a particular site. In these latter cases the information requirements are similar to the more common situation being described here and cover the factors discussed in Parts Two and Three. The main difference is that the site planner has to propose criteria which can be used to run tests to identify best locations or best use within a wider area.

BOX 9.1

Stages in the assessment of site potential

End product
Define the end product of the development in greater detail.

Interrelationships between activities and structures
Gather all the available information about the form and function of any buildings to be located on the site, as well as about the physical elements that will be needed to support outdoor activities.

Assets and liabilities
Work out which of the site's features can be viewed as assets in terms of the proposed development and which are likely to cause problems.

Land and landscape management
Identify the major interactions between the environmental factors which control change in the landscape and identify the critical land management practices in relation to the maintenance of the landscape.

Identification of fit between site and users
Work out which of the proposed activities are fixed in their location because of the site's characteristics and which can be located as the site plan is developed. Indicate the areas which are suitable for each activity on a plan.

BOX 9.2

Information required to define the 'end product'

1. A user-requirements list describing activities, facilities and environmental settings, derived from the type of research described in the Part on The Users.
2. A description of all the buildings to be placed on the site to meet user needs and an agreement on the appropriate level of infrastructure support.
3. A clear statement of intent with regard to the conservation and preservation of the natural environment within and adjacent to the site.
4. Information on who will pay for the implementation of each part of the scheme.
5. Information on who will be responsible for the maintenance of every area and element within the site.
6. A consideration of the cost and time constraints which must apply to each part of the project as well as those that apply to the whole.

THE MAJOR STAGES IN THE ASSESSMENT OF SITE POTENTIAL

The stages which the site planner must progress through are set out in Box 9.1 and described more fully below.

THE END PRODUCT OF THE SITE DEVELOPMENT DEFINED

A statement of the end product for the site plan and design is drawn up; it is the final agreement between the client and the site planning team. It deals with what is to happen on the site and the specifications that can be applied. The client's original brief is expanded into a fixed programme of requirements based on studies of user requirements and the need to conserve the site's natural features. It is a statement which must be agreed by both the client and the site planning team.

Occasionally the original brief received from a client will need no modification, but in many cases the detailed study of the site and its users, which is undertaken as the first part of the site planning process, will suggest either a slightly different or a very different approach to the problem. Any re-definition of the problem must be agreed with the client and a programme drawn up to indicate the factors which the site planner will take into account at the next stage – the decision-making stage. Box 9.2 indicates the information needs of this stage.

To finalize this statement it is normally necessary to progress further into the site potential study so that the problems can be better understood. Once a first draft of the end product statement has been agreed, the site planning team then needs to work through the following issues before returning to draw up a final agreed statement with the client.

INTERRELATIONSHIPS BETWEEN ACTIVITIES AND STRUCTURES

This phase of the assessment of site potential takes the user requirements and facilities list drawn up as a result of the work done for Part Three and assesses its implications for the site layout further. It finalizes the requirements for different types of buildings and determines which of the desired activities can be covered by the site plan.

This is done by taking the description of the required activities, and the facilities and environmental settings required to facilitate them, and translating this into a list of features and elements to be present on the site.

If any of the activities require buildings, these will have to be the subject of intensive research by the architect in conjunction with the site planner. The anticipated form of any buildings, their mass and shape, need to be defined so that the site planning team can be provided with information on the most likely 'footprint' of the buildings. If site planning is to work effectively, the maximum flexibility in the positioning of the buildings is required, so whenever possible alternative solutions should be explored. Buildings are likely to be the most expensive elements on any site. There is, therefore, less flexibility about where they can be positioned and their location on the site will have a major impact on whatever else is planned. Box 9.3 indicates the data required about the buildings.

Once the information about the buildings has been established, the site planner begins to consider the alternative ways in which the layout of the site could be approached (Box 9.4).

When a site has no buildings and few structural elements or they take up a small part of the site, it is still necessary to consider the likely requirements of each of the activities in terms of the features that need to be present on the site and how they are likely to impact on the existing environment. Box 9.5 lists the information required for each outdoor activity.

The information gathered about buildings and outdoor activities

---

BOX 9.3

Information required about the buildings for the site plan

The characteristics of each building
The architects need to provide sufficient data on the likely physical characteristics of the buildings, what people are expected to do in them and how people and goods can be expected to get in and out of them. It is just the same range of information that they will have to provide to allow the client to undertake a proper financial feasibility exercise.

The mass of the buildings, their form and shape, including probable height
This will allow calculations of the likely impact of the buildings on the micro-climate. Areas where there will be problems with wind swirling between buildings can be identified, as can the shadow areas. This also allows assessment of the visual impact.

The structure of the buildings and their weight distribution
This also allows identification of areas where expensive pile driving might prove necessary because of bearing capacity.

The maximum angle of slope that is acceptable before major earth shifting will be needed

On steep sites the assessment should include a consideration of the benefits of using split level buildings. This helps the identification of the areas of the site which are best used for building.

The drainage requirements – surface water and foul water
Large buildings and their associated parking and other hard surfaces radically change the nature of a site's drainage. The site planner needs to know how much surface water will be produced and how the architect and site engineer intend to deal with this so that the environmental implications can be investigated. Alternatives which would use the water on site should be explored. The foul drainage requirements need to be known, so that an estimate can be made of likely disturbance to a site as the trenches are dug for a sewerage system.

Water supply needs
This will allow an assessment to be made of the need to hold water on the site as well as to bring drinking water from outside.

Power Supply
The trenches required for these services can have an impact on the site as their reservations need to be kept clear of trees.Rubbish disposal needs. Rubbish storage areas have to be provided for all buildings, their extent and type depending on the function of the building. The way in which it is anticipated that the rubbish will be collected will influence the system developed for the site.

Lighting needs, including daylight
Many modern buildings have internal light wells and some have few outside windows. The site planners need to know what is envisaged, since window light requirements can determine the distance apart that buildings are placed, which in turn can have a significant impact on the site. The architect's requirements for lighting of the external areas need to be known and incorporated later into a total lighting scheme for the site.

Parking and garaging needs
These can be a significant element in terms of space requirements on many sites and have a strong influence on site layout.

The sunlight and orientation requirements and the need to ameliorate the local climate
These are linked to energy conservation issues and an assessment of the environmental information can identify those parts of a site where it

would be best not to site buildings, for instance, because of the aspect of the slope. The information can also indicate the angles at which it would be inadvisable to place buildings if over heating is to be avoided.

Private space needs
This helps to determine the layout of the space immediately around the buildings and links with the other outdoor activities that must be located within the site.

Security requirements
The site planner needs to know the degree of security required by the buildings. For instance, some buildings housing dangerous chemical processes require large, clear, flat areas around them so that no unauthorized people can approach the buildings; others require high, strong fencing; others blast proof mounds.

Access for the fire vehicles and ambulances
The local fire brigade will provide information to the architect and site planner on their requirements for easy approach to the buildings and the surfaces they are willing to drive over.

BOX 9.4

Alternative means of coping with the buildings need to be considered

The range of possible patterns of layout
Consideration of the different ways in which the buildings could relate to the road surfaces and open areas within the site and adjacent to it is required. For instance, if the buildings are houses, the site planner needs to know both the form of the building (detached, semi-detached or terraced) and how the buildings may be grouped, whether along a street or in various combinations to produce clusters of houses, with the road on the outside or inside of that cluster.

The range of possible construction materials
The architect and the site planning team should begin to consider the range of colours and textures that will fit with the site at an early stage of the development process. Particularly in relation to large buildings using modern hi-tech building methods a consideration of colour should not be left to the end, as there is always a danger that a certain form of building implies the use of certain materials and these may only be available in a limited range of colours and textures. Michael Lancaster's book (1984) on colour in the landscape is a useful guide for site planners considering this issue.

1. The degrees of slope which are acceptable.
2. The need for enclosing structures and information on their dimensions.
3. The types of surface which are suitable for different levels of usage.
4. The extent and shape of the playing surface and the surrounds, where applicable.
5. The safety zones in the case of activities which involve any element of danger.
6. The changing and storage facilities.
7. Which activities are compatible and which are incompatible and the distance which must separate them.
8. Any orientation requirements in relation to the sun.
9. Any requirement for formal or informal spectator provision.
10. The acceptable maximum distance from the homes of the users.

BOX 9.5

Information required about outdoor activities

needs to be translated into facts about the structures to be placed on a site. This allows the site planner to proceed to the next phase of site assessment, which is to work out what all the information that has been gathered about the physical and natural environment means in terms of the opportunities and constraints it imposes on the site development.

ASSETS AND LIABILITIES

The simplest method of ensuring that the site planning team is aware of the implications of the local physical and natural environmental factors is to produce a plan which highlights the important factors. To do this an annotated plan is produced which shows all the assets and liabilities of the site and presents the constraints and opportunities these pose for future developments. This plan is produced by working systematically through all the information that has been gathered about the site and assessing its importance in terms of the proposed future development of the site.

On a small site the process is usually fairly straightforward and the site planning team use their own knowledge of similar projects elsewhere to decide which information is significant in relation to the project. On large sites, assessing which factors should be taken into account is more complex, often requiring the prior definition of goals for the planning process and an agreed system of evaluating the evidence. John T. Lyle (1985) in his book *Design for Human Ecosystems* discusses the various ways in which the problem of developing a vehicle for the design process can be dealt with. He shows the importance of developing different approaches for each circumstance but all the time allowing for a feedback system to develop, which encourages or discourages a certain line of action. Any site planner coping with a particularly large complex site is advised to read the section in Lyle's book on the design process and methods before making decisions on how to proceed.

For the purposes of the present book, which is intended as an introduction to the basics of site planning, a process is described which works well for relatively small projects. In these circumstances, where the problem is not so vast that it cannot be comprehended without the help of systems or models, the site planner's task is to look at all the information gathered during the site inventory stage and decide what it means in relation to making decisions.

The decision about what to record is the site planner's or that of the site planning team. It may be argued that this is just your own opinion but it is worth remembering that that opinion is based on the best evidence available about a site and that you can back it up on the basis of the site inventory. You can, therefore, have some confidence in it, although it is always important to make clear when your decision is based on your own best judgement and when on incontrovertible scientific fact.

The information gathered at the site inventory stage has to be assessed to identify what are the assets and what are the problems. Part Two indicated the types of assessment that should be possible from the information gathered. Box 9.6 summarizes these.

LAND AND LANDSCAPE MANAGEMENT

One of the problems that inevitably arises when considering changes to a site is that changes in one aspect of the natural environment can have repercussions on others. The natural environment is the result of the interactions between all the component parts and man's activities. During the site inventory information is collected separately for each element of the environment and there is always a danger that the information is kept in separate categories. For this reason the site planner has to allocate time to attempt to understand at least some of the more obvious interactions. The aim should be to avoid inadvertently causing damage to an existing habitat or natural feature by a proposed change in the management of another element on a site which you had not understood was related.

For instance, if there is an area of wetland on a site, it might appear sensible to drain the area so that more of the site can be opened up for building purposes. But if this is done it could ultimately lead to the death of an area of trees because of the changed water table. Those trees could

Geological and geomorphological factors
This information will allow the site planner to indicate where it is unsafe to build anything because of instability caused by various factors, where it could become unsafe if certain actions occurred and where building would only be possible in a given way.

Surface and underground water
The information about water allows the site planner to identify areas within which it would be hazardous to develop, for instance because of flooding, which could become hazardous if certain actions were taken and where controls of various sorts will be needed to allow development. It also allows identification of the water bodies which contain high quality water fit for human use and the water bodies from which people should be excluded until the water quality can be improved.

Topography
The information on undulation of the land allows the site planner to identify where the land is too steep to develop in relation to the needs of the proposed land uses and where it is so flat that there could be drainage problems.

Climatic factors
This information allows the site planner to identify which parts of the site are more or less comfortable for human habitation as they are and to indicate the areas that could be made more hospitable by certain actions such as building screens against wind and sun.

Soil
The information about soil in part relates to the bearing capacity of the site, suggesting where it would be best to locate buildings with given foundation requirements. It also indicates the capacity of the ground to cope with changes in surface water flow and land management practice and the range of vegetation that might grow on the site.

Plants
A decision has to be taken by the site planner, on the basis of the information collected a the site inventory stage, about which individual plants and groups of plants must be retained, which could be considered for removal and which should be removed. Where there is likely to be a need for plants to be added to the site, the site planner can ask a landscape architect or plant expert for a list of the plants that could be expected to thrive on the site. If the site is to be developed with

BOX 9.6

How information about the physical and natural environment might be used in the site potential stage

naturalistic planting (Brooker and Corder, 1986 and Ruff, 1979) this list can be arrived at by reference to the data on the soil and other relevant environmental factors and information on local plant communities. If the site is to contain ornamental planting the range of species is wider, but still constrained by the physical characteristics of the site.

Ecology and wildlife

A decision is needed on which habitats must be retained because of their rarity and importance and which ought to be retained if possible. The implications in terms of what can happen on the surrounding land if these areas are kept have to be spelt out. The possibility of developing new habitats has to be considered and suitable areas of land identified. What is possible is determined by the local physical environment. There also has to be an assessment of what this might mean in relation to controlling land-uses on the adjoining areas of land.

Buildings and other structures on the site

The buildings and structures such as walls and tracks which must be retained should be identified, as should the buildings which could be retained and those which can be removed.

Historic and unique features

The historic features and areas should be graded to indicate which must be kept, which ought to be kept and which removed. The unique features should be indicated on the site plan as features to be kept. In addition the area of land around them which is in their field of influence, should be identified for protection from various forms of development. The limitations on development which need to be imposed within those zones need describing.

Views and scenery

The areas of land from which it is possible to experience good long distance and middle distance views need to be identified for special consideration, as do those areas where visual screens will be necessary so that ugly scenes do not detract from the experience of being in the place. In addition any screens that are needed on the site to protect the visual experiences of those that live outside it will need to be indicated.

naturalistic planting (Brooker and Corder, 1986 and Ruff, 1979) this list can be arrived at by reference to the data on the soil and other relevant environmental factors and information on local plant communities. If the site is to contain ornamental planting the range of species is wider, but still constrained by the physical characteristics of the site.

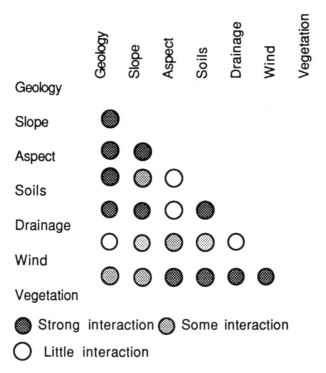

Figure 9.1 Example of the type of matrix which helps identify interactions between the elements of the natural environment on individual sites.

Every site is different, so the site planner has to be very alert to identify what is important for a particular site. The simplest way is to develop a check list for every site in the form of a matrix and to go through this list with the local ecologist or other expert in the natural environment.

The site planner needs to decide how important it is to keep the existing land and landscape management practices unchanged. Many landscapes are held in the state we see them today only by the way each element and each area of the ground is managed: how and how often the hedges are cut, the grass is mown, the ditches and water areas are dredged, the woodlands are worked through, etc.

It is vital to identify any trends in the maintenance and management practices applied to the land and landscape. All changes in land management practice ultimately lead to alterations in the landscape, some faster than others. In particular the landscape types that are susceptible to rapid change if the land management practices change need to be identified. One of the ways that landscape architects carry out this assessment is to use the landscape character zones which were identified as part of the site inventory. These zones can be used as the basis for describing the probable impact on each zone of the proposed buildings and activities and of any changing land and landscape management practices. Before this is possible, time has to be spent considering how the new uses of the land would be likely to lead to change in the related land management practices.

IDENTIFICATION OF FIT BETWEEN SITE AND USERS

Changing anything on a site costs money and unnecessary changes should be avoided. Site planning always aims to make the best use of what is already there; this is one of the reasons that the apparently lengthy process can actually save the developer money in the long run.

This stage of the site potential process looks at the fit between what uses are required to be located on the site and the site as it exists; seeing if there are parts of the site which already have the physical, natural environmental, or other characteristics required by the activities.

If the process proposed here is being followed, information will already be available on the physical and environmental requirements of all the activities to be located on the site. The site is inspected to see whether any of the required characteristics are evident and, if so, where. Any possible areas for that activity are marked on a plan (this stage normally takes the form of mapping on overlays). When there are no obviously correct locations for a particular activity, those areas where some of the required physical and natural environmental factors exist are then indicated. This is not making the final decision about what will happen where, but indicates where an activity can happen at least cost in terms of creating new settings. It is always best to assume that locations might have to change as the planning of the site progresses. This inspection of the site also allows the identification of those activities for which new settings will need to be formed if they are to occur on the site; that is the identification of the activities where the location will be determined by the site design solution as opposed to the site's natural characteristics.

The information on the fit between the site and the user requirements, combined with that on the interrelationships required between different activities and that on assets and liabilities, provides basic input to the site plan. It determines to a large extent the flexibility that can be allowed at the site layout stage.

FINALIZE THE STATEMENT OF OBJECTIVES

The statement of objectives can now be finalized and the production of the site plan can now begin.

Once you have completed this chapter you should follow the programme of survey work described in Step 13 in Part Five. If you have followed the site planning process this far and been working on the related 'steps', you will have all the information required to start producing a site layout. If you are also the designer you can move on after that to the design stage. For those of you who are reading this without carrying out an associated project, remember that not all the factors that have been discussed will always be applicable and what may seem a very time consuming process here can often be quickly dealt with after a short consideration of the issues involved. Again this is where the skill of the practised site planner comes into play, as it allows identification of where short cuts are appropriate. Do not attempt to take short cuts until you are expert, or you could easily leave out a vital factor.

Carrying out the project work

Brooker, R. and Corder, M. (1985) *Environmental Economy*, Chapman and Hall, London.
Lancaster, M. (1984) *Britain in View, Colour and the Landscape*, Quiller Press, London.
Lyle, J.T. (1985) *Design for Human Ecosystems*, van Nostrand Reinhold, New York.
Ruff, A. (1979) *Holland and the Ecological Landscapes*, Deanwater, London.

References

10 Production of the site plan

This chapter suggests one method by which the information gathered and assessed through the application of the site planning process can be brought together to produce a site plan and the associated design briefs. It is a method which follows the sequence shown in Box 10.1.

Throughout this stage of the site planning process, it is necessary for the site planner to work backwards and forwards through a series of decision-making loops, until a best fit between the site and the users needs is arrived at.

Except in rare circumstances, where the form of the layout makes it totally inappropriate, the site plan should always be supported by a landscape structure plan and a site management plan. The former is the means of unifying the disparate elements of the site; the latter deals with all aspects of the future maintenance and management of the site, but specifically with the work that needs to be carried out in the outdoor areas of the site. The site plan and its supporting documents form the basis out of which the design brief is developed for each part of the site.

By the time anyone working on a site plan has reached this stage, they will no doubt have developed a strong sense of what is possible on the site and how the site could best be laid out to meet the needs of the client

BOX 10.1

Suggested sequence of work to finalize the site plan

1. the identification of general strategies;
2. the drawing up of a list of objectives;
3. the environmental guidelines;
4. the concept plan for the site;
5. the evaluation of alternative solutions to the layout;
6. the site plan;
7. the landscape structure plan;
8. the site management plan;
9. the design briefs for each area.

and users. Because it can now seem easy to produce the site plan, there is a danger of thinking that the complicated exercise which has been described in this text as the 'site planning process' is unnecessary. However, if you just worked from your own instinctive feel about what should happen on a site, and failed to carry out a proper site planning exercise, you could not be sure of having all the information to persuade people that your solution would really work. With even small schemes costing millions to implement, the clients want and deserve better than an individual's or group's best guess before committing their money to development.

The client, and the local planning authority responsible for controlling development, need to be sure that the damage to the natural environment is minimal and that the users will not be alienated by the scheme. Local planning authorities are becoming increasingly wary of schemes which create an unnecessary extra long term cost to society due to high maintenance and management costs, just because they were ill thought out by the developer and professional advisers. Developers do not want to waste money on schemes which are rejected on environmental planning grounds by the planning process.

Professionals involved in site planning have a responsibility beyond meeting the client's immediate requirements. They need to ensure that the scheme works within the limitations and constraints imposed by environmental conservation requirements. They must also ensure that the scheme provides a suitable habitat for people, where applicable, and will be approved by the local planning authority.

A systematic approach to site planning is important too, as it allows for public participation. Using the site planning process, the site planners can explain their reasons for taking a certain decision. The site planner should aim to show that all decisions are derived from the site survey and assessment. When this is so, it will be possible to explain which decisions are based on scientific fact and which on subjective judgements. Through the way the site planning process operates, even the subjective judgements are based on best evidence. Therefore, the arguments behind the decisions can be explained as something other than a designer's whim. This way of presenting evidence to support conclusions enables the public to participate in the development of the site plan. They can understand how the decisions have been reached and can argue with the conclusion on the basis of given evidence. Using this process helps to dispel the view that site planning is some mysterious process only understandable by experts.

The financial aspects of site planning

The site planning process is particularly useful for coping with the financial aspects of planning. It allows a full description of all the work that needs to be undertaken on site: the preparation of the site, the construction of the built elements on the site, the planting of the vegetation, as well as the maintenance requirements. This information allows a detailed assessment of the cost of implementation of the scheme and of the design costs and in turn allows the impact on the environment of any cost cutting proposals to be estimated.

Costing each aspect of a scheme allows the site planner to go further than provide information on total cost; it also allows at least a limited attempt at financial evaluations of alternative solutions to both design and management of a site. The reasons that there are limits to the accuracy of these evaluations is that it is nearly always necessary to include an element of subjective judgement. It is not possible to put a quantitative or monetary value on everything in life. How, for instance, could a value be put on the fact that one layout made a space, which would become a small sunny corner of the sort that would attract people to sit out even in the winter, and another layout made no such provision? How could a 300 year old tree beginning to die back but rich in the number of insects for which it was the habitat be valued? It is for this reason that subjective judgements of relative value have to be allowed for somehow.

Providing that the criteria for the subjective judgement are properly set out and can be understood by all involved in using the information, this can be taken as an acceptable method of putting a value on the qualitative aspects of the environment. Residential developers, for instance, frequently use subjective judgements as a reason for designing houses in a certain way. They promote a marketing strategy which sells a certain image to a certain 'lifestyle' or income group. They develop their ideas of an appropriate style on the basis of their experience of market trends and readily change the design of the buildings to meet this image. On the basis of this subjective judgement of what the market wants, they design a variation to their basic house unit and add the required features. The price that can be added on to the sales price because of the change in the design is then calculated; these add-on costs have little to do with the real extra cost of providing the feature but reflect what the market will stand in order to purchase a certain experience. The developer will only be tempted to make the design change if a profit will result.

The fact that the developers already behave this way and commit vast sums on the basis of such subjective assessments should give site planners the courage to attempt similarly based evaluations of different planning and design solutions. They are the best means of persuading the developer, whose attitude is understandably influenced mainly by financial constraints. The site planner has to show that one solution has advantages over another and that providing a certain set of experiences for the user may have long-term financial gains for the developer, even if in the short term it costs more.

As almost every development scheme is subject to financial constraints, an ability to assess the financial impact of making alternative decisions is an important tool for site development. The cheapest capital cost only occasionally coincides with the cheapest site management costs. It is the two costs together which really determine the cost of choosing a particular solution. For instance, the site planner can use a financial evaluation to illustrate to the client the long-term monetary risks involved in deciding to omit to develop a certain environmental setting within the site. This assessment can be weighed against the cost to the client of providing the environmental setting at the time the development takes place. The client can decide which solution to adopt.

The fundamental idea behind these financial evaluations is that there are additional costs associated with user dissatisfaction. In some instances they will be associated with the costs of coping with vandalism and crime, in others only with extra maintenance costs and in others with the cost to society or another developer of providing proper facilities and settings for a particular activity elsewhere. The costs to the developer which come from failing to please the user can be enormous. They can range from the costs involved with borrowing money on buildings which cannot be let or cannot be sold, to the costs of having to upgrade a scheme to make it attractive to users, or the costs of having to knock down a scheme before the loan to build it has even been paid for.

The stages of preparing a site plan

The main purpose of this final phase of the site planning process is to produce a site layout which clearly indicates:

1. what is to be provided on the site;
2. what is to go where;
3. who is to be responsible for each part of the site, both in terms of construction and long-term maintenance.

THE STRATEGIES TO GOVERN SITE DEVELOPMENT

Here the permissible level of impact of the proposed development on the physical environment, the natural habitats, the landscape, the existing land uses and on the existing population is defined. An objective is also outlined for financial viability at different stages of the development.

BOX 10.2

Some of the factors that can be included in area planning statements drawn up by the local planning authority

1. a control on the density of development;
2. the appropriate form of the development;
3. the permitted height of buildings and other structures;
4. the permitted range of land uses;
5. the permitted number of inhabitants or employees in relation to the the social and infrastructure services available locally;
6. the need to preserve certain habitats and areas of vegetation;
7. the need for open spaces to meet both local demand and that of a wider area;
8. the requirement to keep specific groups of vegetation;
9. the requirement to develop in sympathy with certain local historic features.

BOX 10.3

Some of the factors that can be included in topic planning statements

1. greenspace planning in a particular city;
2. recreation standards in a particular area;
3. access to leisure for a particular group;
4. rehabilitation standards;
5. traffic management;
6. social provision;
7. farm management;
8. historic area management;
9. additional land for forestry.

THE MAIN SOURCES FOR INFORMATION TO DETERMINE APPROPRIATE STRATEGIES

Boxes 10.2 and 10.3 indicate some of the local sources of information which can be used to give guidance on appropriate strategies. In the main these derive from Local Plans many of which contain a statement that the local planning authority's intention is to protect and enhance the local environment. This fundamental statement leads to the need to define certain controls and to develop guidelines.

The client's requirements for the future development of the site

The client will normally need to make maximum use of the site to achieve the required financial return. This has to be achieved within the constraints of producing a scheme which will attract sufficient users to make it economically viable.

SITE DEVELOPMENT OBJECTIVES

These usually take the form of unambiguous statements of the objectives for the planning of the site. Box 10.4 lists some of the factors for which a statement of objectives might be required in relation to site development. The list will be different for every site.

---

1. The required land use and infrastructure:
    activities and associated facilities to occur on the site;
    area of land required by each land-use activity;
    the location of the 'fixed' activities;
    the locational requirements of the non-fixed activities;
    the permitted or required level of multi-use;
    appropriate communications system for the activities;
    access control – people and vehicles.
2. Site conservation measures:
    conservation of geological and geomorphological features;
    conservation of soils;
    conservation of water resources;
    conservation of existing vegetation and plant communities;
    conservation of the natural habitats;
    conservation of visual attributes;
    conservation of landmarks and unique features;
    conservation of landscape character zones;
    conservation of historic features and areas.
3. Experiential attributes of the site:
    the appropriate visual characteristics for the total site;
    the means of achieving human scale settings;
    the variations in visual characteristics between the different environmental settings for activities;
    the experiences to be available to the user in each environmental setting;
    the physical environmental controls required to ameliorate the climate;
    the experiences expected to be available on adjacent or nearby sites.
4. Landscape character zones of the site and its parts:
    a description of the appropriate landscape style and spatial structure (on the gradient formal to informal, ornamental to naturalistic, or in terms of an historic style) for the total site or for each of the required environmental settings; this might include a

BOX 10.4

Examples of the factors for which it might be necessary to develop objectives in relation to site development

list of the associated landscape features and elements for each environmental setting;

the landscape management practices required to maintain the existing and proposed landscape characteristics.

5. Financial return requirements:

the appropriate capital expenditure levels for each area and element;

the appropriate revenue expenditure to meet the on-going maintenance;

the appropriate revenue expenditure associated with warden or caretaking schemes required for adequate security.

6. Operational requirements:

the organizational structure to operate the site once it is developed;

the setting up of management or user groups to control and run the site on a day to day basis;

the organizational structure to cope with phased development.

IDENTIFICATION OF THE 'DESIGN FIXED POINTS'

From this stage onwards the site planner needs to work with detailed scale plans of the site. Therefore, before proceeding further the site planner needs to prepare a base plan. This is best done by using the topography plan which will have been prepared as part of the site survey and adding the 'design fixed points' – that is the features and areas which were identified for 'no change' at the site potential stage or were allocated for a specific use. The Case Study illustrates the information that can be included on a base-plan which includes the design fixed points.

APPROPRIATE PLAN SCALE FOR SITE PLANNING

For very small sites such as individual house plots the scale of the plan might be 1:100, for groups of houses 1:200, for housing estates, industrial estates and small parks 1:500 and for more extensive sites, such as large parks and small settlements, 1:1250. Beyond this scale there is insufficient detail on the plan drawing for any site planning exercise; such plans can only be used for more general land-use planning projects.

APPROPRIATE ENVIRONMENTAL GUIDELINES

The selection of appropriate environmental guidelines for the planning and design of the site is a critical stage. It brings together the factual information about the site and its users, linking it with the ideas which the site planning team have gradually developed about the future environmental qualities of the site. It is the stage at which the site planner makes final decisions about how to incorporate the experiential aspects into a site plan.

The information gathered about the experiences that the users might appreciate in the different environmental settings needs to be considered here so that a decision can be made about what should be provided on the site. Box 10.5 indicates some of the factors that might be considered.

As indicated in Part Three the experiential aspects of a development can be those that make the difference between whether or not a site is acceptable to the user. They are, however, particularly difficult aspects to define in detail. One of the ways that the site planner copes with this issue is to draw up guidelines which address the question of what the development will be like to experience as a place, as illustrated in Box 10.5.

An aspect of experiencing the site but one which is normally dealt

---

1.   The appearance.
     What the development will look like from within and without the site. Consideration should be given to:
        the interaction between the edges of the site and adjacent developments;
        the sequence of spaces within the site, the linkages and vistas; the edge characteristics of the spaces and the scale of the spaces. Are spaces to be totally or partially enclosed or should they visually link to the land beyond the site?;
        whether the spaces within the site and on its periphery should look very informal or very formal, or be mixed;
        whether the vegetation should look natural or ornamental, or a mixture;
        whether there is a need to introduce a human scale landscape within the site to counteract the image produced by large buildings or structures within and around the site;
        whether existing landmarks should be incorporated into the development, or whether new landmarks need to be introduced;

BOX 10.5

Some of the experiential factors which might usefully be considered in drawing up environmental guidelines

the need for different visual characteristics in the different spaces, so that visitors are clear about the 'ownership' of territory;

the positioning of screens to close off poor views.

2.   Other experiential characteristics.

What are the other experiences the site planner could consider making available within the site:

using splashing or running water as a means to counteract unpleasant noises and increase aural privacy;

using the rustle of leaves to reduce awareness of unpleasant noise;

constructing noise barriers as a means of reducing unbearable noise;

introducing attractive smells into the site through planting schemes;

using smells as an aid for blind people to locate themselves (too many smells equal confusion – care must be taken);

using plants with edible fruit;

using a diversity of plant material and construction materials to introduce tactile diversity;

using sculpture to add diverse experiences, both tactile and visual;

using a variety of different textured surfaces on the ground to increase diversity.

---

with separately is the overall landscape of the site, its overall image. Except when a site is particularly densely built up, or is in a city centre or other location where a green landscape would be inappropriate, this normally involves developing a landscape strategy for the site.

THE LANDSCAPE STRATEGY

Developing a landscape strategy is of great value to site planning, particularly for larger sites. This is the most effective means of knitting the site together in a coherent whole. The strategy has to allow for diversity within the pockets of space which form most sites, while aiming to produce a landscape with a sufficiently dominant characteristic to give cohesion to the development.

The landscape strategy can rarely be evolved in isolation. In most cases the aim will be to integrate the development of the site into the larger landscape of which it is just a small part. The landscape strategy will be determined by the information gathered on the local landscape character zones as described in Part Two.

Landscapes are so diverse that the site planner will always need to devise a locally applicable method of arriving at a landscape strategy. However, it is possible to identify certain factors that will have to be considered at least where the site in not to be densely developed; these are listed in Box 10.6. The information required to complete this stage will have been collected as part of the site survey.

Sometimes the site planner is working in a situation where there are no local clues as to what features might be appropriate for a new landscape structure, in which case a wider landscape has to be inspected or a local greenspace or landscape plan referred to. In other cases the site planner may be working on a scheme where the intention is not to make

---

1. The characteristics of the local landscape
      the scale of the landscape and how this relates to the configuration of the ground;
      the dominant characteristics of the landscape;
      the contrast between openness and closure – importance of enclosure, importance of ridge-tops;
      the pattern of the old field boundaries or other old features – the shapes of the elements in the landscape;
      the characteristics of the 'edges' delineating the spaces – whether harsh or fuzzy, whether curved or straight;
      the common tree and shrub species, their size, colour and texture;
      the common constructed elements – materials and colours;
      the skyline – whether bare and open, dominated by buildings, dominated by deciduous or coniferous trees.
2. The characteristics of the elements within the landscape
      lines in the local landscape – the characteristics of the lines, whether predominantly straight, diagonal or zig zag, curved or undulating; how do they vary in relation to the lie of the land and the settlement pattern?;
      forms in the local landscape – how are the dominant forms distributed in the local landscape in relation to the lie of the land?;
      textures in the local landscape – is the landscape composed predominantly of fine or rough textures and are these differences related to different areas of the landscape?,
      colour in the landscape – what are the dominant colours: bright and high value, deep hues or neutrals; do different colours occur in different places within the landscape?

BOX 10.6

Factors to consider in the development of a landscape strategy

it blend with the surroundings, but to stand out as a monument; in that case the local landscape still has to be understood so that the contrasting image can be developed. Rutledge (1971) in his book *Anatomy of a Park* describes a useful method for understanding how the factors listed in Box 10.6 have an impact on the way we plan and design landscapes at the site planning level.

Guidelines for the new landscape structure are used during the drawing up of the Site Plan to develop a parallel Landscape Plan for the site.

GUIDELINES ON NATURE CONSERVATION

Closely related to the drawing up of the landscape structure plan is the development of the guidelines on nature conservation. These guidelines are needed for each part of the site. They give details on how the objectives relating to nature conservation can be applied in each area. The habitats to be preserved, those to be restored and those to be created are identified. The range of land management operations required in each area are specified and where necessary the appropriate range of species to be introduced is identified. Readers will find the book *Practical Conservation* by Joyce Tait, Andrew Lane and Susan Carr (1988) contains very useful guidance on the different ways of dealing with nature conservation issues in site planning. Box 10.7 indicates some of the different environments for which guidelines might be developed.

The content of the guidelines will differ depending on whether the natural area already exists or has to be developed, and the scale and complexity of the problem. It is important to work with trained ecologists and landscape managers on the development of these guidelines.

BOX 10.7

Some of the different natural environments for which guidelines might be required in site development are as follows

- woodlands and copses
- stands of mature trees
- hedgerows
- ditches
- ponds
- streams and rivers
- flood meadows
- marshes
- fens
- grasslands
- tracks and their verges
- dunes

As the site plan develops it is worth bearing in mind that each area of land with a different environmental characteristic can be considered a management area. This allows instructions to be drawn up for the future maintenance and management of each part of the site.

GUIDELINES FOR SITE MANAGEMENT

A site management strategy has to be developed which describes in general terms what should happen on each area of unbuilt land within the site. It should be developed into guidelines which describe the immediate actions to be taken in each area to manage the landscape elements.

Box 10.8 indicates some of the site management guidelines it might be necessary to develop for a site. Others could include guidelines on energy conservation, shoreline conservation or historic site conservation. These guidelines allow the following plans to be drawn up, together they form the package of site plans.

THE CONCEPT PLAN

The concept plan normally takes the form of a 'bubble diagram'. It is used to summarize the site planner's ideas about the relative distribution

---

1. it should consider the mechanisms for maintaining any hard surface areas and free standing structures within a site;
2. it should consider the intentions for the future landscape of the area whether it should be formal, informal, ornamental, naturalistic, cultivated or wilderness;
3. it should consider the natural habitats to be preserved in each area, the habitats to be enhanced in their value and the new habitats to be developed gradually;
4. it should consider how each area will be maintained and how frequently and the cost limitations on the operations;
5. it should consider any value that might derive from the management of the land. For instance: timber production, crop production, animal production, fish production, chargeable recreational use;
6. it should be decided whether profit can be ploughed back into the site or taken out;
7. the availability of labour for land management tasks should be considered.

BOX 10.8

Some of the factors it is necessary to consider to develop site management guidelines

of the elements to be located on the site. This initial distribution is modified by the reality of the physical and natural environmental characteristics of the site which force the plan to develop in a certain direction. The Case study at the end of this Part contains an example of a concept diagram.

DEVELOPMENT AND TESTING OF ALTERNATIVE SOLUTIONS

The concept diagram is the key to the next stage, which is to draw out roughly a range of possible solutions. These should be as diverse as possible. These rough diagrams of the distribution of the physical elements on the site, are drawn out on a base-plan. The location and extent of buildings and each environmental setting on the site is defined. These alternative plans are particularly important, as the impact on the environment of each can be tested and the solution which works best identified.

Each alternative is checked for the extent to which it meets each of the objectives and guidelines for the development of the site. It is a process which helps the site planner to identify quickly what works well and what does not. It highlights the degree of flexibility available for the site layout and later the site design. Sometimes there is so little flexibility that the site virtually plans and designs itself, for instance because no alternatives can be found which work within the limitations of the objectives. In other cases virtually total flexibility appears to be available to the site planner and designer, with the exception of course of the financial controls.

THE SITE PLAN

A final site plan is drawn up and evaluated against the objectives and guidelines to identify any remaining problems. The plan goes through a series of modifications until the best fit is reached. See the Case study for an illustration of a typical site plan. During this final stage of the process it is important to involve the client and the users and modify the scheme as necessary.

It is a plan which makes detailed decisions only when necessary, leaving as many as possible to be taken at the design stage.

THE SITE LANDSCAPE PLAN

The landscape plan for the site is developed in parallel with the site plan. On small-scale sites the two issues are normally inextricably linked and the solutions presented together. On large sites where the implementation of the scheme will often be split between different groups, it is useful to have a separate landscape plan which can be used to develop the necessary design briefs for each part of the site. See the Case study for an example of the development of a landscape plan.

THE SITE MANAGEMENT PLAN

The production of the site plan and designs should never occur independently of a consideration of how the land and landscapes will be managed once the scheme is implemented. For instance, the site plan might mark off an area required for the preservation of a particularly fragile natural habitat. However, unless there are strict guidelines on the operations that will be needed within the area of land containing the special habitat, on its boundary and in the immediately adjacent areas, the habitat is unlikely to survive development.

It is the management of the land and elements comprising the landscape which, together with the location and distribution of those elements, determine the appearance of the landscape and whether it survives in its present form or gradually changes. A clear understanding of the relation between practice and the resulting landscapes is important to site planning, linking as it does with the experiential attributes of a site. See the Case study plans which indicate several aspects of site management that might be incorporated in the site management plan.

THE DESIGN BRIEFS

The site plan and the landscape management strategy are used to develop a detailed set of design briefs for each part of the site. These take the form of clear statements on the targets which should be met by the designer and land manager in each part of the site. In effect they define exactly how the objectives and guidelines can be met.

For instance, if an objective relating to soil conservation were proposed which aimed at reducing soil loss, the site plan might indicate that the steeper areas of the site be kept grassed, that the cultivated slopes be contour ploughed and that wind breaks be planted at specific intervals apart. This would result in specific instructions to the site designers for that part of the site needing the special treatment.

Or, if a certain environmental setting were required in a particular location, the design brief would specify exactly the surfaces, structures and equipment to be located and describe the landscape and natural environmental characteristics required for the area in question.

The design briefs are the specific instructions developed from the more general site plan. They set the limits on the designer's freedom of action in each part of the site, and ensure that the overall objectives of the site plan are not lost during the design and implementation process. The design briefs specify exactly what at a minimum must be provided in each part of the site. Such limits do not restrict the designer to a technical role, rather they challenge the good designer by setting a range of fixed requirements to be met. Beyond those requirements the designer has total freedom to impose any design solution that is within the financial and technical limitations.

Designer's briefs are exceptionally varied in style and content dealing as they do with every aspect of development. It is, therefore, unwise to be categorical about their content. The site planner and designer should ideally work together on the drawing up of such a brief.

Carrying out the project work

Once you have read through this chapter you should complete the project work set out in Step 14 to produce the site plan.

Planning for the future

This text has shown how the professionals most involved with site planning – the architect, engineer, town planner, land manager and landscape architect cannot work independently. Effective site planning is only possible if a range of professional expertise is backed up by scientists and social scientists.

At a time when all countries are becoming increasingly conscious of the need to conserve the environment and are beginning to work at international level to develop strategies to limit environmental exploitation, it is worth remembering that it is what happens on each and every small site that in the end has the most impact on the environment. It is a multitude of small sites which forms the environment; it is the cumulative decisions we each make about how to develop, maintain or manage the pieces of land for which we are responsible which determines environmental quality.

Every piece of land, every site which is developed, is linked to another and how development should proceed on that area of land is influenced by that relationship. Every impact on the physical, natural or social environment within a site, resulting from how the site is developed or managed, has repercussions on neighbouring sites. This is why site planning is so important. We all contribute to the quality of our environment by our individual actions in relation to specific areas of land. Whether we own the land, develop it, live on it or only occasionally use it our actions can influence local environmental quality.

Through the proper application of environmental planning to site development, the derelict sites, barren of vegetation, can be rehabilitated. The remaining natural areas can be protected and habitats can be enhanced. It will cost money, but allowing the present rate of destruction of the environment to continue could be disastrous if not catastrophic for mankind.

The approach to site development proposed here is a bottom-up approach to environmental improvement. It can work. As professionals involved in environmental planning for site development we must capitalize on the increasing awareness shown by society for the need to conserve the environment. We can lead by example in promoting the preservation of nature in the development of every site, where appropriate, however small. In Britain we have already seen how the urban fringe and suburban housing areas have become rich in nature (Gilbert, 1989). The greening of individual sites is a simple but effective means of encouraging further environmental improvement. We can aim through our understanding of basic human needs to develop places of sufficient diversity and interest to people that they become satisfying places in which to live, work and play; places which enrich the quality of life.

References

Gilbert, O.L. (1989) *The Ecology of Urban Habitats*, Chapman and Hall, London.

Rutledge, A.J. (1971) *Anatomy of a Park*, McGraw Hill, New York.

Tait, J., Lane, and Carr, S. (1988) *Practical Conservation, Site Assessment and Management Planning*, London, The Open University.

11 Case study of Fort Park

The diagrams contained in this chapter have been derived from a site planning study of an area to be developed as a park. They are intended to indicate to those who have not previously carried out a site planning exercise the type of information that can be presented in plan form. In a book such as this it is only possible to show the information in very general terms.

The site is on the edge of a large northern city. It contains remnants of an iron age fort and several areas of scrub vegetation. The land has not been developed mainly because the slopes are so steep and the site has traditionally been used for informal recreation.

The drawings were produced by Joan Sewell, a landscape architect. They are reproduced with her permission.

Introduction
Areas of overgrown disturbed ground and a generally rundown appearance. Rapid changes are occurring around these spaces with the demolition of old housing and an extensive redevelopment programme. The need to provide a well structured hierarchy of recreation facility to serve local needs and draw in visitors to the area will become very important. The site has been studied in this context throughout. Within the site are many features of interest including an iron age fort and the roman (iron age) rig until now only partly excavated. Views from the site are also superb. Clearly the site is of great local, district and possibly regional interest.

The brief
It is proposed to develop the site as a neighbourhood park with facilities serving local and community needs. The site is set in the context of a round walk with the fort site providing archaeological information and recreational facilities such as picnic areas and car parking to through visitors. It is also proposed to make provision for local needs by establishing a hierarchy of recreational facility within the site and establishing sitting and viewing areas. It is proposed also to establish a community centre serving new housing. The park will essentially be woodland in character.

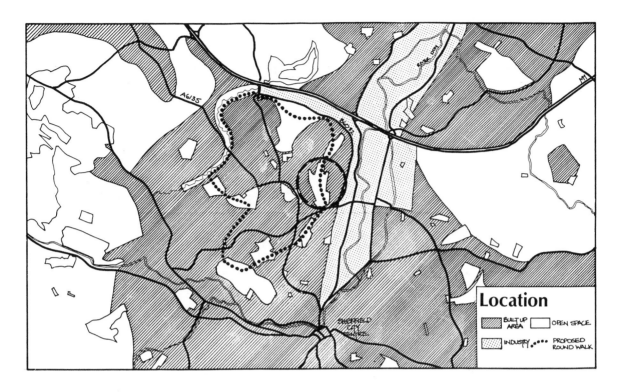

Location

- BUILT UP AREA
- OPEN SPACE
- INDUSTRY
- ●●●● PROPOSED ROUND WALK

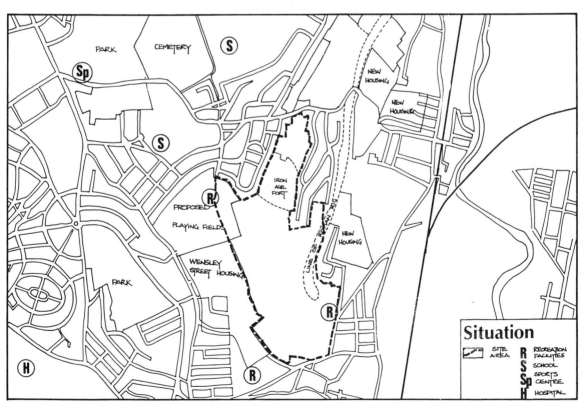

Situation

- SITE AREA
- **R** RECREATION FACILITIES
- **S** SCHOOL
- **Sp** SPORTS CENTRE
- **H** HOSPITAL

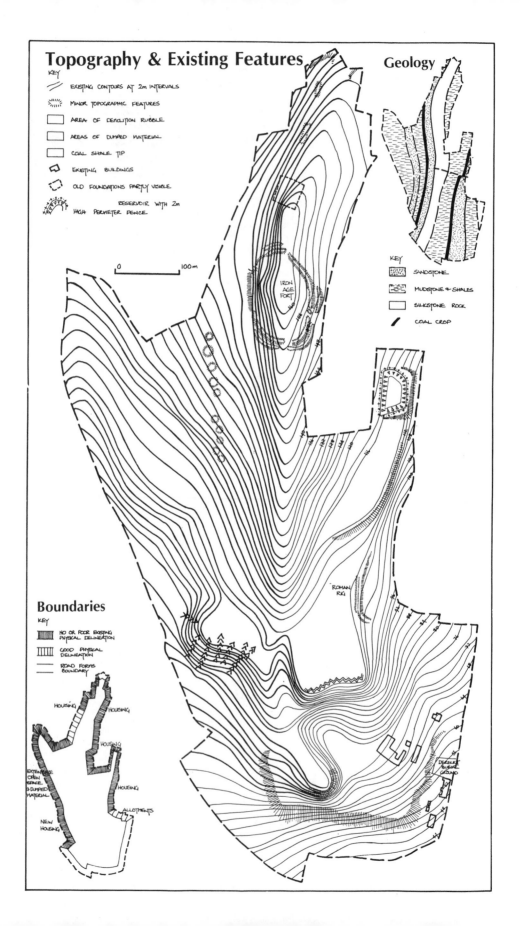

Topography & Existing Features

KEY

~~~ EXISTING CONTOURS AT 2m INTERVALS

MINOR TOPOGRAPHIC FEATURES

AREA OF DEMOLITION RUBBLE

AREAS OF DUMPED MATERIAL

COAL SHALE TIP

EXISTING BUILDINGS

OLD FOUNDATIONS PARTLY VISIBLE

RESERVOIR WITH 2m HIGH PERIMETER FENCE

0   100 m

IRON AGE FORT

ROMAN RIG

Geology

KEY

SANDSTONE

MUDSTONE & SHALES

SILKSTONE ROCK

COAL CROP

Boundaries

KEY

NO OR POOR EXISTING PHYSICAL DELINEATION

GOOD PHYSICAL DELINEATION

ROAD FORMS BOUNDARY

HOUSING

HOUSING

HOUSING

HOUSING

HOUSING

ALLOTMENTS

EXTENSIVE OPEN SPACE & DUMPED MATERIAL

NEW HOUSING

DERELICT BUILDING GROUND

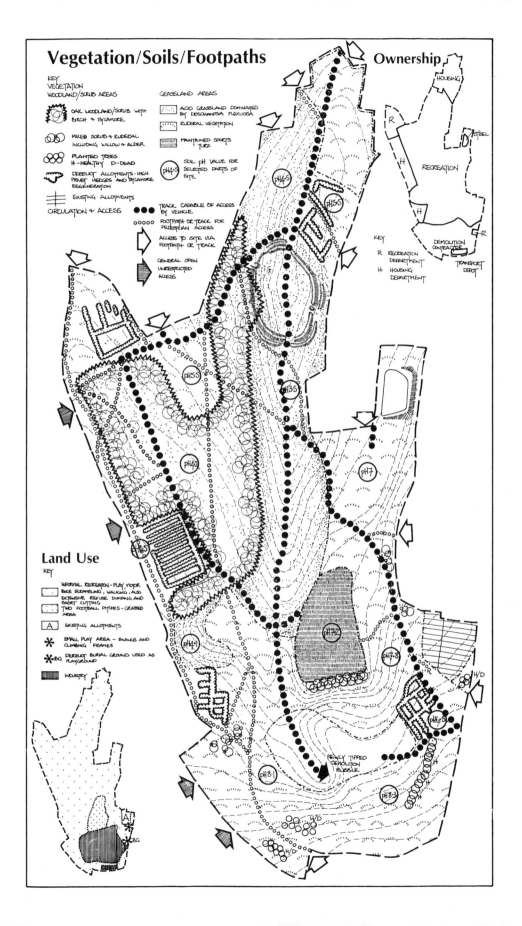

Vegetation/Soils/Footpaths

Ownership

KEY
VEGETATION
WOODLAND/SCRUB AREAS

OAK WOODLAND/SCRUB WITH BIRCH & SYCAMORE.

MIXED SCRUB & RUDERAL INCLUDING WILLOW & ALDER

PLANTED TREES H-HEALTHY D-DEAD

DERELICT ALLOTMENTS - HIGH PRIVET HEDGES AND SYCAMORE REGENERATION

EXISTING ALLOTMENTS

CIRCULATION & ACCESS

GRASSLAND AREAS

ACID GRASSLAND DOMINATED BY DESCHAMPSIA FLEXUOSA

RUDERAL VEGETATION

MAINTAINED SPORTS TURF

pH4·5 SOIL pH VALUE FOR SELECTED PARTS OF SITE

TRACK CAPABLE OF ACCESS BY VEHICLE

FOOTPATH OR TRACK FOR PEDESTRIAN ACCESS

ACCESS TO SITE VIA FOOTPATH OR TRACK

GENERAL OPEN UNRESTRICTED ACCESS

KEY

R RECREATION DEPARTMENT

H HOUSING DEPARTMENT

HOUSING

STEEL

RECREATION

DEMOLITION CONTRACTOR

TRANSPORT DEPOT

Land Use

KEY

INFORMAL RECREATION - PLAY, MOTOR BIKE SCRAMBLING, WALKING. ALSO EXTENSIVE REFUSE DUMPING AND SHORT CUTTING

TWO FOOTBALL PITCHES - GRAZED AREA

A EXISTING ALLOTMENTS

* SMALL PLAY AREA - SWINGS AND CLIMBING FRAMES

*BG DERELICT BURIAL GROUND USED AS PLAYGROUND

INDUSTRY

NEWLY TIPPED DEMOLITION RUBBLE

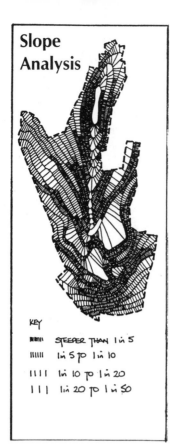

Slope Analysis

KEY

⬛ STEEPER THAN 1 in 5

⦀ 1 in 5 to 1 in 10

|||| 1 in 10 to 1 in 20

| | | 1 in 20 to 1 in 50

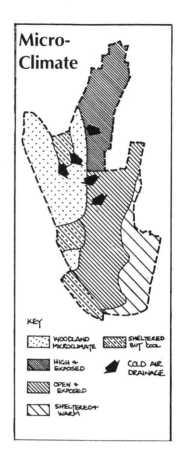

Micro-Climate

KEY

▫ WOODLAND MICROCLIMATE

▨ HIGH & EXPOSED

▨ OPEN & EXPOSED

▨ SHELTERED & WARM

▨ SHELTERED BUT COOL

◆ COLD AIR DRAINAGE

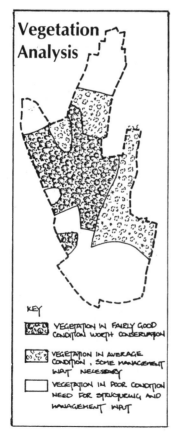

Vegetation Analysis

KEY

▨ VEGETATION IN FAIRLY GOOD CONDITION WORTH CONSERVATION

▨ VEGETATION IN AVERAGE CONDITION, SOME MANAGEMENT INPUT NECESSARY

▢ VEGETATION IN POOR CONDITION NEED FOR STRUCTURING AND MANAGEMENT INPUT

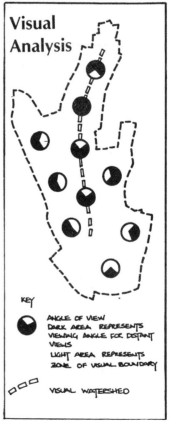

Visual Analysis

KEY

● ANGLE OF VIEW DARK AREA REPRESENTS VIEWING ANGLE FOR DISTANT VIEWS LIGHT AREA REPRESENTS ZONE OF VISUAL BOUNDARY

▱▱▱ VISUAL WATERSHED

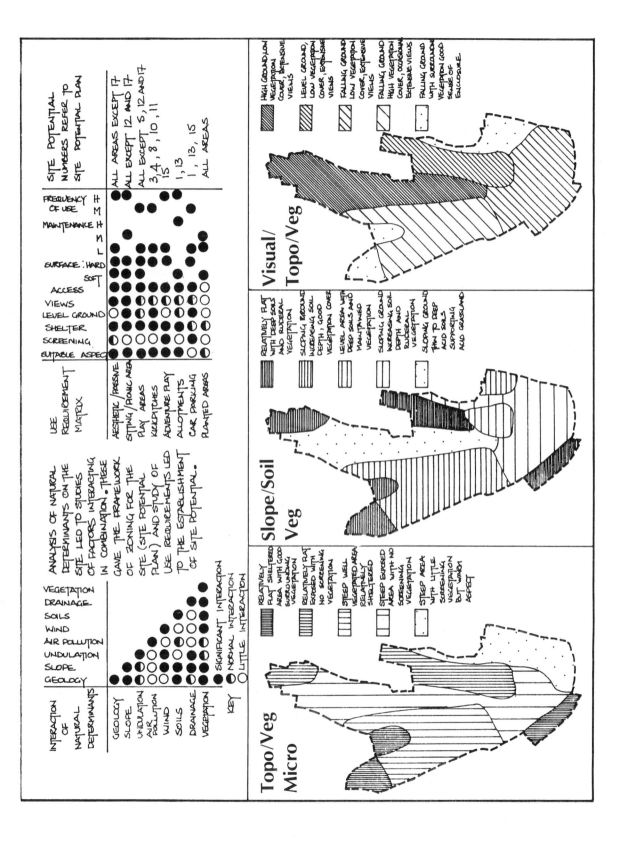

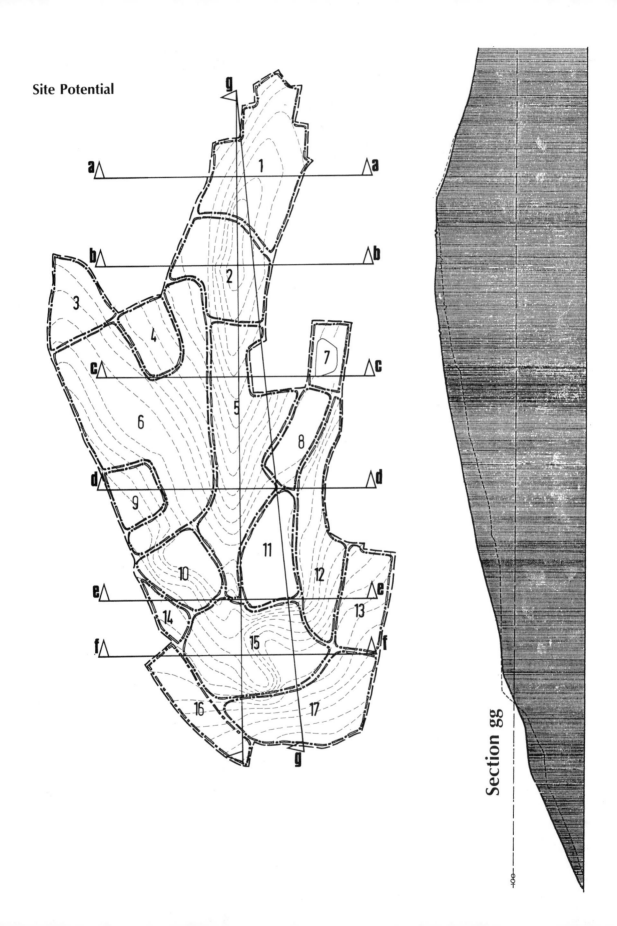

Site Potential

Section gg

Section aa

Problems

PRE WAR AND INTERWAR HOUSING - LACK OF PROPER PHYSICAL BOUNDARY WITH SITE PROBLEM OF PRIVACY | EXPOSED SUMMIT WITH PROBLEMS OF DUMPING AND RUBBLE LEFT FROM OLD ALLOTMENTS, BURNING PROBLEM | HOUSING 1954-72, LACK OF PROPER PHYSICAL BOUNDARY, SOME EXTENSION OF GARDENS INTO SITE

125

Section bb

Problems

GREAT LACK OF PRIVACY AND LACK OF PROPER PHYSICAL BOUNDARY TO SITE | IRON AGE HILL FORT - LACK OF OFFICIAL DELINEATION, PROBLEM OF DUMPING (SUPERB 360° VIEWS) | BUILDING LINE EXCEPTIONALLY CLOSE TO HILL FORT YET NO PHYSICAL OR VISUAL BOUNDARY, PRIVACY PROBLEM

125

Section cc

Problems

CLEARING | LACK OF PHYSICAL BOUNDARY BETWEEN RIDGE AND ADJACENT HOUSING - DUMPING | HOUSING - 1954 to 1972 MASSIVE UNDERBUILDING GREAT VISUAL INTRUSION SOME DISTANCE FROM SITE | RESERVOIR - VISUAL INTRUSION AND SOME DANGER

WOOD - MULTISTEMMED OAK SCRUB GRADATION IN HEIGHT TO EXPOSED SUMMIT

125
100

Section dd

Problems

DERELICT OVERGROWN ALLOTMENTS - DUMPING | WOOD - GREATLY STUNTED NEAR EXPOSED SUMMIT | EXPOSED RIDGE WALK BUT STRONG VISUAL IMPACT SOME DISTANCE FROM SITE | ROMAN RIG - NO DELINEATION DUMPING PROBLEM | HOUSING - VERY POOR PHYSICAL BOUNDARY WITH SITE AND LACK OF PRIVACY

125
100

Section ee

Problems

WENSLEY STREET HOUSING - STARTED 1974 - LACK OF ESTABLISHMENT | DERELICT OVERGROWN ALLOTMENTS - DUMPING PROBLEM | OLD COAL SHALE TIP - COMPACTED ON TOP, SIDES DEEPLY GULLIED, MOTOR CYCLE SCRAMBLING | FOOTBALL PITCHES - EXPOSED BADLY DRAINED, LARGE CRACKS ON SOUTHERN EDGE - INSTABILITY PROBLEM | GROUND FALLS FAIRLY STEEPLY AWAY DESPITE ASPECT RATHER EXPOSED AWKWARD ACCESS TO EXISTING FOOTBALL PITCHES

100

Section ff

Problems

OLD PREFAB FOUNDATIONS | TIP - DEMOLITION CONTRACTOR - IN DEAD GROUND - NOT VISIBLE FROM RIDGE BUT STRONG VISUAL IMPACT SOUTH OF SITE - SOURCE OF NOISE AND DUST POLLUTION | CONTRACTORS' BUILDINGS VIEW IN FROM EDGE OF FOOTBALL PITCHES | ACCESS FOR LORRIES SOURCE OF NOISE AND DUST POLLUTION

100

Informal Recr.

Picnic Area

Play

Play

Archaeol. Info.

Archaeol. Info.

Kickpitch

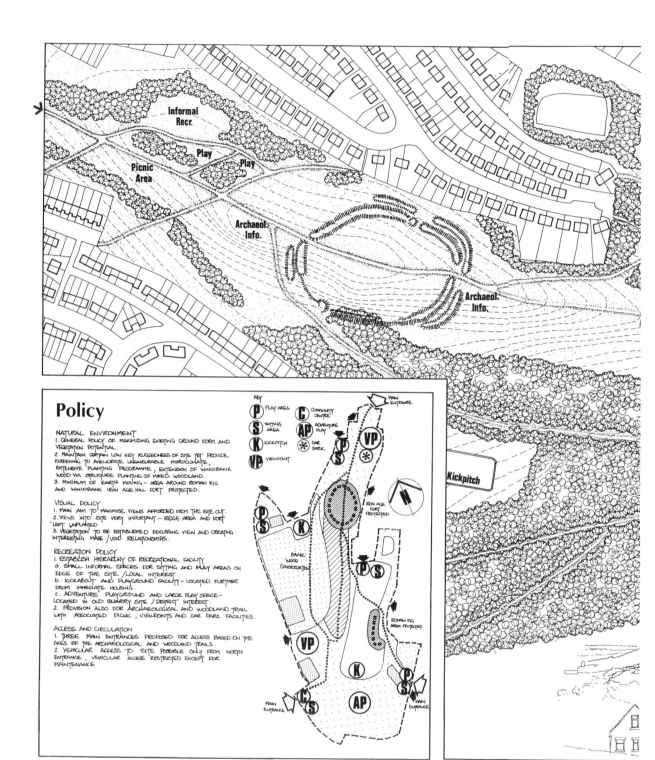

Policy

NATURAL ENVIRONMENT
1. GENERAL POLICY OF MAXIMISING EXISTING GROUND FORM AND VEGETATION POTENTIAL.
2. MAINTAIN CERTAIN LOW KEY RUGGEDNESS OF SITE YET PROVIDE SCREENING TO AMELIORATE UNFAVOURABLE MICROCLIMATE, EXTENSIVE PLANTING PROGRAMME, EXTENSION OF WINCOBANK WOOD VIA STRUCTURE PLANTING OF MIXED WOODLAND.
3. MINIMUM OF EARTH MOVING — AREA AROUND ROMAN RIG AND WINCOBANK IRON AGE HILL FORT PROTECTED.

VISUAL POLICY
1. MAIN AIM TO MAXIMISE VIEWS AFFORDED FROM THE SITE OUT.
2. VIEWS INTO SITE VERY IMPORTANT — RIDGE AREA AND FORT LEFT UNPLANTED.
3. VEGETATION TO BE ESTABLISHED FOCUSSING VIEW AND CREATING INTERESTING MASS/VOID RELATIONSHIPS.

RECREATION POLICY
1. ESTABLISH HIERARCHY OF RECREATIONAL FACILITY
a. SMALL INFORMAL SPACES FOR SITTING AND PLAY AREAS ON EDGE OF THE SITE/LOCAL INTEREST.
b. KICKABOUT AND PLAYGROUND FACILITY — LOCATED FURTHER FROM IMMEDIATE HOUSING.
c. ADVENTURE PLAYGROUND AND LARGE PLAY SPACE — LOCATED IN OLD QUARRY SITE/DISTRICT INTEREST.
2. PROVISION ALSO FOR ARCHAEOLOGICAL AND WOODLAND TRAIL WITH ASSOCIATED PICNIC, VIEWPOINTS AND CAR PARK FACILITIES.

ACCESS AND CIRCULATION
1. THREE MAIN ENTRANCES PROPOSED FOR ACCESS BASED ON THE AXES OF THE ARCHAEOLOGICAL AND WOODLAND TRAILS.
2. VEHICULAR ACCESS TO SITE POSSIBLE ONLY FROM NORTH ENTRANCE, VEHICULAR ACCESS RESTRICTED EXCEPT FOR MAINTENANCE.

KEY

P PLAY AREA
S SITTING AREA
K KICKPITCH
VP VIEWPOINT
C COMMUNITY CENTRE
AP ADVENTURE PLAY
* CAR PARK

MAIN ENTRANCE

BANK WOOD CONSERVATION

IRON AGE FORT PROTECTED

ROMAN RIG AREA PROTECTED

MAIN ENTRANCE

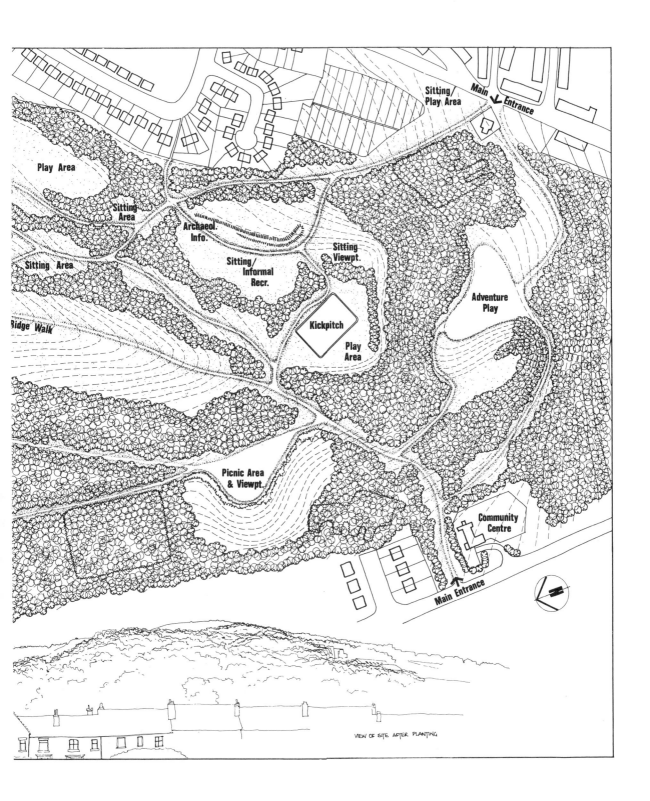

Play Area

Sitting
Area

Archaeol.
Info.

Sitting/Informal
Recr.

Sitting Area

Sitting
Viewpt.

Ridge Walk

Kickpitch

Play
Area

Sitting/
Play Area

Main
Entrance

Adventure
Play

Picnic Area
& Viewpt.

Community
Centre

Main Entrance

VIEW OF SITE AFTER PLANTING

Part Five

A Site Planning Project

This section summarizes the range of work a site planning team has to undertake to produce a site plan based on a full consideration of environmental factors. The programme of events described below can be taken as the base on which to develop a site-specific programme of work.

The steps

For the sake of those undertaking a site planning project for the first time the work required to produce a site plan is summarized here in the form of a series of Steps. Following these will ensure that most of the issues that need to be resolved before a site plan is produced are considered.

As you work through the following Steps and draw the maps and plans, you will find that you gradually collect more details about the site.* As you collect information about each step, you will move from considering the wider area, which forms the setting for your site, to the details about the site itself. This is not just because it is important to be fully aware of the site context as well as the site, but also because information is usually available on different aspects in varying levels of detail.

At each Step of the survey stage your objective is to decide first whether the information is relevant to your specific problem and then to record the required information. It is very common for the site planning team to have to produce multiple copies of its survey and assessment stage as well as the final site plan. Therefore, your drawn plans ought to be produced in such a way that they are reproducible within an acceptable budget.

---

* The suggested order of work has been devised to give you some understanding of the sequence of events that have influenced the development of your site from earliest times. Such an understanding enables a site planner to arrive at proposals for the future which respect the special qualities of the place. These special qualities are often called the genius loci (the 'spirit of the place').

The project begins

As soon as you enter into negotiations with the client you should establish:

1. what the developer wants to do;
2. who will use the development;
3. what they will use it for;
4. when they will use it;
5. the size of site the client intends to develop;
6. any special requirements the client has about the form and type and style and location of the development;
7. if a site has already been chosen or if the site planning project is to help identify a suitable site;
8. how much the client is intending to spend on the development and the associated works;
9. the time-scale of the proposed development and any proposals to phase it;
10. what the client and/or future users might reasonably be expected to contribute in terms of long-term maintenance activities.

If a site has already been selected it should be visited. All members of the site planning team should walk the ground and become familiar with it. If no site has been selected, the site planning team should visit and become familiar with the general area in which the client wishes the project to be sited.

Alternative approaches to tackling the problem should be considered briefly by the whole site planning team. Identify any further information needed from the client to allow the key issues to be examined and any expertise missing from the team to be identified.

Visit the local planners to hold an exploratory discussion of the feasibility of such a project within the strategy and policies governing the planning of the local area. Check in general terms on the need for planning approval for the type of development envisaged in the locations being considered. Check also if an environmental impact statement is required. If there are land use or environmental limitations known to the planners, establish the extent of these. Acquire any planning statements which relate to the locality.

In cases where the planners have no interest or jurisdiction, establish who controls decisions on the detailed layout and use of land and hold the necessary discussions to establish any limitations they might impose.

List the key issues   On the basis of the client's brief, your discussions with the local planners and/or other interested parties, your own knowledge of similar problems elsewhere and of the area within which the development is proposed, compile a preliminary list of key issues to be resolved. This is sometimes called the problem statement. Lynch and Hack (1984) define it as an embryo containing the final design.

To do this:

1. Expand the client's brief (that is expand on what the client said was the purpose of the project); describe what you think might happen on the site in terms of the major indoor and outdoor activities and the minor activities associated with each.*
2. Develop ideas about the main requirements of the different groups of users – the people who may live or work on the project site and the people who may visit it – consider in general terms what they might want the place and its different parts to be like, that is the character of the development.
3. Describe any physical or natural environmental characteristics that might seem to be appropriate to such a project and relate these to any statements of intent issued by the local planning authority in relation to an area's environmental qualities.
4. Describe the building or buildings likely to be required and what may happen in each; if buildings are a major component of the scheme, and you are not an architect, it is vital at the outset to consider the type of buildings and their relationship to each other and the area outside them with the architect member of the site planning team.
5. If the site is known, comment on its adequacy in relation to the above expansion of the brief or, if a site has not already been identified, consider the factors that it would be best to use to identify a possible site.
6. Check that the client's resources are sufficient for the project as it has now been defined.

* For instance, if the client wants to build a restaurant the major activities can be described as eating, preparing the food, delivery of materials and car parking; whilst the minor activities might be eating and drinking outside, waiting for friends to arrive, strolling before and after a meal, keeping the children amused, relaxing in the sun, having photographs taken, waiting for taxis.

If no site has yet been selected, use the criteria established above and knowledge of similar schemes,* to develop a list of the acceptable characteristics of a site suitable for the type of project envisaged. List any other locational requirements defined by the client or the local planning office. Carry out a desk and site study to identify possible locations. Assess each site for the extent to which it meets the criteria and advise the client of the best location or locations. The client has to take the final decision.

The site planner comes to an understanding of the possible links between the site and the users through applying the site planning process. The normal practice is to first examine the site in detail (Part Two) and then the users (Part Three) The limitations and possibilities these create for the development are assessed by studying the interaction between the two, prior to the preparation of a site planning proposal (Part Four).

Most of this information will be recorded in general terms for a site context area and in detail for a project area. If a first general look at the implications of any of the following factors seems to indicate that it is irrelevant, then do not waste your time pursuing it at a detailed level†. Where a factor appears to be particularly important, any information relating to it should be plotted on the detailed project area plan.

Site planning cannot be undertaken by using the written word only. If the information you gather is to influence the design directly, it must be produced in the form of plans or maps.‡

If you are working on a small site you may find it is possible to record

---

* If you do not have this, make an attempt to identify similar projects elsewhere and visit them, observing how sites are used and how people react to the external areas.

† For instance, if your check of the geological data for the site context area reveals no sign of any problems that might inhibit development (Part Two) then you need not spend time gathering more detailed site specific information on this factor and instead you can probably concentrate on a sub-soil survey within the site which will establish the composition of the materials immediately underlying the surface.

‡ If you find drawing difficult, do not worry, it is something that rapidly improves with practice. By working through this project you will rapidly become familiar with using drawn plans rather than words to explain your thoughts. Many microcomputers can now be used for storing information in mapped form and you could consider using a basic Geographic

all the site survey information on one or two plan drawings.* It is only for clarity that it is suggested that the basic information is recorded on a series of plans. It is up to you to decide how to present your findings – the key factor is whether other people can understand what you have done and how you have arrived at your proposals.

Base plans   Normally three base plans are required:
- a location plan
- a site context plan
- a project area plan.

LOCATION PLAN

Although the client and all members of the site planning team will be absolutely clear as to the location of the project area, it is easy to forget that others will need to know exactly where the site is located. Any proposals for the site are likely to be viewed by planning officers and planning committees, without anyone from the site planning team being present. Therefore, it is vital to include a location map as the first piece of information in your portfolio of information about the site.[†]

North point, scale and title panel[‡]
Draw a north point on every plan you produce, including plans that you trace. Also add a scale (otherwise plans are meaningless).

Information System (GIS) for the site plan. You will find that a different scale and type of map may be appropriate to record each item of information, as the amount of detail available will vary so much. However, for efficient use of your time you should restrict yourself to a limited number of different scales.

* You have three main alternatives for recording your information on a plan: the first is to draw it straight on to base maps produced by photocopying from a hand-drawn base or from a topographic base (be careful to check for any copyright problems before reproducing); the second is to use tracing paper or layout paper overlays on top of a base map. You can also scan a plan into a microcomputer and add data to that.

† Make a tracing from the 1:25 000 or other appropriate map. Prepare a diagram showing the position of the site. Add sufficient information about place names, topographic features, land uses and the communications systems around the site to identify the location clearly.

‡ All Ordnance Survey (OS) maps are printed so that the north point is at the top of the sheet and it is good practice, but not essential, if you draw your plans in the same way. All plans submitted in relation to a site should be orientated in the same alignment in relation to the north point, as it helps those who have to read the information to interpret them correctly. Use a scale-ruler to draw a scale bar. On 1:500 plans you may show 10 metre intervals and on 1:1250 it may be 100 metre intervals and on plans of larger areas kilometre intervals (most maps have a scale that you will be able to trace). If you are unfamiliar with metric measurements and prefer to think in feet and inches (imperial scale), add a mile scale to the kilometre one and mark off in ¼ mile units. You may think all this seems unnecessarily detailed when all you are trying to do is to learn about the site planning process, but good office practice is an essential part of being a good site planner. Clear labelling is needed

You should label this first drawing and all subsequent ones and preferably give it a code number, for example Plan 1, so that you can refer to it in any separate written text.

BASE PLAN OF THE SITE CONTEXT AREA

You will first have to determine the size of your site context area. Consider the type of site planning problem before determining the boundary; you have to decide the appropriate scale for the plans. If this is your first practice run use a boundary about 500 m distant from the edge of your site.*

The topography (the lie of the land) around the study area
You can find out how your study area sits in the landscape by looking at the topography around the site. In Britain such information is shown on the 1:25 000 Ordnance Survey (O.S.) plans on which contours are marked. Does your site lie on a slope, in a hollow or on top of a ridge – such factors can determine how you plan the project area.†

Height above sea level
If you are working in a country where detailed contour plans have not been produced, gather as much information as is available on the height above sea level and mark the location of any spot heights within the site context area (that is the height above sea level at a given point) on your plan.‡ Also on your site context plan mark where you have identified the highest and the lowest points. Remember to note whether the heights are in metric or imperial (feet and inches) measurements. For site planning it is more often the relative height that matters, rather than the exact height above sea level.

because plans can get mislaid, you can change jobs and other people can be co-opted into site planning teams and will need to be able to find specific information quickly without your help.

* The scale of the base plans will relate to the size of the site and the complexity of the planning problem. As a rough guide, if this is the first time you have done a site plan, it is suggested that for a small site you should first try to work at 1:500 for the project area and at 1:1250 for the site context area. If the site is large, work at 1:1250 for the project area and 1:2500 or 1:5000 for the site context area. When buildings are involved the scale should be 1:500 or 1:200.

† If you have not used maps in the past, try to become familiar on this walk with what a map can tell you about the lie of the land and the limitations of such plans. For instance, you will find that they are often insufficiently detailed to show the small breaks of slope that are so important in determining the detailed layout of a site.

‡ In Britain, and some other countries, you will find bench marks cut into rocks or posts. These indicate an exactly measured height. If you find one of these on or near your site, this will be useful to establish its height above sea level. Bench marks are much more accurate than the contour lines, many of which are interpolations (rough estimates) of the height above sea level.

BASE PLAN OF THE PROJECT AREA

Produce an outline plan of the project site to a suitable scale such as 1:500 or 1:1250, the scale depending on the complexity of the site*. Add any information about height, paths, tracks, roadways, buildings within and immediately adjacent to the site. Make sure you draw the site boundary on the plan and include details of the adjoining land. As you work through the sequence of activities outlined in this book you will add many details about the site to this base plan – it might look a bit bare to start off with.

* If you are working in an area for which no maps or plans are available, it is important that you advise your client that a properly measured plan of the site should be produced. Such plans are normally produced by surveyors. They mark out a grid on the site, the size of the grid depending on the complexity of the problem, and then work out the height differences across the site and indicate its boundaries exactly.

Geology and geomorphology

Geological data

Locate the best source of published information on the local geology.[*] The information about the surface geology is likely to be most immediately relevant. Note the main rock types found in the area, and indicate on the plan any special features such as faults or outcrops. Look out for evidence of mineral workings.

After recording any published information on the geology within the site context area, discuss the implications of the rock types with expert geologists.

For the site context area you should then record:

- the type and strength of the rock at or near the surface
- any evidence of subsidence or landslips
- the presence of mineral deposits.

Within the project area record any evidence of outcrops of rock:

- record whether any rock is hard or friable
- record the depth at which solid rock is encountered.

If any substantial structure is to be built, boreholes are needed to a depth of about 6 m initially.[†]

In particular, any area which has been subject to glaciation should be examined in detail, as unexpected problems can be found beneath the surface soils. These are mainly due to the random deposition of boulders of a variety of sizes as the glaciers retreated, as well as pockets of running sand or clay. In such areas make sure extra boreholes are drilled if anything is to be built as part of the project.

---

[*] If you are working in Britain it is relatively easy to find out about the geology of your area. Large-scale OS-based maps have been produced for the Geological Survey of Britain. In other countries you will often find data available from government offices.

[†] This survey must be done by geologists or civil engineers.

**Make an assessment
of the implications of
the geological data**

BEARING CAPACITY

If the help of geological experts is not available, inspect Figures 4.1 and
4.2 for preliminary guidance on the extent of any problems with bearing
capacity within the project site. They give some basic criteria on the
relative bearing capacity of different materials. If there are any areas of
friable rock or other loosely consolidated materials or peat on the site,
mark these on the project base plan. They will be unsuitable for certain
types of building and other engineering structures.[*]

GEOLOGICAL FAULTS

If the geological plans show there is a geological fault running through
or near the site, record the location. The problem of the impact of such a
feature on the future development of the site should be assessed with the
help of experts.[†]

OUTCROPS OF ROCK

Record where rock outcrops on the project site and describe the type of
outcrop. If areas of hard rock or boulder strewn land occur on or near
the surface of the site, this can limit certain forms of development.[‡]
Assess too the recreational potential, if any, of any of the outcrops.

AQUIFERS

The water that accumulates on your site can directly enter a near surface
ground water storage area. Establish if any water is drawn from this
level for human or industrial use within the site context area and establish if it surfaces as ponds, lakes or springs anywhere near your site. If
the water is used or comes to the surface, this should limit what can be
done within a project area.

Talk to the local water board or the local geologists to establish
whether the project site lies over a recharge area for a deep aquifer. If so,

---

[*] Lynch and Hack suggest the presence of peat can add 85% to the cost of improving a site for
development.
[†] Those working in countries with no or few earthquake problems should still check for faults.
Such faults are always liable to be associated with some movement.
[‡] Lynch and Hack (1985) suggest that rocky land can add 25% to the cost of improving a site
for development.

this severely limits what can happen within the project site, implying that no potential contaminants should be allowed to enter the soil, or any cesspits built.

WATER TABLE

If no local wells or other holes exist on site, dig a test pit at the wettest time of the year to establish if a high water table exists. Record any information about the water table under the project area and gather evidence on the extent to which it normally fluctuates. Note in particular any evidence of a high water table which might limit how the site could be used unless expensive drainage measures are part of the development.

Record any evidence of running water under the site. The land over such natural features should not be built over unless special and costly structural measures are taken.

IMPERMEABILITY

Note if the project site is underlain by any impermeable material which could cause drainage problems, making it difficult to construct buildings or even to plant the site. In such situations note how the site is presently drained. This drainage must not be disrupted by the development unless a new drainage scheme can be financed as part of the scheme.

WASTE TIPS

Record the extent of any waste tips within the site context area. Establish if any over or underground water from those tips enters the project area. Arrange for a chemical analysis to be carried out, to see whether the effluent could in any way contaminate the project area. With the aid of these experts establish if any of the tips contain elements hazardous to human or animal health.

Old waste tips may not be contaminated with modern chemicals but can still contain toxic substances. Other waste tips may be the remains of household waste only and if sufficiently old can be of interest to archaeologists – look out for evidence of old artifacts as you walk the area and record these (also Step 10).

OLD MINE WORKINGS AND QUARRIES

Establish whether the project area, or the area around it, has been worked over or under for mining or quarrying. Show the location of any old mine shafts, capped or uncapped, and with the help of experts establish whether it is safe to build over the area. Note the location of any waste heaps from mining operations on the site, as these can contain toxic waste. Some old tips can be re-worked economically by modern methods. Establish the possibility of this by having a chemical analysis carried out.

MINERAL RESERVES

Are the rocks, gravel deposits or sands underlying the project area of any economic value? Check the geological survey and discuss with local experts. On very large development sites the presence of building materials on site can substantially reduce the development costs associated with bringing in sands and gravels, but on small sites the preparation costs normally outweigh the advantages.

INFORMING THE CLIENT OF PROBLEMS

If as a result of your investigations you spot any possible problems in relation to the proposed development, however minor, it is essential that you advise your client to call in expert help.

Geomorphological factors which could influence the development of a site

Note if any of the following processes are operating on or near the site:

1. Erosion and deposition along rivers; these can result in rivers changing their course and making it ill advised to develop near them, or less spectacularly in the slow eating away of the land along parts of the river, while along others the silt is slowly deposited.
2. Erosion of cliffs by the sea which can reduce the area of safely developable land.
3. Rocks breaking away from mountainsides because of frost action, which can in some circumstances make it dangerous to build on the mountainsides.
4. Landslips occurring where slopes are not yet at a stable angle in relation to their composition. Areas with a high tendency to slip are unsafe for construction or even recreational use.

Talk to someone who has studied the geomorphological processes which operate locally. Identify with their help any that could be at work on your site and could influence its use. Look in particular for evidence of water erosion and landslips. Look also for evidence of unconsolidated material held by vegetation.

Consider if any of the operations involved in the proposed development of the site could accelerate erosion of those parts of the site that in nature are relatively stable.

Lynch, K. and Hack, G. (1985) *Site Planning*, MIT, Cambridge.   **References**

STEP 3 Surface water

Surface water systems Prepare a base map of the site context area showing:

1. the total surface drainage system and any areas of still water;
2. the water catchment area that feeds the local surface water; in many circumstances it will be necessary to look at maps covering a larger area to identify this.

This preliminary plan should indicate the position of all the water courses containing running water (rivers, streams, ditches) within the site context area and within the project site. Within and on the periphery of the project area, look at all the water courses and make notes on how wide and deep they are and the flow rate across each stream.*

Water quality Record any official information available on water quality and advise on what this means in terms of how the water can be used.† Is it safe to drink, is it safe for swimming and water sports. Add to this by local observations:

---

* This can be done with the aid of a flow meter. If you do not have access to one, you can crudely calculate the flow by measuring the time it takes for a float to travel a given distance of 10 metres. Water speed needs to be timed at several points across a stream to find the area of fastest flow.

† If you are working in Britain on a site planning project, it is suggested that you contact the local Water Board office.

Where there is no information on the water bodies, try to find out yourself how polluted they are: does the water smell, is there a lot of algae (the green slime that settles on the top of the water when there is not enough oxygen in the water) or does it, at least at first glance, seem an attractive area of water associated with plenty of wildlife and plants? When you make notes about this, remember to indicate that you are making a subjective judgement. In these circumstances do not spend too much time on the water bodies outside your study area, but concentrate on gathering information within and immediately around the project area. For smaller sites with minor water bodies, it will often not be necessary to call in hydrologists to help assess the problem. In Britain you can check how safe the water is for people to use by consulting Public Health officials. In other areas find out who analyses the water quality and acquire the necessary information. If none is available a proper water quality analysis will have to be carried out by experts if the water is to be used.

1. does the water smell* and if so how foul?
2. does algae or weed grow on the surface?
3. note by taking a sample how clean the water looks, look for foreign material held in the water – soil, bits of vegetation, dirt;
4. record whether the water is slow and sluggish or fast and bubbling over rocks and pebbles.

Assess the water body's capacity to be self cleansing under the present circumstance and in relation to what is known about the proposed development. If the evidence seems to imply a doubt about a water body's ability to cope with pollution and remain self cleansing, experts should be consulted.

Flood problems

Check whether there are dry valleys affecting the project site. Find out from local people how often, if at all, water flows through it.[†]

On the site context plan outline the major and minor valleys so that you have a feel for how the project area fits into this larger system. This will help you to establish whether the site is in any danger from flooding, or other water problem such as flash flooding, or whether it is located well away from areas where problems might be expected to occur.[‡]

Where a project area is liable to flood it is essential for you to establish how regularly such floods normally occur in the local river system and the area of land commonly affected.* If your site is on a valley floor, near a stream susceptible to flooding or on land divided from water by levees (the mounded banks beside streams which occur either naturally or because man has built them to protect land from flooding), then establishing the likelihood of floods is particularly important.

Show on a plan the maximum extent of the yearly flood, the maximum it averages over a five year period, a ten year, a twenty year and a fifty year period. If the flooded area has been known to be larger, then map the maximum known extent of flooding. If no information is available, yet it appears from your study of the river system that there might be a problem, talk to local people to establish which, if any, houses have been inundated in the recent and distant past.

---

* Remember that temperature and water availability conditions can be different at different times of the year and these natural fluctuations will affect the likelihood of smells becoming a problem.

† In certain climates flash flooding of valleys, which remain dry for decades, is a major human hazard. It is essential to discuss the local patterns with the local people as well as the local experts on climate and hydrology before proposing any development of valley bottoms.

‡ In Britain the Water Board can tell you about the likelihood of flood problems in or near your project area, so that you can quickly establish whether it is an issue which might influence the way a site is developed.

* You might find that the local governmental body responsible for water has produced a plan showing the likely extent of flooding and how often it occurs. You should assess this information in relation to your project area and indicate clearly the limits of flooding.

In areas with flood problems note what has been done to control flooding and what, if any, measures it is intended to implement in the future.

Canals, ponds, lakes and wetlands

It is also important for site planning purposes to know where all the still water is within the project area. Detailed information needs to be gathered on the water quality of all still water. An assessment needs to be made of the wildlife value, recreational value and permanence of the feature.

Record how each water area is fed by water and drained. Make notes on the condition of the edges.

Topography

If you have kept to the sequence of work suggested here and considered the geology, geomorphology and the present surface water system of the area within which the project site is located, you will by now know enough of the major factors which have determined the form of the land to be able to understand why the local topography is as it is. You recorded the detailed information on contours when you produced the original base plans of the project area and the context area. Look at those plans now to check that you have gathered information about all the major physical features on each plan.

You will have visited the project area on sufficient occasions to have developed a 'feel' for the lie of the land. This understanding of the hummocks and hollows and of the general shape of the area is vital to the success of site planning at the later stages of the process. It is a major part of the understanding of the local area needed by the site planner, if proposals are to be developed in sympathy with the local landscape and the sense of place. Detailed information about topography can also reduce unnecessary expenditure by indicating the best positions for buildings and other structures.

Recording the lie of the land

If you were able to draw a fairly accurate contour map of the project site when you produced the base maps for Step 1, you won't need to spend much time on site now. However, if your base plans are vague, you should now spend time walking backwards and forwards through your site recording how the land lies.

If the project is not in a densely built up area, you will find it useful to draw several cross sections through your site and the land which surrounds it. The more complicated the site the more cross sections are needed to understand how it sits in the local landscape. Cross sections should be drawn across the contours and also along them. Draw the cross sections to scale, with no vertical exaggeration.

Even when details about the topography within the site are available, it is essential to walk over the site with a copy of the base plan and check that it records all the breaks of slope.

On a base map for the project area you should show:

1. the extent of any flat areas; note if these coincide with waterlogged areas indicating poor drainage;
2. the extent of any steeply sloping areas and all sudden breaks of slope (no matter how short) within these major slopes as well as the flat land;
3. the position and extent of any high points on the site which link together to form ridges or hill tops. It is important that you record even very minor ridges as these can help you to make the final decisions on the best location and extent of the different land uses;
4. the location, angle and extent of any vertical or near vertical faces, such as cliffs or quarry faces. If no detailed measurements are available, roughly estimate the height of these objects above the general ground level around them.*

You should make sure that the information on the topographic plan shows accurately the width of any water courses and indicates the position of any weirs, dams or waterfalls. Take care to record the way the land lies along the edges of all water bodies on the site – show where it goes gently down to the water's edge, where there is a sharp break of slope, or a vertical face at the junction between land and water. Record on your plan the height difference between the normal water-level and that of the land immediately surrounding it.

Visual enclosure

As you walk round the site identify the extent of any areas within which you are aware of feeling totally or partially enclosed. Indicate the areas on a base plan of the site. Write notes on your plan to describe the different types of enclosure experienced in different parts of the site.

Slope analysis

The information you now have about the lie of the land can be used to produce a diagram to highlight the site's main features with regard to slope. It is useful for the site planning process to produce a diagram which shows the location of the vertical and near vertical banks, the very steepest land, the steep land, the moderately sloping land, the gently sloping land and the flat land.

If this is the first time you have done a slope analysis, and you are as yet unclear about the implications of slope in relation to the proposed use of the project area, you could use the following categories to prepare a slope analysis diagram:

- less than 1:100
- 1:40–1:100

---

* Those without any training in surveying will find a dumpy level quite easy to master and this will give sufficiently accurate information at the preliminary stage of a site planning exercise.

- 1:20–1:40
- 1:10–1:20
- 1:7–1:10
- 1:5–1:7
- more than 1:5.

Indicate the direction of slope on the diagram.

STEP 5 Local climate

In order to have some idea of the variations that could be expected in the local climate and the problems that these might cause the site planning team, you should acquire the climatic data for the most recent ten year period from the nearest weather station to your site.

From this data note:

1. the average temperatures for each month of the year;
2. the average number of hours of sunshine in each month;
3. the cloud cover expected at different times of the year;
4. the average rainfall for each month;
5. the average number of days when frost occurs;
6. the average number of days when fog occurs;
7. the average number of days when snow lies and the expected depth;
8. the average number of days drought conditions are to be expected;
9. the lowest and highest temperatures experienced;
10. the humidity level throughout the year;
11. the diurnal range (the daily fluctuation in temperature); this is only necessary in hot/dry countries.

If a wind-rose has been drawn up for the weather station, copy it. Otherwise note any information available on direction and strength of winds.

Apply the information gathered Work out the likely climatic differences across the site context area. The following categories should be indicated on a plan:

1. identify all the slopes that face south and south-west;
2. identify all the slopes that face south-east and west as well as the flat areas;
3. identify all the slopes that face north-west;
4. identify all the slopes that face north, north-east and east;
5. identify all the areas exposed to the most common cold winds; that is the ridge tops and open slopes where there is no protection

from landform, tall vegetation or structures; consider in particular whether the landform of your study area will accentuate the cold winds and direct them towards the project area;

6. locate potential frost hollows;
7. locate where fog is likely to accumulate;
8. locate areas where there might be a problem with drifting snow.

Assess what this might mean for the future development of the project area. It is up to you to work out what the information means in relation to your knowledge of the local situation.

Look at wind patterns, shade and shelter as well as direction of slope and aspect, to establish an understanding of the micro-climate within the site. You will find that the diagrams and plans that you produce at this stage can be a very useful guide at the decision-making stages.

Microclimate within the project site

Show on a diagram how winds behave on the site. If there are buildings on the site at present, which are to be retained, carry out wind tunnel tests to establish the patterns of flow. This exercise will have to be repeated when the location of any new buildings has been agreed.

If the site is presently undeveloped, record how the local topography influences wind flow.

Wind

When you are considering which areas are likely to be shady, you might find it helpful to produce a quick diagram of the shade cast by trees and landform as well as buildings and walls. The diagram should show morning shade, mid-day shade and afternoon shade. Knowing where these shady areas are is very useful at the decision-making stage.

Shade

Indicate which parts of the site already have the climatic conditions required to provide satisfactory settings for the various users' activities and where money will have to be spent to improve the local climate and make it more suitable for the envisaged activities, particularly those that take place outside.

Consider too how the location, size and form of any proposed buildings on the project site might be expected to affect the local climate immediately around them. You will have to come back to this again when decisions are finally taken on the site layout, so that you can check the implications of the layout.

On a base plan of the project area indicate the information listed

Shelter and aspect

below. You will find it useful to pay particular attention to the small localized topographic undulations of the site. You will have identified these when you gathered information about the topography of the project area, so refer to the relevant drawing as you locate any of the following categories:

1. Very warm areas: those parts of the site that are particularly sheltered and are sunny for most of the day, or are sunny in the afternoon; they should also slope towards the noonday or afternoon sun or be flat.

2. Warm areas: those parts of the site that are sheltered but only sunny in the morning; they should slope towards the noonday and morning sun or be flat; they are shady in the afternoon; they are sheltered.

3. Cool areas: those parts which are always exposed to winds but are never in the shade; those parts which are exposed to winds and are in the shade for part of the day; slopes which face the morning sun but are not sheltered; slopes which face away from the sun but are sheltered.

4. Very cool areas: areas always in the shade; those parts which are exposed to winds and are mostly shaded; areas with no protection from the coldest winter winds.

Add any categories of your own which are appropriate to your site.

Soils

The identification of soil types

If any published soil information is available, you should plot it on a site context plan; it is unlikely that such information would be in sufficient detail to be worth recording on the project area base plan. If you have no access to a soil scientist for an interpretation of the information, you will probably find it most useful to talk to the local farmers. If the context area is built up, talk to the people who work any local allotments or gardens about the quality of the local soils.

How to gather basic information about the soils

You will need to consult the experts about the capabilities of the different soils on the project site, if any part of it is to be cultivated for crops. If the scheme does not involve any crops it is possible for the non-expert to do some useful mapping work in relation to soil types.

No doubt as you have walked over the project site you will have noticed that surface conditions vary from one part to another. You should now plot the boundaries of any obviously different areas. If you are working on a site within which no variations can be identified, this stage will not be necessary. It is also unnecessary if the site has been developed previously and is now totally covered by a recent layer of rubble. In this latter case you would not need to spend time on gathering information on soils, but instead obtain expert advice on what could grow in hostile conditions similar to those prevailing on the site. Find out whether it will be necessary to import expensive topsoil to allow any areas of new planting to become established, or if the existing conditions will produce an adequate vegetation cover (Bradshaw and Dutton, 1982).

Now carry out the following surveys and make a brief assessment of what the findings mean in relation to the future development of the site.

Soil profile and topsoil

If the site is large enough, or has sufficient variations in surface conditions, it is important that you select several sampling sites. They should relate to the different conditions that you have observed. Visit each of these areas to look at soil samples. If possible, you should take a spade to the site and dig a small pit at least two feet (600 mm) deep at your sampling points and then look carefully at what you have uncovered.

For your work as a site planner you should concentrate on what the pits can tell about the topsoil and soil water content and soil fertility. Look carefully at the section through the soil by looking on the sides of the pit you have dug; this is the soil profile. First make a note of how the profile changes in any way from the top to the bottom of the hole you have made. Does it look darker at the top and do the colours change as you look towards the bottom of the pit; if so, at what depths do the colours change?

The dark layer at the top is the topsoil; record its depth. If the site is to be developed, this layer will need stripping off and storing. It can be reused elsewhere on the site and space should be allowed to store it on site through the development phase.

Soil water content, impermeable layers and the subsoil

By looking in the soil pits and observing site conditions as you walk over the site, establish if there are any areas of poor drainage. Refer too to the information you gathered under the geology section.

You should note if your soil is:

1. Waterlogged: the hole that you dug fills up with water quickly;
2. Moist: the clay or peat seems wet; the soil obviously shows signs of containing plenty of water;
3. Dry: the soil looks and smells fairly damp but there are no signs of water;
4. Very dry: the soil does not show much sign of dampness and there is no sign of water.

It is important to note whether the weather has been exceptionally dry or wet over the last three months, as this can distort the information available from the pits.

SOIL TEXTURE

There are official systems used by experts to record soil texture (Courtney and Trudgill, 1984). The following is a very simple version but has been developed as a useful way for amateurs to classify soils and identify different types.* Take up a handful of soil, make sure it is

* From information in Weddle (1967).

moist, then rub it through your fingers and note which of the following categories it seems to fit best:

1. Sandy: it feels gritty and does not make a mess of your fingers. You can probably see sand particles in it.
2. Sandy loam: it feels gritty but sticks to your fingers so that they look soiled. You can probably press it so that it stays in a ball.
3. Clay loam: it feels sticky and makes a mess of your hands. You can easily make a ball of it and it will hold together when you mould it. It feels quite slippery in your hands.
4. Clay: it is very sticky and solid, yet also plastic so that you can easily roll it into a thin shape without it falling apart.
5. Silty loam: it feels soapy or even silky and although you can press it into a shape, it does not stay like that but falls apart.
6. Medium loam: it does not feel gritty, sticky or silky.
7. Peat: it is full of small fibres and feels spongy.

SOIL ACIDITY

Record any differences across the site using the following classification:

1. an extremely acid soil: pH of less than 3.4;
2. a very acid soil: pH of 3.5–4.4;
3. an acid soil; pH of 4.4–5.9;
4. a neutral soil: pH of 6.0–6.5;
5. an alkaline soil: pH of 6.5–8.4;
6. an extremely alkaline soil: pH of more than 8.4.

SOIL FERTILITY

If accurate information is required because the site will be used for growing crops, soil scientists have to be consulted. If only general guidance on relative fertility is necessary, a useful but very rough estimate of the relative soil fertility within a site can be made by non-experts looking at the information available from the soil pits.

There are two easily identifiable indicators of high fertility and if these are present it is likely that the soil on your site will be a good growing medium:

1. Fertile soils are characterized by high numbers of earthworms; these create a good crumb structure in the topsoil so that when it is handled it breaks down into a mass of small crumbs or granules.
2. Fertile soils tend to have merging boundaries between the different layers in the profile.

In contrast infertile soils have few earthworms, an amorphous structure and tend to be strongly layered.

In Britain an additional guide to fertile soils on any disturbed or untended site can often be gained by plotting where nettles grow, as they indicate fertile soil. In other climates you will probably find similar indicators exist by asking the local farmers.

SOIL EROSION

The information that you have collected on local soil textures will indicate the extent of the wind erosion problem on your site. Soils with the fine light particles will blow most easily. Surface wash erosion will be a problem where there is any bare soil, which is always likely to be eroded by heavy rain and by the associated surface wash, particularly if the land slopes.

TIPPED MATERIAL

Check if there is any evidence of tipped material on or near your site. Where no records of the content of waste tips are available, either because the tips have not been used for some time or because you are working in a country which has not kept records, it is only close observation of a site which will highlight the problem.

Indicate any areas that you are concerned about on a project area plan and have a check of the chemical composition carried out.

References   Bradshaw, A.D. and Dutton, R.A. (1982) *Land Reclamation in Cities: a guide to methods of establishment of vegetation on urban wasteland*, HMSO, London.

Courtney, F.M. and Trudgill, S.T. (1984) *The Soil, an introduction to soil study*, Edward Arnold, London.

Weddle, A.E. (ed.) (1967) *Techniques of Landscape Architecture*, Heinemann, London.

Plants

Do not worry if you are not familiar with the names of plants; you will find that you can still do some useful preliminary survey work. You will, however, have to get an ecologist or botanist to help with the assessment stage.

On a project site plan:

Position and extent of vegetation

1. plot the position, height and spread of all free standing trees and shrubs on the site;
2. plot the extent of the woodlands and note their maturity;
3. plot the hedge rows and note their size and width;
4. plot the position, as accurately as possible, of all the individual trees (the trees that stand alone) and outline the boundaries of all the clumps of trees and woodlands and show the areas where shrubs predominate.

Unless you are fortunate enough to have access to a plan on which surveyors have accurately plotted the position of all the trees, and such surveys are rarely available at the beginning of a project, make a best guess as to positions by site observation or preferably by using air photographs. Once the detailed site layout stage is reached, a proper survey of the position of the vegetation will be required.

Even if you do have a surveyor's carefully measured plan of the project area, it is quite common to find that it has only recorded the position of the tree trunk. In most circumstances, but particularly at the preliminary site planning stage, it is more important for you to know the extent of the canopies of the trees and the height and condition of the plants than the exact position of the trunk. You will need to walk round your site systematically and make notes about the individual trees and groups of trees.

You should:

1. note tree height for individual trees and the general height of the canopy in woodlands;

2. plot the spread of crown for individual trees and small clumps; (mark on the plan if you are working at 1:500 scale or make notes if working at 1:1250 scale; at the latter scale you will only be able to outline the area within which the free standing trees are found);
3. plot the area within which shrubs predominate and note size and density;
4. plot the position and spread of the hedges and note height;
5. plot the spread of the canopy edge around woodland and note its edge-type;*
6. note tree maturity in very general categories (whether they are very small young plants like transplants and whips, standard trees, young mature, mature or old trees). Note too if you think they have been recently planted and are not yet fully established;
7. note tree condition (whether it looks healthy, a bit unhealthy, very unhealthy, is dead).

Knowing about the condition of the vegetation is particularly important for the site planner, as it allows decisions to be taken as to which trees must be kept and which could reasonably be felled. It takes many years of training as a forester or arboriculturist to identify how old a tree might be[†] and whether it is in good or bad condition, but you will find that it is possible for the amateur to recognize certain signs which indicate that a tree is beginning to die back because it is diseased. When trying to get an idea of the condition of the vegetation, look for dead branches at the extremities of the trees, look for trunks that appear to have been damaged so that the tree's food supply has been interrupted and look for signs of fungoid growths (lumps which do not normally appear on healthy trees). All these will be signs that the tree is dying back.

If you see signs of die back, it is vital to talk to an expert. Try to find out why the trees are dying back. Is it because of old age? (Different species live to very different ages.) Is it because the ground has become waterlogged or has dried out? Is it because they have been infected by some disease, or is it because man has been disturbing or polluting the ground around the trees or lighting fires? (Adding even 150 mm of soil

---

* Edge type. Define these as edges where:
  the trees suddenly stop with bare tree trunks facing open land, as they do when woodland is being managed for timber;
  there is a well vegetated edge with many shrubs, smaller trees and herbs;
  the edge occurs in clearings within the woods.
  Note: an edge with a high degree of diversity can be of great importance to the ecology of an area, as it increases the diversity of habitats.
† The age of a tree can be accurately established by drilling out a core of the wood from the trunk and counting the rings (each ring equalling a year of growth) but such accuracy is rarely required by site planners.

around a tree can cause it to suffocate, as trees breathe through the roots near the surface).

In particular, if you find more than a small number of trees on your site looking unhealthy, it is essential that you call in an expert to look at them. You need advice on the cause of the disease and the remedy.*

Record the tree and shrub species

This has been left to the second stage as not all of those working through this text will be able to do it themselves.

You need to be able to establish:

1. the species of the individual trees and those in clumps;
2. the range of shrubs and trees in the different parts of any woodland, including its edge; indicate the boundaries of any different zones that you find on your plan; it is not necessary to establish the species of each plant in the woodland for site planning purposes.

If you cannot recognize at least the native species yourself, get help. It is important for the future planning of the site that you identify the species which thrive locally and any variations in species which seem to relate to localized environmental conditions. Reflecting such variations in your own proposals for the future use of plant material on the site will help you to produce a plan and later a design which builds on the special character of the site. Soil, ground water and microclimatic conditions can all influence vegetation, so note any factors that seem to have an impact on the distribution of species across the project site (for example, in many parts of Britain you could expect an area of wetland to have many willows and/or alders).

Look carefully at the hedges and try to establish approximately how old the hedges are, as this will help you to decide whether they are a special feature worth keeping or not.

The age of a hedge can be very roughly estimated by counting the number of woody species occurring in 30 m (100 foot) lengths. For each different species you find in a hedgerow you can estimate about one century and so if you find five different species, you can very roughly estimate that the hedge was planted as a single species hedge in the fifteenth century. To do this part of the survey properly you would need several sampling sites.

It cannot be a totally accurate method but it does help to identify the

---

* In Britain many local authorities employ arboriculturists in their parks departments and they are often very helpful to the public as well as public agencies. In most other countries you will find tree experts either in the forestry departments or employed by government departments. They will know the specific local problems and how to deal with them. Their help is invaluable to site planners both at the survey and assessment stage and at the stage of deciding what should be done in the future.

older hedges. They are the hedges which tend to be of more ecological interest, carrying a wider range of wildlife. If you do find a hedge with a great diversity of species it might be a forest remnant and in that case will definitely be worth preserving as a wildlife habitat if not for historic purposes. You ought to talk to an ecologist about any hedges you find which seem to be diverse in the number of species before deciding which to fell.

Record the way in which the trees, shrubs, hedgerows and woods are being managed

Write brief notes about how it appears that each area of landscape is managed, note too how frequently the management occurs. For instance, in Britain you would note if the hedges were untended, obviously cut by a tractor-powered cutter, or have been treated in the traditional way and carefully laid by hand. (Laying a hedge is the process where the stem of each plant is partly cut through at the base and then the top part of the stem is laid along the hedge, almost but not quite parallel to the ground. The hedge then grows into a stock-proof mass as the new branches interweave with the stem and each other).

Find out how the vegetation on the project site has been and is being managed. Assess whether the management will continue once your site plan is implemented; if not then what arrangements is the client going to make? If it is likely to be retained, assess the long-term implications for the landscape of the present land management pattern.

Almost all landscape in Britain is managed in some way, even if that management is infrequent. The management of most countryside landscapes is done by farmers as part of the daily running of their farms, by woodland owners as part of their requirement to make profit out of timber and by public agencies looking after the relatively small parts of the landscape which are used for recreational or military purposes. Even remote upland hills can turn out to be managed, being grazed by sheep, or having the heather burnt off at regular intervals. As site planners we need to know in detail how each part of our landscape is managed, so that we can predict how the landscapes will change as the land management practices change. Recent research into the man hours involved in managing and maintaining different types of planting and different landscapes has produced some useful ideas for site planners (Groundwork Trust Foundation).*

An ecologist or botanist will be needed to advise you if there are any

---

* Groundwork Trust Foundation, Birmingham.

rare or otherwise important species on your site.* It is very important to try to arrange for them to look over the site, even if you think there is nothing of interest. Rare species can be so easily and quite unintentionally damaged. For instance, by proposing a site plan which increases the use of an area which has only kept its special range of plants up to now because few people have visited it.

Plotting other vegetation

Gather the following information about grass, ruderal (weedy vegetation), scrub and wetland areas:

1. Plot all areas of regularly mown short grass, anything that looks like a lawn or playing field.
2. Plot the areas of grass that appear to be cut only once or twice a year.
3. Plot 'rough grassland', that is all the areas of grass that appear never to be cut. Note if you can the relative level of diversity of species.
4. Show separately all the areas of grassland which are dominated by tall herbs. These flowering members are good for attracting all kinds of insects.
5. Plot all areas of bramble, ivy and low scrub. These too are areas which support a wider range of wildlife than grass can by itself.
6. Plot all the areas of marshy land. Note which seem to carry a single species of plant and which seem to have a lot of different plants.
7. Plot all the water margins in which plants grow and again note the level of diversity.
8. Identify areas of ruderal (that is the weedy type) of vegetation which comes in when ground is intermittently disturbed. It will tend to be rather open in character, contain annual plants and in towns probably also garden escapes, that is flowering plants and shrubs which are most normally grown in gardens.

You need this level of information so that you can decide if there are any areas which could be encouraged to go 'wild' at the site planning stage, so reducing maintenance costs and creating more visual and ecological diversity on the site.

Wildlife

The presence of wildlife in any area is inextricably linked with the plant species that live on the area of land, although many other environmental factors will determine which wildlife actually inhabits the area. These

---

* In Britain most local authorities have an expert who may be able to spend some time checking out a site, but you cannot rely on this. The client will probably have to hire help for a short period.

other factors include the environmental change caused by man's activities. It is possible to predict that if you find particular plant association in certain environmental conditions, certain wildlife could be encouraged.

If you spot any wildlife on your walks around the site, or you have been told that wildlife inhabits the site, try to identify it. Note if the site appears to be relatively rich in any particular species. When a site is wasteland it can still support wildlife.*

Many wildlife species do not like disturbance and will abandon a site when it or adjacent land is developed.

Some wildlife is not appropriate to have in or near a site occupied by people because of the safety aspects. The presence of such wildlife implies that a decision has to be taken not to develop the site, or alternatively to accept the loss of yet more wildlife.

Outside the milder parts of western Europe, and a few other areas, insects can be a major problem which deter people from living near certain trees and shrubs, and plant associations. It is important that the site planner understands what happens in different seasons in relation to insects and does nothing to make people's life on the site intolerable. In areas where the malarial mosquitoes breed, the problem of malaria has to be examined and if the pools in which they breed cannot be drained, then the question must be raised as to whether it is safe or sensible to use the site.

---

* For instance, in Britain one of the best known links is between butterflies and the Buddleia shrubs which so often thrive on urban wasteland. In Britain too thistles, nettles and brambles are particularly good for attracting wildlife in urban areas along with shrubby willows. If you are working elsewhere, find out from ecologists about the local links between plants and wildlife.

Relative ecological value

Any assessment of ecological worth should be made only by a fully trained ecologist. However, it is possible for the non-expert to obtain some idea of the relative worth of the different vegetation types within the site by using the method outlined below.

Using such a method does not suggest that one vegetation type is more valuable than another, for instance that woodland is more valuable than grassland. It only allows you to spot which areas, within a vegetation type, are most likely to be worth trying not to disturb during the site planning process. However, there is no substitute for expert advice. Should anything be found that appears to be of value or in any way unusual, the client ought to be advised to employ an ecologist.

It is not necessary to visit the site for this Step, as you should have recorded all the information that you need by completing the previous seven steps of the site planning process.

Plot the major vegetation types

Using the information that you gathered in the vegetation survey, you should now plot the different vegetation types and classify them. If you are not an expert ecologist you could use a system like the one outlined below, but it is very simplistic and will need modification for local use.

WOODLAND

Indicate on the plan any different types of woodland that occur on your site – deciduous, coniferous, mixed woodland and young woodland or scrub. Then consider each wooded area in turn and decide which category it comes into:

High value
Areas of woodland with a mixture of different native tree and/or shrub species. To be in this highest value category the plants in a wood should also be of different ages and there should in most cases be a dense

understorey (lots of herbs and low-growing shrubs on the woodland floor). If you can recognize the main species in this mix, list them.

The mature beech woods of Southern England are also in this high-value category, but they do not have a dense understorey (because of the level of shade produced by that species).

Include in it also any areas of woodland edge and glade edge which have a dense understorey.

Valuable
Woodlands with native but with no dense understorey (this category excludes the mature beech woods).

Lower value
These would be woodlands where all the trees seem to be of the same species. State which species and if they are native plants.

GRASSLAND AND RUDERAL (WEEDY) AREAS

High value
These are the areas of grass and herbs with a high level of diversity. They include the areas where individual trees grow in the grass. These are the areas you identified in your vegetation survey as being rarely, if ever cut and being composed of many different species. Areas where a few shrubs are established may be included but not the areas where the shrubs are beginning to develop to the extent that they suppress large numbers of herbs.

Valuable
These include the areas where you found that the herb layer was composed of diverse species and cut once or twice a year.

Also included are the areas where native shrubs and pioneer trees are invading the grassland in substantial numbers.

Lower value
The areas of grass which are infrequently cut but where you found little variety in the species. Also the areas where non native shrubs and trees are invading the grass.

Very little value
This includes close mown, relatively recently sown grass, such as found in lawns and playing fields.

HEDGES

High value
All hedges with more than five different woody species in a 30 metre length, no matter how they are at present managed.

Valuable
All hedges with between three and five different woody species in a 30 metre length which are managed by layering, hand cutting or are overgrown.

Lower value
All hedges with only one or two species which are layered, hand cut or overgrown. Also all hedges which are machine cut but still allow for a mass of herbs to grow at the base.

Very little value
This includes the single-species hedges kept cut right down by machine and where the herbs are regularly removed from underneath.

WETLANDS AND WATER MARGINS

These can be very important to the local ecology, mainly because so many of them have disappeared as man has drained the land for development or to improve agricultural or forestry productivity. So if you do have any areas of wetland on your site, you can designate them as worthy of preservation and conservation (even if they look a boggy mess to you!).

Indicate all wetland and water areas on your ecology map as a valuable or potentially valuable resource.

You now have a very crude guide to the relative ecological value of the different parts of your site which can be used to decide what should happen in each part of the site. However, you must remember its limitations and in particular that this method will not identify the very special and rare habitats and groups of plants which it takes an expert botanist to identify.

STEP 9 Land use and people

Use a copy of the site context area plan to record the general information on how the land around the project site is utilized. Then use the project area plan to record the detail of land use within your site and immediately around its edge.

Land uses within and around the project area

For the project area and its immediate surroundings it is best to gather the information on a site visit. For the more general information about land-use in the surrounding site context area air photographs will give sufficient information (although if you are not familiar with using them, you should check your interpretation at several locations on site). Indicate the extent of all the different land uses within the project site and around it. For instance, for those areas where the land is at present unbuilt and for rural areas.

UNBUILT AND RURAL AREAS

For the site context and project area:

1. Show any areas of pasture land; note whether grazed or mown for silage or hay.
2. Show any arable areas within the project area and the site context area; indicate the present range of crops used in the area.
3. Show any managed forests or woodlands within the project area and the site context area and indicate crop.
4. Show any unmanaged forests or woodlands within the project area and the site context area.
5. Show the location of any other major land uses (for example mineral extraction, industry, recreation) within the project area and the site context area; describe the use.
6. Indicate any areas of derelict land within the project area and the site context area.

In addition, add the following information on the project area and the land immediately around it:

1. Show any areas used for horticulture within the project area and immediately around it; indicate the range of crops.
2. Show any areas used for fruit growing within the project area and immediately around it (excluding fruit-trees). Indicate the type of crop.
3. Show any area of orchard within the project area and immediately around it and describe the type of fruit tree.
4. Show any areas at present left fallow (not used for any particular crop and only to a limited extent for pasture) within the project area and immediately around it. Indicate whether the area is part of a land use pattern or land which is surplus to requirements.
5. Show any irrigation or drainage systems within the project area and immediately around it which are associated with crops.
6. Show the location of any housing within the project area and immediately around it and if possible indicate whether used by those involved in agriculture or others.
7. Show the location of any farm storage buildings on and immediately around the project area.
8. Show the location of any buildings presently used for other uses on and immediately around the project area.
9. Show the location of any derelict buildings on and immediately around the project area.
10. Show all tracks and roads on and immediately around the project area and indicate the nearest point of access to the public road network.

AGRICULTURE

As part of the work you did for Step 6 you should have established the relative quality of the local agricultural land. Note now the relationship, if any, between that and the local agricultural land use pattern. Talk to local agricultural experts to find out whether agriculture in the area is thriving or marginal.

Record the farm holding boundaries, if this is appropriate and possible, and the subdivisions into fields or other units. Find out from local experts what has been happening to the size of holding and the size of fields. Identify any changes or trends which are the result of governmental or other policies, or market forces.

Discuss the range of crops with local farming experts to establish if the present range is static. Find out if the choice of crops is related to a special economic policy, is the result of international market forces or is decided by local market forces, so as to assess the likelihood of change.

If the site planning project will retain a substantial area of agricultural land, establish which crops are most likely to be grown and assess the environmental consequences. Local agricultural experts could be asked about this as well as local farmers.

IF THE LAND IS BUILT OVER OR IN AN URBAN AREA

For the site context and project area:

1. Indicate the position of any houses on the project site and immediately around it. Outline any major areas of housing in the site context area. For the area immediately around the project area and within it indicate the type of housing, its age and its condition.
2. Mark the location of any industrial units, warehouses or workshops within the site context area and for the area within and immediately around the project site record details of the use of the buildings. Note any noise or air pollution associated with the use of the buildings.
3. Record any areas of public open space inside and within 400 m of the project site.
4. Record the other areas of open land accessible to the public inside and within 400 m of the project site.
5. Mark on the site context plan the location of any social facilities within the wider study area. Indicate the service provided.
6. Indicate any major roads within 0.5 km of the edge of the project area; if there are none indicate where and how distant the nearest major road is. Record all possible access points to the main road network that would be accessible from the project site.
7. Indicate any footpaths adjacent to or within 400 m of the project site on which the public has a right of way.
8. Indicate all the places within 400 m of the site where the present public transport systems have stopping points. Mark the routes taken by buses.

In addition add the following information on the project area and the land immediately around it:

1. Indicate any positions where the present minor road system would allow access to the project area.
2. Indicate any roads or tracks used by vehicles in and immediately around the project area.
3. Indicate any noise problems affecting the project site.
4. Indicate any footpaths through the project site or on its periphery. State if their use must be continued after development.

5. Mark the location of any major parking areas within walking distance of the project area.
6. Indicate the walls and any other man-made structures within and on the edge of the project area. Describe their initial and present use and make notes of their structural condition.
7. Mark the location of any road accident blackspots on or near the project area.
8. Mark the location of any services – sewers, water, power supply, communications cables – which would be available for use on the project site without having to be specially laid on.

HOUSING

When making notes about the housing, record information on the relative density of any housing developments, the form the development has taken (is it built along streets or clustered etc.), the size and type of housing (small, medium or large sized; terraced, semi-detached or detached houses, bungalows, or flats in tower, slab or low blocks, etc.) in each different area. In most instances it will be sufficient to gather general information on the housing within 400 m of the edge of your site, but more detailed information will be needed for the area immediately surrounding the project site.

OPEN LAND

Note the extent and type of space (formal parkland, playing field, grassland, wasteland).

SOCIAL FACILITIES – SCHOOLS, COMMUNITY BUILDINGS, CLUBS, SHOPS, INDOOR SPORTS AND SWIMMING FACILITIES

Note the location and type of facility and the area it serves. In Britain most facilities are marked on the Ordnance Survey maps, but elsewhere or where the maps are not up to date you should talk to the local social planners, or you may have to make an on-site investigation of the social facilities within walking distance of the project area.

INDUSTRY, WAREHOUSING AND WORKSHOPS

Note in detail what happens in the industrial premises on or adjacent to the project site. You should also attempt to find out, perhaps with the help of the local public health authorities, whether there are likely to be any environmental problems associated with those industrial premises. Nuisance can be caused by noise from delivery lorries or machinery, by smell, air pollution or even because those who work in them might start to use any additional open spaces or facilities provided as a part of the site plan. When the latter is likely to occur it is necessary to adjust the site plan to allow for the extra usage, or design the site in a different way.

COMMUNICATIONS – ROADS, FOOTPATHS, BUS ROUTES, BUS STOPS, RAILWAY STATIONS, CAR PARKS ETC.

Pay particular attention to the location of access points for vehicles to major roads and the location of safe pedestrian crossing points.

If traffic noise is a problem obtain expert advice on its extent, the parts of the site affected and the means of combating it.

Establish if there is any flexibility in the routes taken by public transport which might allow the project site to be better serviced.

If you are working in an area where road traffic is heavy, discuss road safety with the local authority and establish where the black-spots are.

SERVICES

Note whether there are services available to the project site and establish if these have any surplus capacity or not. Sewerage systems, water mains, gas and electricity as well as telephone and other communications cables are all normally required if a site is to be built over.

The people who live on and around the project area

THE LOCAL POPULATION

Indicate approximately how many people live within about half a kilometre of the edge of the site. If possible break this information down so that it relates to any different land-use areas around the project site. The site planner often has to rely on observation and best guesses in relation to populations around an area. For many projects this is acceptable, but any assumptions should be checked with the local experts – the town or rural planners or others responsible for collating population information.

If there is any likelihood of a local population using the project site when it is developed, more detailed information should be collected on the social characteristics of the population. The age and sex structure should be recorded and the information grouped into appropriate categories. For instance: children, young people, adults and older people. When detailed information is needed about the local population, employment and unemployment trends are useful in assessing how the external areas might be used.

If the site is for public use, gather information on the local social and cultural mixes and find out what you can about how the differences affect the various groups' reactions to the external environment locally.

HOW PEOPLE USE THE PROJECT AREA AT PRESENT

If casual or unauthorized use of the project area has been observed during the site visits, or particularly if part of your brief is to produce a site plan which will work for present as well as future users, you should note on a project area plan:

1. Which tracks people use and the regularity of use. Where do they enter and leave the site?
2. What people do on the site and where. This information needs to be exact, to show where they sit, run, sun bathe, play, congregate, stroll.
3. How long they stay in each part of the site.
4. Indicate if you have observed people of different ages using different parts of the site. Are there any differences in which parts of the site men and women use? Are there any differences in the proportions of men and women in different parts of the site? If you observe differences can you work out why they exist?

Land ownership and planning controls

Note on the plan everything that you have been able to find out about the present land ownership pattern immediately around the project area. If it appears that there could be difficulties with negotiating access to the project site, discuss this urgently with the client and the local planners.

Record any possibility of the adjacent land uses changing in the foreseeable future.

Identify any special planning controls, such as tree preservation orders or conservation area status which apply to the project site and the land immediately around it.

STEP 10 Landscape

Landscape character of the larger landscape

You should attempt to work out what constitutes the special characteristics of the area of landscape within which your project site lies. In particular, make notes about the characteristic spaces, forms, shapes, colours and textures and look for the special patterns of the local landscape. Look too at the scale of the landscape. Supplement the notes with a photographic record.

In many urban areas the land uses strongly influence the landscape character, although even within a land-use such as housing you will find many different landscape character zones. In rural landscapes it is often the landform and the way it is clothed with vegetation which determines the different landscape character zone.

Once you have identified the different landscape character zones you should spend a short time thinking about the visual attributes of the area in which you are working. Try to work out why the area looks like it does. Try to analyse the extent to which this appearance reflects the way in which the physical features interact on that area of land, or is dependent on the way in which man is managing the landscape.

For each landscape character zone list the factors which you think detract from the landscape and the factors that enhance it. Pay most attention to the landscape character zones abutting the project area and within the project area.

Looking at the site and its surroundings in this way could help you to identify what, as well as the addition of more plants, can be suggested as a means of enhancing the landscape – make a summary list of these for the project site and the land immediately surrounding it.

Landscape types and their maintenance and management

There is no particular format for you to record information about landscape types and their maintenance regimes. You have to work out what is appropriate to the specific problem. It is, however, very helpful at the decision-making stage of the site planning process to be able quickly to define the landscape types that could with benefit be changed within the project area and which should be conserved. Knowing how each of the landscape types which comprise a landscape is at present managed and what its visual impact is, enables us to make positive proposals to change the method of management as well as the landscape type, should that prove necessary.

You should devise your own scheme for recording landscape information within the site. John Handley of the St Helens Groundwork Trust devised the following categories:

1. grassland (natural, naturalized, amenity, production, ornamental lawn)
2. scrub (native, naturalized)
3. mature woodland (native, naturalized)
4. young woodland (naturalized, production, amenity)
5. wetland (native, naturalized)
6. hedges (naturalistic, amenity, ornamental)
7. individual trees and those in small groups (native, naturalistic, amenity, ornamental, productive)
8. shrubs (ground cover, ornamental)
9. herbaceous (naturalized, ornamental).

If a similar classification seems appropriate for your site, you will find that the information you recorded for Step 6 will provide most of what you require. For each of the categories on your site find out how the landscape type is maintained and managed, describe in detail the operation carried out and how frequently (such as grass cutting, hedge cutting).

ENCLOSURE AND INTER-VISIBILITY   **Views and scenery**

Refer to Step 4 for the information you have already collected on zones of visual enclosure related to landform. If visual intrusion is likely to be a problem in relation to your project and this will be an issue when it comes to organizing approval by the planning authority, a landscape architect must be employed to carry out a full inter-visibility exercise using a recognized technique (University of Aberdeen, 1976). However, if the project is less visually significant, a short cut can be taken by the site planner. First choose a number of viewing points regularly spaced out through the project site and add to these the places where you know, from site visits, that the most extensive views are available. Visit each of these positions and record what you can see in the foreground, middleground and distance looking north, west, south and east. From the same point make a note of the direction and quality of the most interesting view. This method of walking round the site works well in open landscapes but of course does not work for densely wooded or dense urban areas; if these exist on your site you need to go out into your wider study area and try to establish which, if any, parts of your site can be seen from different parts of the wider study area.

VISUAL QUALITY OF THE VIEWS

Use the same viewing points as for the inter-visibility exercise and when you do that exercise, note which views or parts of views can be considered to enhance or detract from the scene. Recording the views by taking photographs or doing drawings provides a useful aide memoire at the planning stage.

If it will be necessary to make decisions about which views to keep open and which to screen, you might find it useful to add the following assessment. If time is short it can be based on your subjective judgement about how much the view pleases you, as long as you make it clear that this is the only basis for the assessment. Preferably involve local people and those who might use the site in the future in the assessment.

Categorize the views as:

1. very good views, which must be kept open
2. good views, which ought to be kept open
3. moderately good views, which could be used with advantage
4. poor views, which ought to be screened
5. very poor views, which must be screened.

QUALITY OF VIEWS INTO THE PROJECT SITE

Do not neglect to walk around the edges of the project site looking inwards. Try to identify the best views into the site. You are once more trying to establish which areas need screening and which could be opened up to view, but this time from the point of view of the people outside the site.

References   University of Aberdeen, Department of Geography (1976) *Assessment of Major Industrial Applications: a Manual, DOE Research Report 13*, DOE, London.

Unique objects

This Step brings together the information that you have already recorded about unique physical and natural areas as well as objects, and supplements it with information about the historic features and landmarks.

These include the unique physical, natural and man-made features of the project area and the land immediately adjacent to it. Refer to the work that you have already done on the physical and natural environment and plot on a plan the most memorable features that occur in the local landscape, places that would appear to be of recreational, educational or scientific value.

Unique features

LANDMARKS

Add the local landmarks to the plan. They can be a rock of a particular shape, an outcrop of rock forming a cliff, a group of rocks, a clump of trees, an individual tree of a different sort or shape from the others in the area, a church tower or any building different from the others around it. The list is endless and psychologists have shown that in our local neighbourhood even small scale objects, which to an outsider seem insignificant, such as a shop on a corner, are the landmarks that make up our mental map of the area in which we live (Lynch, 1972).

If you have time it is useful to understand how local people remember their area. Carrying out the following exercise helps to illustrate this.

Ask local people to draw from memory a map of the area which they would describe as their neighbourhood, that is, the territory in which they feel most at home. They should include all the features that they are aware of using to orientate themselves as they walk round (the buildings, the trees, the walls). If they cannot think what to do, ask them to describe a walk round the area to an outsider, perhaps someone who is blind. Ask as many people as possible to do this exercise and see if there is any consensus as to the most memorable landmarks. This will give you an idea of the features which should be retained as you develop ideas for the future of the project area.

HISTORIC FEATURES ON AND AROUND THE PROJECT SITE

Plot any features of historic interest on the unique features plan. Do not neglect the walls, embankments, ditches, old trees, old burial grounds or even old rubbish tips. Unless your site and its surroundings are very simple, you may have to use a separate plan to indicate these. Information would also be useful on the age of the structures and their physical condition and also expert opinion as to the historical value of the features and areas identified. The classification you use to indicate age will differ from country to country depending on historical development. In Britain you could use the following classification to indicate roughly when the structure was built:

- In the twentieth century
- In the nineteenth century
- Between the fifteenth and eighteenth centuries
- In medieval times
- Before the eleventh century (state period).

Find out from the local archaeology and history experts if any of the man-made features on or near your site are officially classed as historic monuments (in Britain information is kept in the local museum or library in the form of a list of historic buildings and monuments). However, remember that not all historic sites are known and you could unearth something of importance on your site.

Is there anything else on your site which suggests how man used the land in the past? Have you noticed any curious earthworks (any shaping of the land which would seem not to fit with the way most of the land lies)? To refresh your memory look again at the detailed topographic survey you did as part of Step 1. If there are changes of level across the site which have so far not been explained by your survey work, ask the local archaeology and history experts whether these could be old field systems, evidence of early industrial activities or of old settlements and whether they are worth retaining for their link with the past (Hoskins, 1955; Rackham, 1986).

References   Hoskins, W.G. (1955) *Making of the English Landscape*, Hodder and Stoughton, London.

Lynch, K. (1972) *The Image of the City*, MIT Press, Cambridge.

Rackham, O. (1986) *The History of the Countryside*, J.M. Dent, London.

User requirements

This Step is designed to provide you with the basic information about the people who will use the site. This information is required before you can undertake an assessment of the site potential leading to the site plan. You will already have information from the client about the main land-uses to be located on the site; this Step allows you to translate that into the facilities and equipment you must locate on the site and the environmental settings you ought to provide for the users.

1. User requirements – activities:
   (a) Describe the users and the reasons why they will use the site.
   (b) Work out what major and spin-off activities they will be involved in on the site.
   (c) Work out the facilities and infrastructure needed to allow each activity, work out the environmental settings needed to support each activity.
2. User requirements – locational requirements, related activities and compatibility:
   (a) List the locational requirements of each activity.
   (b) Work out which of the above activities are related and need to be sited together.
   (c) List which related activities are compatible and can use the same land.
   (d) List which related activities are incompatible with others and will need discrete sites.
   (e) List any activities which are independent of other uses.
3. User requirements – movement patterns:
   (a) Work out the likely movement patterns to and from the site.
   (b) Work out the likely movement patterns within the site.
   (c) Note any movement through the site but not linked to the use of the site.

THE USERS

Describe the population characteristics of those who will live on, work on or use the site for living, leisure, commerce or any other function.

Identification of activities

Gather information on age and sex of the users and when possible make an estimate of the numbers of people involved in each category. You should also collect information about the social and economic characteristics of the users. In many cases this is available from the census data.

To identify the users that you should plan for on the site you could prepare a chart such as that shown in Figure 12.1 and if there is no detailed information make a best guess at the numbers of people you have to plan for.

Function	Number of people by age group			
	Children	Teenagers	Fit adults	Less fit
Housing				
Cafe				
Youth club				
Nursery				
Total				

Figure 12.1 People by age group

Gather information on the buildings that will be required for each use. Work with the architect involved in the scheme to describe these in as much detail as is possible at the early planning stage. If there is a mixture of uses on the site which will result in different demands of the outdoor areas, describe these differences in some detail as they will be important at the site layout stage.

THE ACTIVITIES

Using whatever information you have been able to gather about the people who will use the site, construct a chart of activities. Your information will preferably come from a thorough investigation of user needs as described in Part Three, but if the users cannot be fully identified it may have to be a best guess based on your own understanding of how people behave. Make sure you indicate clearly the source of your ideas as to which activities should be allowed for on the site.

As each site is different you will have to construct a different series of charts each time. It is useful to use charts as they will act as a check list and you will be able to assess easily quite how many of the activities you have provided for as you develop the site plan.

The first chart will probably be very simple, containing a limited range of information such as indicated in Figure 12.2.

Major activity	Spin-off activities
Housing	Gardening
	Car parking
	Children playing
	etc. (see Section Three)
Cafe	Car parking
	Outdoor eating
	Waste disposal
	Areas to wait for friends
	Private sitting area (staff)
	etc.
etc.	

Figure 12.2 Activity chart

This first attempt at an activity chart is then expanded by looking at each activity (major and spin off) separately. The facilities that will be needed are listed and the environmental settings that would best suit the activity are described. The list below shows an example of the type of information it would be useful to set down in relation to young children's play in a housing area:

1. Activity: Housing
    Spin off activity: Children playing (doorstep play)
    Facilities and equipment required:
    something to scramble on, nooks and crannies to hide in, steps and curbs and small walls to sit on and climb on, rails to balance on, smooth surfaces to play on with wheeled toys.
    Setting required:
    Spaces on or very near the doorstep of the home with diverse sights, sounds, textures, smells to stimulate the child. Mixed surfaces. Visible from the home.

The locational requirements and the relationship between the activities

Knowing that areas and facilities for activities must be provided is not by itself enough. The site planner also needs to know whether the activity has any particular locational requirement, or should always or sometimes be linked to another activity.

For instance, it normally works best if gardens can be adjacent to and directly accessed from the homes of the people who will use them. Even where the housing takes the form of apartments, many people, particularly those on the ground floor, still like their bit of land directly outside their home. So as you develop a housing layout, you do not just have to concern yourself with the house, but also with how to make the area around the house usable by the owner or tenant. If you decide there must be gardens to satisfy the user's requirements, you are then involved in a whole range of decisions: the suitable size, the need to be totally private or only partially, whether they can just be accessed from the house or whether they need a gate to give access to another area, the amount of shade that is tolerable, etc.

Some activities cannot take place in combination with others for reasons of danger, for instance archery. Others are best on separate pitches, for instance team games. Others such as strolling happen everywhere. You have to consider each activity in turn and decide if there are any particular constraints to its location. For instance, whether it requires a particular area and extent of land or any special feature such as a steep slope for tobogganing.

Making up a list of all the requirements for each activity will help you decide whether or not it can in fact be provided as part of the site plan, within the developer's cost constraints.

Activities that happen everywhere such as walking and jogging have few constraints, but if they are to be a pleasant experience for the participant they need to allow diversity of experience. A walk which takes you through a wooded area, to a rose garden, past a children's play space, to a pond, along a stream, to a nature area, past a view point and back home along a street; a walk such as that with a mixture of experiences is much preferable to one through a monotonous landscape with little or no diversity of experience. The site planner has to think hard how this can be achieved for the users of a site.

Movement patterns

Constructing roads and other hard surfaces is, after the construction of the buildings and retaining walls, the most expensive item on any site. It is, therefore, important to understand how people will enter and leave the site and move around and through it. It is also important to limit the use of hard surfaces for nature conservation reasons, as it is best to keep as much earth unbuilt as possible.

It is only by understanding the movement patterns, people's desire lines, that a proper balance can be achieved between hard and soft surfaces. As you study this aspect do not neglect to consider the people who already use the site and have established routes through the area. Such movements are unlikely to disappear because of the new development and will have to be catered for.

You should be careful to do some 'future gazing' about the linkages that might develop between the activities you are proposing to place on the site. You will not get all the linkages right, but you should at least try to. For instance, you must consider the routes that people going to bus stops, going to the shops, going to the post box will take. The servicing of the site too must be considered. How is the postman, the milkman and any other delivery or collection service to move round the site?

At this stage, you may find it useful to construct a rough diagram of the various uses, showing how they relate to each other and the need for physical or visual links.

STEP 13 Assessing the potential of the site for development

This Step is designed to allow you to determine what your information about the site and its users means in terms of what can happen within the site. It can be a straightforward or a complicated process, depending on the site and its proposed use. The method suggested here is most suitable for a medium to large site with a low density of usage, but it can be adapted to others; you will have to devise a best method for bringing the information together in relation to each site, as they all have such different problems. The process is described in more detail in Part Four.

There are a series of stages which need to be completed for every site. These are listed below:

Identification of assets and liabilities

You will find it easiest to use a base map to record this information and may even find it helps to use a simple colour coding for the good and bad points.

ASSETS

Using the vast knowledge of the site which you have by now gathered, go back quickly through each category of information and note in relation to each which aspect you think is going to be a useful feature for the proposed development. To do this look at the information you have on geology, soils, vegetation, ecology, scenery, zones of enclosure, unique features, etc., while referring to the list of required activities, facilities and settings drawn up for the previous Step.

LIABILITIES

Do the same for the factors that it now appears might create problems.

THE CONSTRAINTS AND OPPORTUNITIES FOR DEVELOPMENT

Consider also how the site and its features impose constraints or opportunities on the proposed development, either on the location of a particular activity or its extent. This is a useful step towards preparing a site plan. You will find that drawing up brief notes of your reactions to what constitutes an opportunity and why, will be useful at the next stage.

It is at this stage that you identify the physical and natural environmental factors which must be safeguarded and depending on the type of development project, you will see these as constraints or opportunities.

THE LINK BETWEEN MANAGEMENT AND THE QUALITY OF THE NATURAL ENVIRONMENT

You should have as clear an understanding as possible, within the limitations of present knowledge, of the influence of the interactions between the physical environmental factors within your site. You should work out which factors can be changed without damage to the site and which cannot. This establishes whether this adds a further layer of constraints also exists. Understanding these linkages also helps to determine which land and landscape management practices must be maintained on the site and which can be changed with no ill effects.

First identification of best location for activities

The assessment of the opportunities and constraints will enable an immediate identification of the best location for at least some of the activities. These are the activities for which the right conditions exist in parts of the site. Working on the assumption that it is likely to be cost effective site planning if the site is changed as little as possible, the site planner searches for a match between conditions on the site and the facilities and locational and environmental setting requirements of an activity. There will be some activities which can happen in many areas and others for which there is only one possible location.

This is a first step towards determining the form the site plan will finally take.

LANDSCAPE TYPES AND SITE POTENTIAL

On larger sites, you will often find it useful to use the landscape character zones that you identified during the site survey, to record the site potential. These same zones can be used as the basis for the first distribution of uses and activities across the site. This is a good way of ensuring that the diverse character of a site is respected and retained through the development process.

Preparing the site plan

This is the final stage of the site planning process, when the site planner or the site planning team finally decide what will happen on a site. Proposals are prepared for the distribution of land uses and activities. These are supported by a landscape structure plan and a site management plan and, if the client is proceeding directly into the implementation stage, the preparation of design briefs for each part of the site.

The process is described in detail in Chapter 10 of this text, so only a checklist of what you must do is included here.

Identifying the planning strategies to govern the development

These are in effect the outside controls. You will be able to determine what they are through contact with the local planners and by reference to planning documents. The opinions and needs of the local community too can be very important determinants of the strategies which should be adopted.

For instance, the strategies may determine that as part of a city wide policy the area must have a naturalistic character, or because the site is within a conservation area its buildings must have a certain form and scale and be constructed of certain materials. In other circumstances there may be a requirement for a certain range of recreational activity which relates to a wider planning strategy.

Listing the site development objectives

Using both the strategies and your knowledge of the site and its possibilities, list the most important objectives for the development. These objectives will relate to the specific site and not be general. It is the possibility of achieving these objectives which guides our selection of a particular layout and design solution. See Chapter 10 for guidance on the factors which might be considered, but note that it is at this stage that you determine how conservation measures will be applied to the site.

Objectives frequently conflict and the site planner has to come to some decision on the relative importance of meeting each objective; the strategies are usually some help in deciding this.

This stage includes the drawing up of guidelines on the experiential aspects of the development of the site. These deal with what the place should be like to be in and the environmental qualities of its parts and spaces. The work you completed on the environmental settings for the site potential phase helps in drawing up these guidelines, as do the studies of the landscape within and around the site.

A concept for site development

This is meant to allow you to sort out your ideas. Draw a bubble diagram of how you think the general relationships of the different objects and areas on the site should develop. Remember to take account of the design fixed points that you identified at the end of the site potential stage when you do this.

Testing alternative site layout solutions

You will find that three is the minimum number of alternatives worth exploring. Even if you are sure that you know how you are going to lay out the site, it is still worth testing out possible alternatives, as this will help widen your perception of the different ways of coping with the site. These alternative plans should be drawn out very roughly with just sufficient information to allow you to evaluate them against the objectives and the guidelines.

The site plan and landscape plan

The site plan and the landscape plan are best developed together, although in some circumstances it is preferable to separate the two and consider the landscape plan first. How it is done will be determined by the strategies which govern the site and the type of problem.

The landscape plan develops out of the objectives and guidelines. It determines the massing of the site in most cases. Outside city centres it is rare that the buildings themselves are sufficiently massive and cohesive to give an overall structure to a site. The landscape plan indicates the main areas of enclosure, defining whether landform, vegetation or structures form the edges of the spaces as well as defining the main characteristics of those spaces – for instance, hard surfaced and edged and formal in appearance, well vegetated but formal, well vegetated and informal, or an open clear space with a transparent edge formed by vegetation. The combinations are countless and will depend on the character you want to develop on the site. The landscape plan indicates all vegetation to be kept, the areas of vegetation that are to be enhanced and the areas of new vegetation. It also defines the range of species to be planted in each area.

There are occasions when it is inappropriate to produce a landscape plan; these occur particularly in highly developed sites where the local planning proposals allow for no or little space to be left after the buildings are completed.

The site plan must define all the existing features to be retained and those to be modified. It also indicates a location for all the required buildings and structures. The position of the roadways and footpaths are defined, as well as the possible routes for the underground services. Where they are developed separately it should reflect the proposals in the landscape plan.

Once the site layout has been developed it should be tested against the objectives and modified as necessary. Then it should be presented to the client and users in draft form for their comment. After final approval a joint site and landscape plan should be prepared.

Site management plan

Depending on the site this can be very complex or simple. For each different area of the site describe the maintenance operations and their frequency.

You should define who is responsible for the maintenance of each area and check that they have the resources allocated both for the implementation and maintenance phases. If they do not, then it is necessary to go back to the site plan and change it until the long term management problem is solved. There is no point in attempting to develop a site unless this issue is decided in advance. Maintenance is as crucial as implementation; without it the users will never be satisfied.

DESIGN BRIEFS

If a site is to be designed as one area, then the site plan and the supporting landscape and management proposals are in effect the design brief. If the site is to be designed by several designers, a separate design brief should be prepared for each part of the site.

You should draw up a design brief in as clear terms as possible and ensure the designer is aware of all the work that has gone into the site plan and how the individual site relates to the whole. The brief should be clear as to what are design fixed points within a particular zone and leave as much scope as possible for the designer's talent to operate. On small sites the designers will have been part of the site planning team and this can be a great advantage at the design stage. When the designers have not been part of the site planning team, a mechanism needs to be developed whereby they can put their proposals before the site planners and client and enter into a constructive discussion of how the ideas relate to the brief for the site; this should happen regularly and not just when the designer has fixed the scheme and insists that it is too late and too expensive to change anything.

The site plan is a mechanism for dealing with both short and long term problems. It can be particularly useful when a site is to be developed over a number of years by disparate groups of people. The process explained here would work as well for small settlements as for an individual site.

References

Lynch, K. and Hack, G. (1984) *Site Planning*, MIT Press, Cambridge.

University of Aberdeen, Department of Geography, Project Appraisal for Development Control Research Team (1976) *Assessment of Major Industrial Applications: A Manual, DOE Research Report 13*, DOE, London.

Lynch, K. (1972) *The Image of the City*, MIT Press, Cambridge.

Conclusion

The site planning process described in this part will enable those at the beginning of their careers as students or practitioners to produce a first attempt at a site plan. For those more familiar with the process the information in the part can act as a checklist. It is, however, worth re-stating that every site is different and will need a slightly different approach. As you become more skilled at site planning, it will be possible to identify short-cuts which will speed up the decision-making process.

Index